Food for Thought

Parallax Re-visions of Culture and Society
Stephen G. Nichols, Gerald Prince, and Wendy Steiner,
SERIES EDITORS

Food for Thought

Louis Marin

Translated,
with an Afterword,
by Mette Hjort

The Johns Hopkins University Press
Baltimore and London

This book has been brought to publication with the generous assistance of the French Ministry of Culture.

Originally published as *La parole mangée et autres essais théologico-politiques*. © Librairie des Méridiens, Klincksieck & Cie, 1986. This English language edition © 1989 The Johns Hopkins University Press

Chapter 10, "Recipes of Power ('Puss-in-Boots')" was previously published as *"Puss-in-Boots:* Power of Signs—Signs of Power" in *Diacritics* (June 1977): 54–63.

The Johns Hopkins University Press, 701 West 40th Street, Baltimore, Maryland 21211
The Johns Hopkins Press Ltd., London

The paper used in this publication meets the minimum requirements of American National Standard for Information Sciences—Permanence of Paper for Printed Library Materials, ANSI Z39.48-1984.

Library of Congress Cataloging-in-Publication Data

Marin, Louis, 1931–
    [Parole mangée et autres essais théologico-politiques. English]
    Food for thought / Louis Marin ; translated, with an afterword, by Mette Hjort.
        p. cm. — (Parallax : re-visions of culture and society)
    Translation of: La parole mangée et autres essais théologico-politiques.
    Bibliography: p.
    Includes index.
    ISBN 0-8018-3476-7 (alk. paper).

    1. Body, Human, in literature. 2. Human figure in art. 3. Body, Human (Philosophy) 4. Power (Philosophy) I. Title. II. Series: Parallax (Baltimore, Md.)
PN56.B62M3713 1989
844'.914—dc19   88-29342
                                                              CIP

For Judith

Contents

Part IV: The King's Body

Illustrations

Introduction to the English-Language Edition

In bringing the Augustinian tradition to its culmination within the Cartesian *épistémè*, the *Logic of Port-Royal* (1662–83) sums up a long chapter in the history of Western semiotics. In this crucial text, the logicians define the very structure of signification as representation. Following such a conception, ideas represent things to the mind, and signs are the representations of these ideas for other minds. This representation of a representation is the meaning of a sign, and this meaning is true to the extent that it corresponds to the idea and, thereby, to the thing signified. The ideal of the sign, if not its ideality as well, involves a process of self-effacement that leaves it transparent before the thing, an effacement that is all the more easily achieved and justified by the conventional nature of the sign when no mimetic relation obtains between the sign and its signified.

If, then, the whole structure of signification consists of a doubling, we may note that this duplication is accompanied by a substitution of the thing for the sign or, alternately, by a reduction of the sign to the thing. Indeed, it is precisely this reduction that is, ipso facto, constitutive of objectivity: here is the object's true foundation. We may well question the coherence of this reductive process because it appears to annul the first moment (the doubling or duplication). It is the purpose or function of the sign and of representation to guarantee that individual minds may communicate being and truth to one another. Indeed, the sign as representation is functional, and this characteristic of the sign defines its objective structure. The converse is true in the case of the object, which manifests its structure in the sign's representation, that is, in its function; this very function constitutes the pragmatic dimension of the sign.

By the same token, a community of minds wholly transparent to one another and embodying a kind of rational sociability establishes itself within the reversibility that lies at the basis of their intercommunication. Such, then, would be the essential structure and function of the linguistic sign. Thus, we understand that this representational theory of the sign finds *(thesei)* its authority and justification in the particular de jure or conventional relation that it bears to an absent entity or thing. If representation means the substitution of an *x* for an absent *y*, then it is the juridical conformity of what is present to what is absent—in other words, the isomorphism—that justifies the substitution. Optimally, the transparency of the representation affords the sign its transitive dimension. To represent is to represent something. The operative character of this formal relation between what is present and what is absent ensures that the former functions in the place of and assumes the function of the latter. Representation carries the effect of an object.

Yet this substitution between things and signs, a substitution generally characteristic of all representations or signs, is itself an oriented process. Replacing the sign with the thing can achieve an effect of objectivity within the rational universality of a discourse of knowledge.

The process may also be inverted. Then signs take the place of things, representation substitutes for being, and the world of signs achieves an autonomy that allows it to deploy itself as a screen displaying the entire universe of things. This world is all the more deceptive or seductive precisely because it betrays its imitative nature *(phusei)*. In it, the universal objectivity of true knowledge, systematically elaborated and enhanced within a rational discourse, comes to be replaced by the subjective infinity of individual desires. These desires find a bond or connection in an ever-deferred and differing satisfaction realized in the various pleasures of the imagination and sensibility. A different society develops as a result, a society that no longer espouses the fundamental value of what Augustine calls *uti*. As opposed to valorizing the use of signs, this society prefers the *frui* or intense thrill that underwrites a system of values that privileges hedonism and a pleasure that perpetually falls short of its complete realization.

This line of reasoning readily reveals one of the well-known themes of Augustinian and Jansenist thought. At the same time, however, the excesses and failings of these themes testify to the power of mimesis. Representation as image, and no longer as idea, is at once self-sufficient and ornamental. It proves to be the seductive and deceptive image before which the aporias of mimesis vanish through the effacing of the referential relation to the object.

As a result of the effects that it exercises on the senses and the imagination, however, this form of representation, which we here associate summarily with the image, also perverts the other dimension of representation. Each and every sign presents itself as representing something. In its very presentation, every sign redoubles or reflects the operation of representation, thus revealing the reflexive dimension that may be summed up as the gesture of presenting oneself representing something. Every sign produces an effect of a subject. The sign may constitute the subject as an *ego cogitans;* as Kant said, the "I think" accompanies all of my representations.

Yet certain signs have the particular characteristic of being able to exercise an effect on the subject. They have the potential to constitute the subject as a "pathetic I" or, alternately, as the "I" of intense pleasure.* Better still, to represent is, as Furetière indicates in his *Dictionary,* to exhibit or display a presence. In other words, the ostentation of the act of representation constitutes the identity of what is represented. Through theatrical display, the effects of a subject are consolidated into an "I" and assume the identity of a self who experiences and carries affect. In theatricality, the effect of a subject finds its own particular substance and value.

In their theoretical model of signs as representation, the Port-Royal logicians found a way of elaborating a set of articulations between conventional form and natural form, transitive transparency and reflexive opacity, representation and presentation, invisibility and visibility, and absence and presence. These articulations allow the members of Port-Royal to salvage eloquent dis-

---

*I agree with Stephen Heath's rejection of "bliss" as a translation for *jouissance.* I adopt his convention of "thrill" or "climactic pleasure" for *jouissance* and "pleasure" for *plaisir* (Barthes 1977, translator's note, iv).—*Trans.*

course and the charms of the voice, along with painterly representations and their rigorously intelligible purposes or ends. To be
persuasive, the discourse of moral truth must aim at pleasing its
listener. With the help of the specific means offered by discourse,
the speaker necessarily aspires to move the hearer's sensibility by
imitating the movements of desire, by setting them in motion
and allowing them to find their realization in a beautiful form.

Thus we witness the use of a vast number of figures of speech
that were made the object of normative description by the logicians, themselves eloquent preachers who tended to use these
same figures. Most perfect among the tropes are hypotyposis and
harmony, both of which were deemed to function as stylistic
figures by virtue of their imitative dimension. Here language
evokes things so vividly and so energetically that, in a certain
sense, it makes them present to the eyes, turning a group of sentences into a veritable painting.

At the same time, the specific workings of this kind of deceptive imagery are such that these figures make known the essence
or structural truth of the thing. Images can, then, regain legitimacy, for their force can be given an ethical justification. Is not
the drawing in the painterly representation the invisible yet visible element that discloses the rational truth of pictorial mimesis to the eye of the mind? Thus the drawing is set in opposition
to the visible coloring of painting, that is, to the elements that
infuse it with its power of seduction and pleasure.

Thus, the *Logic of Port-Royal* describes a *chassé-croisé*, or back-
and-forth movement, between language and the image. Language
acquires from the image its force and mimetic form, while the
image acquires from language its normative and juridical form.
However, we also note that this movement finds a motive, if not
a basis, in a specific sign and in the utterance that produces it—in
the eucharistic sign and its consecratory utterance. By virtue of
its very production and as a result of the pragmatic nature of the
context in which it is uttered, this sign plays on both registers,
although it is always excessive vis-à-vis the one as well as the
other. With respect to language, the excesses of the eucharistic
sign are evident when the utterance that produces it ("This is my
body") is uttered by an authorized individual under appropriate
circumstances.* The sign then has the power to transform a thing

---

*Following Heath, I have translated *énoncé* as "utterance" and *énonciation* as "the

that is shown by means of the demonstrative *this* into a body that is signified by the word *body*. This body belongs, not to the person who utters the formula, but to Him whose words are cited in it, that is, Jesus Christ.

In relation to the image, the eucharistic sign is excessive in the following sense. The linguistic operation that I have just mentioned does not exercise its effects on what can be seen, touched, or felt. These effects do not make themselves evident at the level of appearances or secondary qualities, nor in the field of the visual or visible. On the contrary, the effect of the eucharistic sign is invisible. It contacts the level of being that underwrites and supports its appearances and qualities. These effects concern the substantial and opaque nature of the flesh and are realized in the mystery of the real presence of the divine body.

Elsewhere, I believe that I have shown that, in the *Logic of Port-Royal*, the issue of "real presence"—of the sacrament of the Eucharist—and of the mystery of transubstantiation is intimately connected with the problem of the sign and language. Similarly, Pietro Redondi, to cite only one source, has shown that this very same question was at the heart of the modern, scientific, and epistemological mentalities that found expression in the atomistic theories of Galileo. In both instances, although for somewhat different reasons, the relation to the theological issues is occulted for political and ideological purposes. At most it is present only obliquely, in the form of a digressive discussion of an example or as an illustration of a general analysis.

Thus we are faced with a surprising situation, one that I have studied at great length in an earlier work. In what is essentially a charter for a rational and bourgeois modernity, the problem of the sign and of language is broached only indirectly, appearing in the context of theological debates concerning the Eucharist. In addition, as a result of an inverse and symmetrical movement, the issue of real presence is raised only indirectly through a reflection on signs and words. What emerges is something like a dual evasion that itself designates a site essential to the theory of Port-Royal.

Yet the designation in question is almost entirely effaced. The

---

act of uttering." In cases where *énonciation* combines with other terms to form a phrase, the specific emphasis on the act of speaking has been preserved (Barthes 1977, translator's note, 9).—*Trans.*

problem of language and the mystery of the Eucharist, the material presentation of the idea and the incarnation of God, all
proved to be enigmatically linked to a human art of thinking. As
a result, the logicians seemed to be incapable of speaking about
either issue explicitly. Even though it was impossible for them to
thematize these questions in their work, in a certain sense, they
never stopped speaking about them.

Is the Eucharist, then, a particular instance of the problem concerning signs and words in their relation to things and ideas? Is it
not true that the problematic nature of signs and words only
acquires the status of a theoretical question by virtue of the mystery of the incarnation and as a result of the miracle of transubstantiation that is effected by the eucharistic consecration?
These questions evoke the absolutely crucial task underwriting
the project and discourse of the logicians of Port-Royal, a task to
which they nonetheless appear to have been blind. In the *Logic*,
the Eucharist makes the problem of language appear to be a particular instance of a general problem surrounding the signifying
body and the word as an efficacious force by means of which
things may be brought to articulation and transformed.

At the same time, however, the logicians were obliged to sever
their theory from its theological and mystical origins in order to
secure its full rational force. More precisely, they included this
origin within their theory and discussion, but only as an illustration of the problem that, in fact, could not have been articulated
without it. By the same token, this simultaneous effacement and
integration allowed the problem surrounding the Eucharist to
benefit—at the very least for the purposes of its polemical
solution—from the potency and generality of the theoretical
model for which it was a condition of emergence. Thus it was possible to make the eucharistic utterance appear to be nothing but
a particular application of the more general model.

I believe, then, that it is wholly appropriate to rewrite the
Logic of Port-Royal in such a way that the double effacement of
the problem of language and the eucharistic mystery will itself be
effaced, and both of these issues, as well as their relation to each
other, will be reinscribed critically and clearly within two crucial sites. One site is the altar, where signs and the divine body
are connected to each other and interlock (see Part One). At the
same time, we must not overlook the importance of all those
figures that expose and transform this mysterious relationship by
means of travesty and an altered temporality.

Ideally, in a representationalist philosophy, language does not constitute a problem. The signs are transparent with respect to the ideas that they re-present, just as the latter are translucent in relation to the things of which they are ideas. Yet this clarity of language only appears immediate and self-evident on the condition that one forgets or fails to understand that signs are also forces. They are nowhere more powerful than in the sacramental word of the Eucharist; the proposition that is uttered as part of the ritual of this institution effects the transformation of an existing thing into a produced body. It is this ontological transformation, which is at once a mystery and a miracle realized by the words of the consecration, that we shall encounter elsewhere in stories and images. Having undergone a process of displacement, metonymy, projection, or metaphorical reversal, this transformation resurfaces in the play of the voice, in the play of space, and in the complex logic of discourse and writing.

Signs re-present, but they present themselves as representing something. They are forces (see Part Two). What is the nature of this force within representation? What is the nature of the particular transformations effected by representation? Elsewhere I have characterized the particular relationship between force and representation as power. An appropriate question now is, how and following what modalities does force become power in and through representation?

Power is first and foremost a matter of being in a position to exert an action on something or someone; it does not necessarily reside in the performance of an action, in a doing, but in having the capacity to act, in having the force in reserve so that one may later be in a position to expend it. Power is also primarily the institution of strength as law, strength being construed as the capacity or potential to exercise force. It is the valorization of strength as an obligatory constraint. Representation plays a role with respect to this particular point.

Strength finds in representation at once the means of its display as well as its foundation. Yet how can representation transubstantiate force into power, except by putting force into signs and by signifying it in the discourse of the law and its institutions? In representation, the external act—in which a force manifests itself in order to annihilate another force in a struggle unto death—is replaced by signs that are so expressive and explicit that they enable the force that they signify or represent to be seen and thereby believed.

This particular understanding of how force is transubstantiated into power leads to the discovery of the philosophical and historical workings of the eucharistic model within the structuring of the imaginary and political symbolics of the absolute monarch. As a heuristic hypothesis, I propose that we consider historical narratives, panegyrics, paintings, medals, or portraits as extensions of the utterance "This is my body." Proffered by the mouth of the prince, these various representations, in their diverse modalities, are transformed into so many signs of the political sacrament of the state, as it is really present in the monarch. Furthermore, one could also imagine a kind of application of the utterance that produces the divine body as the food of the eucharistic banquet. At the court, which the members of Port-Royal considered to be largely the Church's opposite, a discourse is proffered, the only function of which is to transform language into goods, that is, money, pensions, and boons. This language addresses itself to the King, who responds with words that, within the state institution, will produce the consumable or accumulable goods.

In the final analysis, it is precisely this vast theologico-political operation that concerns me in my analyses of Perrault's tales. In my readings of these stories, I have tried to detect and construct one of the rhetorical figures for this transformational process by exploring the manifestations of what I have called the culinary sign. This sign forges a space between the image of the King and his inverted reflection in the figure of the Ogre. It opens onto a field of ingenious activity, where fairies and men interact through strategies and tactics of power and representation (see Part Three). Written toward the end of the century profoundly marked by Louis xiv, these tales seem to me to offer the most precise and most suggestive narrative expression of the theologico-political issues raised above.

To remain faithful to the Augustinian origins of the Cartesian linguistics of Port-Royal, however, we must point out one crucial aspect pertaining to the semiotics or the general science of signs that is part of this linguistic theory. It appears in the semiotics of Port-Royal by virtue of a series of oblique encounters with the motif of the Eucharist, the latter being the site in which the church institutes the miracle of an edible, divine body. As a result, this semiotic theory is intimately connected with an erotics, even if the logicians never cease to play on the Augustinian opposition between a generalized use of signs and the indivi-

dual thrill of the ultimate Good to which they refer by degrees.*
What does this imply? The body of stories underwriting the institution of Christianity, the discourses that account for its origin,
insist at one and the same time on the Incarnation and the Passion, on the oblation and the withdrawal of the divine body. As a
result of this gift and this loss, the founding divine body is posited as an object of desire. The Church, the institutional and instituted site of belief, has always thought and conceived of itself in
terms of a body that is at once a real, socio-historical body and a
mystical, divine body. Thus the body of the Church proves to be
the substitute, the delegate, the representation of the divine body
that was given and lost. By re-presenting it, the Church construes
the divine body as absent. When it is made to return or be present
once more, this body is placed in exile.

The configuration of belief surrounding the Church body thus
constitutes the latter as a desire for the real presence of the body
of God. The particular movement, force, and orientation of this
desire ultimately trace the contours of this absent presence. It is
noteworthy that the Church's canonical text casts its story about
the resurrection of the Body of Christ in the form of a discourse
that says that he is alive, but elsewhere. In this sense, we may say
that, for the members of Port-Royal as well as for Saint Augustine, the communicational usage of signs and representations is
nothing short of the manifestation of an irrepressible desire for
the intense thrill to be derived from the heavenly and divine body
that is both replaced and realized by these very signs and representations.

Once again it is apparent that the mystery of the Eucharist and
the miracle of transubstantiation are the erotic core of Port-Royal
semiotics. The displacements and transformations of the culinary sign in Perrault's *Tales* may be viewed as the figurative
traces of this desire for the divine body. This desire operates on
the borders between Logos—the word and utterance—and Eros—
pleasure and love—between a need for preservation, which is
satisfied by food, and a desire realized through the pleasures
offered by a dish or a meal. Similar observations are pertinent
with respect to the quite different domain of politics. Here we
encounter the monarch's portrait of state, a portrait that betrays
the feminine traits of a body of love through the representation of

---

*See translator's note, p. xv.

the state's power. It discloses the erotic features of a body of pleasure that is represented and proffered for the sake of sensuous
pleasure. The king's portrait is thus marked by its dual nature,
allowing politics to intertwine with aesthetics and enabling politics to function erotically.

This dual character becomes manifest, however, only when
the king of representation or the representation of the king is subjected to critical studies. Consonant with Freud's analysis of
smut, a ferocious nineteenth-century English caricature figures
within the first of our two critical essays in Part Four, even
though the caricatural image is ultimately more revealing of the
bourgeois and liberal individual's encounter with the theologico-
political body than it is of the *arcana imperii*. The second essay
explores the revelations of the *Journal of Louis xiv's Health*, a
journal containing the diagnostics of the royal doctors. This document made it possible to affirm that melancholy is the governing principle of absolute power. It reinforces historically and
medically the philosophical hypothesis that the desire for absolute power is but one type of death drive. It allows us to consider
the divine body within the royal body, in terms of an untenable
desire for a generic, psychological, pathological, and metaphysical indifference, a desire that the representation of the Sun King
never ceased to deny or occult by means of the simulacrum of
pleasure's glorious eruption.

It seems to me that the issues I have briefly sketched above provide *Food for Thought* with a guiding thread and a unity that
transcends the diversity of the essays. I have not been primarily
concerned in these readings with erecting a general theory of
power, language, or representation; that task has already been
admirably undertaken in several disciplines — psychoanalysis, history, anthropology, semantics, and philosophy. I have instead
sought to transmit the surprise and amazement that may be
derived from a careful and attentive description, summary, or
reading of certain texts and images. The essays provide the occasion for writing about my encounter with drawings, paintings,
and texts. This encounter is necessarily dialogic in nature, since
it is informed by earlier and still vital interests in speculative and
practical philosophy. This is to admit, by way of an advance
response to potential questions on the part of the reader, that the
imperatives of theory-building have sometimes been ignored and
abandoned to the pleasure of reading or writing fictions. My hope

is that these fictions will incite others to discover the paths of their own reflection.

Some of these essays have already appeared in French journals or anthologies, in some cases, quite some time ago. I would like to thank the editors who initially published them for allowing me to include them in this volume.

Last but not least, I would like to express my deepest gratitude to Mette Hjort, my translator and interpreter, who has had the delicate task of transubstantiating a French "thing" into an English "body." I am pleased to say that her performance amounts, if not to a miracle such as that of the theological sacrament, then at least to the kind of marvel that figures in the world of the fairy tale.

Louis Marin

One

Food For Thought

I The Body of the Divinity Captured by Signs

1.1. In this essay, I shall be looking at a particular moment in the history of theories that concern the nature of the sign. The moment may seem strange from the perspective of contemporary scientific attitudes. Nonetheless, since the instance in question definitely amounts to more than an ordinary event or a pure accident, it raises some important issues concerning the theory and history of semiotics. Thus, I would like to discuss the theologically inspired elaborations that were added to the fifth edition of the *Logic of Port-Royal* in 1683. Referring to these new sections in a prefatory note expressly composed for this purpose, Arnauld and Nicole are careful to point out that the appendages by no means constitute elements that are adventitious or extrinsic with respect to the *Art of Thinking*. That these elaborations were articulated in 1683 is, from a historical point of view, entirely coincidental, since the additions were inspired by some of the contentions set forth by the Protestant ministers. This does not, however, make these additions "any less essential or natural a part of Logic. And they might have been undertaken even if the world had been entirely without the Protestant Ministers who were out to obscure the truths of faith by means of false subtleties" (Arnauld and Nicole [1683], 1970, 33). The logicians of Port-Royal also insist that "these clarifications will show that reason and faith are in perfect agreement, both being streams issuing forth from a common source. Thus it would be impossible to stray from the one (that is, from reason) without also straying from the other (that is, from faith)" (Arnauld and Nicole [1683], 1970, 33).

1.2. What doctrinal issues are thus in question? Crucial aspects of Catholic dogma are at stake: the Eucharist, transubstantiation, and consubstantiation, that is, the real presence, in the form of bread and wine, of the body of Jesus Christ during the celebration of communion. At a theological level it is a matter of how we understand the main ritualistic formula that is spoken during the sacrament of the Catholic mass: "This is my body"—"*Hoc est corpus meum.*" We need to have a clear grasp of this consecratory utterance if we are to determine exactly what its effects are. The Catholic interpretation is that it miraculously and substantially transforms the nature of something—the bread and wine—without, however, altering its appearance. Elsewhere, I have tried to show that this theological model of the Eucharist had far-reaching implications in the political sphere at a time when the French monarchy was headed straight toward absolutism and the concomitant ideology of Louis xiv. I pointed out the extent to which certain ideas concerning the bodies of the king and of the state (or royal history) were indebted to the theological thrust of an utterance that finds its full effectiveness in the telling of a story, the repetition of a discourse, and the reproduction of a law. These three enunciative modalities are part of the canon of the Catholic mass at the time of consecration. The first modality finds expression through narrative representation: "Then Jesus took the bread and giving thanks, he broke it and gave it unto his disciples. . . . " The second involves a discourse of assertion: "This is my body which will be given for your sake." It is, however, the prescriptive discourse that institutes the space of the ecclesiastical community: "Take . . . eat . . . drink . . . do this in memory of me, the new Covenant of my blood."

1.3. The prefatory note to the fifth edition of *The Logic of Port-Royal* calls a specific issue to the attention of the reader of 1683, as well as to that of modern ones such as Michel Foucault and Noam Chomsky, among others (although they have not taken sufficient note of its message). The preface seeks to convey the idea that what is theological about the eucharistic utterance is also a perfectly "essential" and "natural" part of logic. In other words, that which founds belief and provides it with its instrument and its communion, the theory of the sacrament as sign, meaning, and institution, proves to be wholly compatible with logic. The theological elements in question are an essential part of the theory of the sign and of representation, of representation construed in terms of signs, and of the sign construed as representation. They are a natural part of a semantic theory, the object of which is the activity of a speaking subject who engages in the conjunctive or disjunctive construction of propositions by means of signs and representations. Finally, the theological elements are an essential part of a theory that seeks to account for the effects of meaning and of a theory of discourse in general, with specific reference to the function of discourse in relation to persuasion, belief, and the institutionalization of belief.

How is it, then, that the model provided by the consecratory utterance—"This is my body"—can be construed as co-natural with, and proper to, the logic of meaning as this logic is understood by Port-Royal? In what sense is this model an essential part of semiotic theory (a theory of semantics and pragmatics)? I would like to begin to answer this question by taking the references to "essential" features to imply the reciprocal adequation and appropriation of theology and semiotics. Thus, one might paraphrase the text from the prefatory note cited above (1.1) and suggest that history and theory harmonize perfectly since they are streams springing from a common source—it is impossible to stray from the one without straying from the other. It is, therefore, appropriate to consider the theological additions to the fifth edition of the *Art of Thinking* against the background of the logico-grammatical semiotic theory that constitutes the object of this text.

2.1. The elaborations in the fifth edition are never presented as being theological in nature. Evidence bears this out. The first section of the *Art of Thinking* is dedicated to the first of the four main operations of the mind—the act of conceiving—and to its products—representations or ideas. Chapters 4 and 15, inserted into the text of 1683, deal with both products respectively, with representations of signs as compared with representations of things, as well as with the representations or ideas that the mind adds to those which are precisely signified by words. The second section develops a theory of judgment which is construed as "the action by means of which our mind brings together diverse ideas and then either asserts that some idea is the same as another or negates this identity" (Arnauld and Nicole [1683] 1970, 59). Four

additions appear in this section, two of which are imported, with
some novel elements, from the *General Grammar*. Chapters 1
and 2 are entitled "Of Words in Relation to Propositions" and
"The Verb." The two other additions, like those of the first section, stem from the *Great Perpetuity of Faith*. Chapter 12 is entitled "Of Two Different Subjects Confounded with Each Other"
and chapter 14 is headed by a somewhat enigmatic title, "Of the
Propositions in which the Names of Things Are Bestowed on
Signs." This last chapter was already said to be important at the
end of chapter 4 of the first section which dealt with the idea of
the sign.

2.2. In each case the theological motif of the consecratory utterance appears only in an incidental way. It is invoked purely in the
manner of a random illustration, as though it were a supplement
to the semiotic definitions and typologies and to the semantic
demonstrations and pragmatic descriptions. The motif is explicitly mentioned only in chapter 12 of the fourth section, "Of What
We Know by Virtue of Faith, Be It Human or Divine," which is
dedicated to methodology and the order of reasoning in demonstrations. Thus it is in the methodological prescriptions of the
volume that the Port-Royal logicians intend to demonstrate the
way in which "theology" pertains to "logic," a claim that they set
forth in the prefatory note to the 1683 edition. More polemically,
this is where they take on the Protestant ministers and argue that
religious heresy is nothing but a particular form of rational error.
Yet the way in which theological and logical issues are articulated in the discourse of the logicians gives rise to a diametrically
opposed reading. The theological model that makes it possible to
construe the consecratory utterance according to its Catholic
interpretation turns out, in fact, to be nothing short of a royal
road leading to an understanding of one function of the sign. This
model sheds light on how the sign functions as a representation
during the act in which the speaking subject articulates a judgment. It clarifies the propositional statement in which a subject
claims that some *x* is the case about some *y*, and it elucidates the
structures pertaining to the general discourse by which a social
community of speaking subjects is instituted. In other words, the
Port-Royal logicians undertake an analysis of the utterance "This
is my body," which turns out to occupy two of the most important floors in the edifice of the *Art of Thinking*—that of representation and that of judgment. The fact that this analysis concerns

precisely this utterance, as well as the religious institution that is its context of utterability, has important consequences. For it makes possible a marked progress in general semiotic theory. This is not, however, to say that this theoretical progress could be formulated or theorized independently of this domain.

3.1. In chapter 4 of the first section, "Of the Ideas of Things and the Ideas of Signs," the Port-Royal logicians begin with a twofold definition of the sign: it is an operation by means of which the mind (that is to say, a subject) considers some object exclusively from the point of view of its representing some other object; a sign is also defined as the product of this operation that is, as an object considered uniquely with respect to its representational function. This object is called a sign. This sign, which is in fact the sign of a sign, has a corresponding representation—the idea of a sign. It is quite striking that the logicians emphasize a particular type of icon in the examples that they give of signs: "This is how we usually look at maps and pictures" (Arnauld and Nicole [1683] 1970, 80). In reformulating their definition, they once more insist on the dual aspect of the sign, on its being at once an object and an operation. The object is the product of its own operation and therefore inseparable from it—this is the first definition of the sign. The object also gives rise to the operation in question— this is the second definition of the sign. "Thus the sign includes two ideas, one of the thing that does the representing, the other of the thing represented, and it is its very nature to stimulate the second idea by means of the first" (Arnauld and Nicole [1683] 1970, 80). The essence of representation by means of signs resides in this "stimulation," as a result of which the mind is transported, or transfers itself, in the relation of representation from one pole (what represents) to the other (what is represented). The very essence of the sign is to be found in this operation, in this "metaphor" of the subject who is carried from one idea to another idea, the latter being itself contained within the first. The sign can only be thought in operation, indeed as an operation.

3.2. The logicians then go on to divide signs into three groups based on three criteria. The first is an epistemic criterion pertaining to certainty and probability. Sure and certain signs must be rigorously distinguished from probable signs; otherwise, an effect could be attributed to one cause when it is actually the effect of another. The second criterion concerns continuity and

discontinuity: some signs are conjoined with the things they signify while others are separate from them. This second classification gives rise to four maxims to which we shall refer again later.
The third criterion distinguishes between what is natural and
what is instituted: some signs do not depend on the imagination
of the human mind, while others are created, which means that
they bear no relation to the thing they represent. The words that
represent thoughts are of this order. Linguistic signs appear only
in the last few lines of this important chapter dedicated to the
ideas of signs. The chapter opens with examples typical of the
logicians of Port-Royal, with the maps and pictures that recur in
chapter 14 of the second section as the map of Italy and the portrait of Caesar or Alexander. Chapter 14 is, in fact, already announced in the last line of chapter 4: "In discussing propositions
we shall explain an important truth about these kinds of signs
(natural and institutional signs)—how it is that, on some occasions, these signs allow us to assert the reality of the things they
signify" (Arnauld and Nicole [1683] 1970, 82).

3.3. Underlying these three groups of signs is another network
consisting of a series of examples with a dual coherence. The first
type of coherence is obvious and has to do with the three binary
typologies that the examples illustrate: sure and probable; conjoined and separate; natural and institutional. The other level of
coherence is no less operative, though less conspicuous, than the
first: it concerns the theological model of the Eucharist, which
motivates and gives meaning to the series of examples. This
model is typically located between each of the three sections
mentioned.

3.4. To recapitulate, the first group consists of signs that are certain in the way that breathing is a sure sign of animal life, and
signs that are probable in the way that paleness is a probable sign
of pregnancy. The two examples involve indexical signs of the
body, the one being a sure sign, the other probable. To these examples the logicians might very well have added the one that
appears at the end of their work, in chapter 12 of the fourth section, entitled "Of What We know by Virtue of Faith, Be it Human
or Divine": "What we see clearly—by virtue of reason or the faithful recordings of the senses—when we consider things carefully
[that is, when we avoid those bold judgments that confound sure
signs with probable ones] is never contrary to what we are taught

by our faith. . . . For example, in the case of the Eucharist, our senses clearly show us whiteness and roundness" (Arnauld and Nicole [1683] 1970, 411). Yet, are the latter to be taken as sure or probable signs of the substance bread? To judge boldly would be to consider these qualities as the *temeria* of bread, rather than as its *semeia*. "Our senses do not tell us whether it is the substance of the bread that makes our eyes perceive roundness and whiteness in it; and thus our faith in no way runs contrary to the evidence provided by our senses when it informs us that these features do not belong to the substance—the body of the bread—that only previously was present, having now been changed into the body of Jesus Christ by the mystery of Transubstantiation" (Arnauld and Nicole [1683] 1970, 411).

3.5. The second group concerns signs conjoined with things. A facial expression, which is a sign of the movements of the soul, is conjoined with the very movements that it signifies. Symptoms are signs that are conjoined with the illnesses they signify. Our authors then add the following: "To employ more important examples, Noah's Ark, a sign of the Church, was conjoined to Noah and his children who at that point were the true Church; our earthly temples are signs of the faithful and frequently conjoined with them; the dove is a figure for the Holy Ghost: baptismal ablutions are a figure for a spiritual regeneration and are conjoined with this regeneration" (Arnauld and Nicole [1683] 1970, 81). The gradual transition effected in the series of examples is significant: we begin with bodily symptoms of the hidden movements of the body and soul; we are then presented with the sacred figures that reveal or effect their own meaning, as in the case of the baptismal ablutions where the effect of the sacrament is immediate, although secret. As in the previous examples, the complex and unitary space of the eucharistic model is organized in such a way that the binary oppositions pertaining to the classificatory criteria are dissolved into a mysterious unity that provides the theological and theoretical origin of their diversification. The only example of signs separated from things displays the immediate operations of the sacramental sign, that is, its hidden effects. Moreover, the example does this at the level of sacred history and its diachronic typology: "Just as the sacrifices of the ancient law, the signs of an immolated Jesus Christ, were separated from what they represented" (Arnauld and Nicole [1683] 1970, 81).

3.6.1. The four maxims that follow from this classification probably contain even more interesting examples of the sacred,
secret, and sacramentary coherence of the series. In a sense the
first maxim again takes up, though in a more precise way, the initial dichotomy between certain and probable signs: it is always
impossible to conclude with any real precision as to the presence
or absence of the thing signified on the basis of the sign's
presence. "It is necessary to judge according to the specific nature
of the sign in question" (Arnauld and Nicole [1683] 1970, 81). The
presence of the tangible signs of bread should not lead to a hasty
conclusion about the presence of the substance bread. Nor
should the presence of the signs that evoke the historical
sacrifice of Jesus on the cross lead us to conclude that he is
absent *hic et nunc* at the altar above which this history is narrated. The second maxim states that, in some cases, a thing can
do the signifying or figuring, while in others the same thing may
be what is signified or figured—although a thing in a particular
condition cannot be a sign of itself in that same condition: thus a
man in his room can represent himself preaching. This example
introduces the reflexive dimension of representation, which
implies the temporal or ontological distance between the present
moment and that of the past or future on the one hand or
between actuality and fiction or mere possibility on the other. As
a result, the same thing may be quite different now from what it
is otherwise—on the condition that this thing embrace a distinction between what represents and what is represented, thereby
giving rise to two distinct immanent states. We may add that this
is the case with the bread that figures on the table of the Last Supper and on the Church's altar, a point to which I shall return later.

3.6.2. The three examples for the third maxim reveal the possibility of such a temporal and ontological distance. The maxim
states that a thing can simultaneously hide and reveal another
thing; since a thing can be at once a thing and a sign (two different states), it can hide the very thing that it reveals in the form of
a sign. Thus the warm cinders hide the fire—that they reveal in
the form of a sign. Similarly, the forms adopted by angels concealed them as things and revealed them as signs. The eucharistic symbols, bread and wine, hide the thing that is the body of
Jesus Christ and reveal it in the form of a symbol. These three
examples—the fire, the angels, and Jesus Christ—bring together

in a single stroke a physical thing, a bodily form, and the body of the Eucharist. The result is a kind of escalating oxymoron that brings together cinders and fire, evokes the powerful symbolic connotations of death and life, and binds together the bread and wine, the body and blood of Jesus Christ. In each of the three cases, the identity of the thing is split twice. The first time, it divides into a thing and a sign; the second time, the nature of the sign requires a distinction between the thing that does the representing and the thing that is represented, even as the thing being divided is supposed to remain what it is. Moreover, the aporia—constituted by an absolute difference within an absolutely maintained identity—can only be overcome by modeling the structure of the sign-representation on that of the secret: something is indeed hidden, but not totally, for then the secret would disappear. It is crucial that some traits or marks signify, or rather indicate and signal, the fact that something is hidden. It is crucial that the secret secretes its presence: one might even say that the secret's secretion constitutes the reality of its presence. These remarks raise the question of whether or not the structure of every operative sign is derived, in one form or another, from the structure that characterizes a secret. This is so in the case of the cinders that possess the property of heat and thus reveal the fire that is hidden within them. Similarly, a dazzling gown and sudden manifestation is revelatory of a celestial messenger. But what are we to make of the eucharistic bread and wine? Is there in this case a particular mark or sign that discloses the presence of the sacramentary secret—other than the specific utterance that accompanies them and repeats another more ancient and originary utterance? What sign is there other than the accord between this repetition and the injunction to repeat the original utterance issued on that distant occasion? Does the originary utterance not found the institution of the Eucharist and render legitimate the discourse of repetition?

3.6.3. The examples for the fourth maxim provide an answer to the above questions. The essence of the sign is assumed to reside in the establishment of a scission or difference within an identity, and the idea of the sign is assumed to be a tangible and manifest metaphor, a transfer of thought from the thing that plays the role of a figure to that which is being figured or represented. Then, "as long as this effect subsists . . . the sign subsists, even if the nature of this thing is destroyed" [Arnauld and Nicole [1683]

1970, 82). Previously the opacity of the thing, the physical nature of the body, was said to hide the thing that it revealed in the form of a sign. At this point, however, the thing can cease to exist according to its true nature, as long as its image subsists. As a result of this twofold nature, this ephemeral appearance will give rise to the metaphor or transfer of thought that allows the signifying function to be achieved. Thus, "the colors of the rainbow which God gave as a sign that he would never destroy the human species in a deluge" might not exist in reality. This would not matter, however, "on the condition that our senses always receive the same impression of these colors and employ it in the conceptualization of God's promise" (Arnauld and Nicole [1683] 1970, 82). It would matter then if the bread of the Eucharist were destroyed at the level of its true nature, "as long as it always stimulates our senses in such a way that we perceive an image of bread. For this image helps us to conceive how it is that Jesus Christ is the food of our souls as well as the way in which the faithful are united amongst each other" (Arnauld and Nicole [1683] 1970, 82). The fact that this bread is a eucharistic symbol is probably not marked by anything other than the consecratory utterance which transforms it into the body of Jesus Christ. Yet the image of bread subsists, and the faithful, kneeling before the communion table, eat this bread as the body of a truly present Jesus Christ. This manducation is itself a sign, although this does not mean that the bread is taken to be a figure for the body of Jesus Christ. Rather, it is a sign that the body of Jesus Christ is food for the soul, that He is the mystical body of the Church and of the community of the faithful—their social body.

3.6.4. The eucharistic model does indeed reveal the profound coherence of the network of examples illustrating the semiotic theory of Port-Royal—at least as this theory is outlined in the general definition of the sign as representation and in the classifications which categorize the signifying function. I have been trying to articulate the eucharistic model on the basis of this network of examples. We saw that the model possesses an astonishing semiotic productivity, since it can function on all registers pertaining to signs, as well as on the borders between the registers. Yet it is striking that while this model turns out to be an exceptional semiotic matrix, it leaves what is essential indeterminate. That is, it leaves undetermined the linguistic utterance by which a thing is destroyed as a thing in order to become something else, even as it maintains its outward appearance during the entire process. The process in question involves yet another dimension: it allows the thing that is being transformed to become at once a sign of the transformation that its own specific substance undergoes, as well as a sign of the symbolic and real effects that it produces with respect to those individuals who consume it and with respect to the communal group that they form.

3.7. The third group includes natural and institutional signs, and establishes an opposition between specular images and the words that make up language. It is not surprising that the text refers only to specular images and words: the specular image is present as the typical example of the natural sign, of which maps and pictures had initially been proffered as derivate examples; and words are presented as primitive semantic and lexical units, as the component elements of the minimal discursive unit that we call the sentence (the proposition or judgment). Yet the problem that is raised in the last few lines of the chapter, only to be set aside for the second section, is none other than that which the consecratory utterance of the Eucharist presents for the logical and grammatical theory of Port-Royal. Much like the eucharistic symbols, this utterance situates itself on the boundaries between various sign typologies. It operates and produces its meaning on the boundary between those utterances that involve natural signs and those that involve institutional signs and on the boundary between the discourse that produces icons, such as the map and the portrait, and that which produces the tropes of language.

Now we will establish more precisely the matrical space of the theologico-semiotic model before proceeding further with our analysis of the consecratory utterance.

4.1. Chapter 15 of the first section treats "Of the Ideas which the Mind Adds to Those which are Precisely Signified by Words." These ideas are derived from what the logicians called "accessory ideas" in the previous chapter. Arnauld and Nicole had taken note of the fact that, when words are employed according to the common usage that makes up ordinary discourse, "they often mean more than they would seem to mean" (Arnauld and Nicole [1683] 1970, 130). "When the meaning of a word is to be explained, the totality of the impressions to which it gives rise is not recalled. . . . It is frequently the case that a word, besides giving rise to the main idea that is considered to be its specific meaning,

also stimulates several other ideas that might be referred to as
accessory ideas. We do not pay attention to these ideas, even if
the mind does receive their imprint" (Arnauld and Nicole [1683]
1970, 130). Accessory ideas not only include the connotative meanings "which come to be attached to words by virtue of ordinary
usage" (Arnauld and Nicole [1683] 1970, 130), but also the meaningful impressions that accompany the tone of a voice, facial expressions, gestures, and so on. In short, these ideas refer to a level of
meaning that could be said to mark the emergence of the body
within the functioning of language and of bodily practices within
linguistic exchanges. The Port-Royal logicians, who are also moralists, elaborate an exceptionally subtle and poignant analysis,
with great theoretical import, of this aspect of language.

4.2. Chapter 15 tends, however, to develop the notion of an accessory idea along different lines. Unlike chapter 14, it does not orient its analysis toward linguistic connotation and its "unhinged"
semantic structures; instead, the discussion focuses on deictics,
particularly on those which are demonstrative. In the category of
demonstrative deictics, the neutral "first person" deictic is
brought to the fore. An example of this is *hoc*, or *this*, its English
equivalent. The Port-Royal logicians undertake a study of one of
the crucial elements of the formal apparatus of speech which, in
turn, is the basis of any semantico-pragmatic theory of discourse.
Their analysis is not, however, motivated by linguistics alone. It
is quite clear that the specification of the nature and meaning of
neutral deictics was important to a theology of the Eucharist in
which *hoc (this)* figures as the first term in its formal ritual. In
other words, the Port-Royal logicians lay the bases for a theory of
speech while simultaneously developing a linguistic theology of
the Eucharist.

4.3. Even if accessory ideas were to insinuate themselves into the
functioning of the demonstrative and neutral deictic, into *hoc*, or
this, it would clearly have to be in a different sense than that of
connotative meanings. In the system of language, it is probably
true that *hic, haec, hoc* and *iste, ista, istud* all belong to the
formal and functional class of pronouns like *ille, illa, illud*, much
like other nominal or verbal forms. Yet *hoc* is to be opposed to
both referring nouns and lexical notions, for there exists between
these elements a fundamental difference derived from the very
process of speaking itself. As in the case of personal pronouns—*I*

and *you*, the signs of the first and second person—an utterance that contains *hoc (this)* belongs to the type of speech that includes a reference to the sign-users within the signs themselves. More precisely, to cite Benveniste, in the case of a demonstrative pronoun, "the identification of the object is effected by means of an ostensive indicator that is concomitant with the discursive instance containing the personal indicator. The latter will be what is designated ostensively at the very moment of speaking, the reference that is implicit within the form (*hoc* as opposed to *istud*) of the utterance and which connects it to an *'I,'* or a *'you'*" (Benveniste 1966, 253). The only point of contact between a theory of neutral demonstratives and that of the ideas that the mind carelessly adds to the meaning of words is to be found in what the Port-Royal logicians call the notion of usage.

4.4. "It frequently happens that the mind, having conceived of the precise meaning that corresponds to a given word, nonetheless does not settle on this meaning if it is too confused or too general. Looking more closely, the mind avails itself of the possibility of considering once more the other attributes and other aspects that are present *in the object that is represented to it* [my emphasis]. Thus the mind may conceptualize the object by means of ideas which are clearer" (Arnauld and Nicole [1683] 1970, 136). Thus *hoc (this)*, the meaning of which is "the thing present," "is a very confused and very general attribute of every object, for it is only to nothingness itself that the word 'thing' cannot be applied" (Arnauld and Nicole [1683] 1970, 136). Consequently, "when the word 'this' is used to show a diamond, the mind is not content to construe it merely as a thing that is present, and it adds the idea of a hard substance and that of brilliance" (Arnauld and Nicole [1683] 1970, 136). The logicians pursue their analysis by underscoring the different ways in which these various ideas might be construed. The idea of a "thing that is present" is construed as the specific meaning of the word *this*, while the other ideas are "supplementary and additional." For the latter vary, depending on "the different substances to which the word *hoc* is made to refer" (Arnauld and Nicole [1683] 1970, 137), examples being a diamond, wine, or bread. The idea signified in the mind is probably given rise to by the word *this* in, for example, its application to a diamond, just as are the ideas of a hard substance and brilliance. While the latter ideas may be sparked by *this*, "they are not indicated with any precision by the pronoun *hoc*, for the

mind simply conceives these ideas as being connected and identified with the first main idea" (Arnauld and Nicole [1683] 1970,
137)—that of a diamond. In every instance in which it is used, *this*
has as its meaning "the thing which is present." The accessory
qualities attributed to a diamond will, however, vary from case to
case. On this point the logicians oscillate between two alternatives: drawing a metalinguistic distinction between the meaning
and the reference of an utterance on the one hand, and integrat-
ing or equating the two psycholinguistically on the other. This
oscillation betrays their desire to ensure that the speaker has at
his or her disposal the knowledge necessary for speaking. It simultaneously gives expression to an observation that this knowledge
can be had only once speech has been made the subject of an analysis. At that point the elements that make up speech can no
longer be said to subsist uniquely in speech or in thought.

4.5. There exists, however, an exception to what was said about
the pronoun *hoc* above. It is in the use to which *this* is put in the
utterance "This is my body." The two strata of meaning constitutive of "this" are, in fact, revealed by the proposition in which it
is uttered. For "this"—which means "the thing which is present"—
is subject to two successive determinations: at the beginning of
the proposition, it is clearly determined as "bread" and, at the
end, as "my body." The contradiction to which the Protestant
ministers point and which they seek to resolve through metaphor and heresy, turns out not to be a contradiction at all. From
the beginning to the end of the utterance of the eucharistic formula, the word *this*, which is the subject of the proposition, maintains its general and confused meaning as "the thing which is
present." At the outset of the utterance, however, an additional
meaning attaches itself to the primary meaning. The word *this*
receives the additional determination of "bread," thanks to the
unique context in which it is uttered. By the end of the utterance,
this additional determination has been replaced by another, that
of "my body." Elsewhere I have tried to analyze the semantic and
pragmatic problems that arise as a result of this particular interpretation of the eucharistic utterance. The most important is probably the replacement of the thing bread, which is only indicated
in the context of speech, by the word *body*, which is actually signified by the utterance. The problems raised by this substitution
are not discussed by the Port-Royal logicians. Is the copula ade-

quate to the task of bringing about this surreptitious assimilation of what is signified to what is merely indicated? Does not the analysis elaborated in the *Logic* ultimately tend to suggest quite the opposite? It seems to imply the effacement of what is indicated—of this "other" to language—by a reversion to language in its capacity of representing things. In the second part of the proposition, the word *body* appears, and thus what comes to replace the indexically indicated bread is a body in the form of an uttered term. It would seem that the body as word is given to be eaten. Thus in the case of this Christian utterance, we would be confronted once again with the aporias that surround the idea of a language attaching itself to the things that it signifies, aporias already encountered by the Pre-Socratics: "When you say the word *chariot*, a chariot comes out of your mouth." However, I now believe that it is the presence of the first person possessive adjective—the word *my*, which refers to the very moment of speech—in the second part of the proposition that allows the Port-Royal logicians to circumvent this critique. While the word *body* does indeed remain an uttered word and a lexical signified throughout, the word *my* or *mine* is a deictic term which points to the person who utters the proposition, "This is my body," in the here and now.

5.1. The foregoing remarks make it clear that the Port-Royal logicians must undertake their construction of a theologico-semiotic model at the level of an analysis of predicative propositions. For such propositions involve judging, which is the second and perhaps most crucial of the mind's operations. In a proposition, one idea or representation is predicated of another idea or representation. In the present context, however, we cannot discuss at length chapters 1 and 2 of the second section of the *Art of Thinking*, which is where the logicians elaborate a theory of propositions based on their *General Grammar*. They focus on precisely what constitutes the active core of a proposition: the verb, "a word which is used primarily in assertions, that is, in order to indicate that the speech in which this word is employed is that of a subject who not only conceives of things, but also judges or makes assertions about them" (Arnauld and Nicole [1683] 1970, 150). In the theory of Port-Royal, all verb phrases are subject to a triple reduction: the first reduction involves limiting them to the verb *to be*, the second, to the present indicative; and the third, to the third person singular. Thus, *it is* becomes the primary core of the propositional phrase, and all other determinations of person, time, gender, and number are grafted onto this basic phrase. All other modalities of speech and all other semantic features become grammatical derivates of "it is."

5.2. At any level of analysis, this triple reduction reveals an extraordinary logico-grammatical attempt on the part of the Port-Royal logicians to seek a Cartesian transcendental deduction of the truth of being, which would be based on the representation of a thinking subject and its representations. They seek this deduction within the structures of language and the actual functioning of signs and speech. Through its exclusive concentration on the verb *to be*, the first reduction indicates that every propositional occurrence of the copula serves a dual purpose. It signals the conjunction of two representations, and it effects an operation whereby the phrase acquires a truth value and the weight of an ontological thesis. And behind these propositional acts and operations is a subject speaking in the here and now. This is the thrust of the second reduction, which makes the present indicative the model for all the other temporal modalities that a verb can take on. The present indicative form signals the presence of a subject "who not only conceives of things, but also judges or makes assertions about them" (Arnauld and Nicole [1683] 1970, 150). On the other hand, the third reduction of the verb—to the third person of the present tense—effaces the asserting and judging and allows being in general to appear or emerge suddenly through the neutrality of an *it is*. Thus the determinations asserted by this subject cease to figure as the mere representations of a judging mind and become instead the articulations of things in their full objectivity. At this point the following will be obvious: the consecratory utterance "This is my body," as it is articulated within a Catholic religious community (that is, universally), provides the model, paradigm, and matrix for every other sentence (for all propositions and judgments). This much is clear from the way in which the Port-Royal logicians analyze what constitutes the active core of every sentence—the verb.

5.3. Two points discussed in chapters 12 and 14 of the second section are worth emphasizing. The first concerns the function of the third person in the present indicative of the verbal form *is*. The second concerns the metaphorical and, more generally, the figurative capacity that is inscribed within the semantic and syntaxical structures of language. These two issues are potentially contained in the definition that the Port-Royal logicians provide for the act of judging: "The action by means of which our mind brings together diverse ideas and asserts that some idea is the same as another." What status should we accord to the *is* in "This is my body"? Is it a figure of speech or reality?

6.1. The issue raised in chapter 12, "Of Two Different Subjects Confounded with Each Other," seems to be straightforward and ordinary. It concerns a common use of language and has to do with the subject of a proposition. The same term can often refer to two different subjects. "This water, we say in speaking of a river, was muddy a few days ago and now it is clear as crystal. But is it really the same water?" (Arnauld and Nicole [1683] 1970, 194). In response the logicians cite Seneca (who cites Heraclitus): "We never set foot in the same stream twice. The same name 'stream' remains; the water, however, flowed by" (Arnauld and Nicole [1683] 1970, 194).

6.2. The elegant solution of referring to what is permissible in ordinary speech, as well as to the authority of common usage, gave rise to one of Pascal's most striking reflections: "A town or a landscape from afar are a town and a landscape, but as one approaches, it becomes houses, trees, tiles, leaves, grass, ants, ants' legs, and so on, *ad infinitum. All that is comprehended in the word 'landscape'"* (my emphasis) (Pascal 1966, 48 [no. 65]). The relation between the noun phrase—*landscape*—and the thing—landscape—is such that the former designates the latter in a single word. Yet what is designated by the noun gradually dissolves into an infinite proliferation of signifieds that ought to have analytically determined the noun's meaning. Asking what a given sign means thus involves a certain risk. It may turn out to be impossible to specify its meaning because the sign designates and loses itself in an infinite flux of being. By virtue of its "comprehending" ability, a word can put a stop to this flux and capture it in a single signifying term which, in ordinary speech, roughly signifies what is presented in perception from a distance. The *Art of Thinking* replaces Pascal's metaphysical analysis with a descriptive assertion: "It sometimes happens that two or more things, bearing some resemblance to each other, pass through the same place in succession. And particularly when these things exhibit no visible differences, people do not, when speaking about them in ordinary language, distinguish between them. Although these things might be distinguished by speaking metaphysically [like Pascal], people bring them all together beneath a single common idea which neither reveals their differences nor indicates what they have in common. Thus these things are spoken of as though they were the selfsame thing" (Arnauld and Nicole [1683] 1970, 194).

6.3. At bottom, the object of Pascal's reflection is quite different from that of the citation from the *Logic*. Pascal considered the infinite analysis of a thing within a field of reference that is signified by a single noun. The Port-Royal citation, on the other hand, deals with a temporal succession that occurs in the same place. All the examples given by the logicians dwell equally on some kind of change, a coming into being and passing away, or a succession in time: a cold wind that becomes warm; the river's water, muddy two days ago and clear now; the body of an animal, which was composed of certain bits of matter ten years ago and is now composed of quite different bits. "One says of a town, of a house, or village that it was destroyed at one moment in time and rebuilt at another" (Arnauld and Nicole [1683] 1970, 195). Thus "Caesar said that he had found a Rome built of bricks and that he left it in stone. . . . The word 'Rome' seems to be a single subject in the sentence, but it does nonetheless refer to two which are actually distinct [the Rome built in brick at the outset of Caesar's reign and the Rome made of marble at the end of his reign]. Yet the word brings both subjects together beneath a confused idea of Rome, which has as a consequence that the mind does not detect any difference between these two subjects" (Arnauld and Nicole [1683] 1970, 195). Two different subjects that bear the same name successively occupy the same place. The shared noun is a sign representing a confused idea that, to a certain extent, neutralizes the real time pertaining to the genesis and transformation of things. This temporality is, however, very precisely accounted for by the utterances that are given as examples.

6.4. Now, what of the chapter's last example, the proposition "This is my body"? This phrase is at the origin of all the other examples. The logicians want it to be the abbreviated equivalent of the proposition, "This is what is bread at this moment is my body at another" (Arnauld and Nicole [1683] 1970, 196). Is the latter proposition, in turn, comparable to "this water that was muddy two days ago is clear today"? I do not think that this is the case. The temporalities in question are not homogeneous. The proposition in the last example describes a temporal succession of states pertaining to the same thing. This is also true of the rewritten form of the consecratory utterance which the logicians propose. On the other hand, the proposition "This is my body" describes the unique condition of a thing present in the here and now. It describes a single present moment of "real" time.

6.5. The *Art of Thinking* does not, however, discuss the temporal simultaneity of the consecratory utterance. Instead, it emphasizes the time that it takes to utter the proposition "This is my body." Saying these four words occurs over a period of time that has a beginning ("this"), a middle ("is"), and an end ("my body"). By the time the speaker utters *my body, this* will already have been uttered at some past moment. *This* begins to slip into the past precisely when *is* is uttered, because *is* orients itself toward a future utterance, *my body*. As a result, the *is*, a tiny slice of the present that figures in the speaking of an utterance, becomes much more than a mere copula connecting two representations, the indicator by means of which a proposition acquires a certain truth value and quantification. It is an infinite slice of actual presence. At the moment it is uttered, it destroys the *this* (which is bread) and allows for the advent of the divine body.

6.6. If this interpretation is correct, then it follows that in the case of the proposition "This is my body," and only in this case, the time that it takes to utter the phrase generates the real presence that it describes. The temporality in question involves a past *(this)* and a future *(my body)* which respectively figure before and after the *is* that constitutes the central part and present tense of the utterance. The time that it takes to speak the consecratory phrase—this tiny and yet infinite slice of presence—produces the real presence of the divine body in what it also destroys—in what is indicated by *this*. In this sense, and only this sense, the logicians are right to assimilate the time that it takes to speak the utterance "This is my body" to the real time of the utterances that figure in their preceding examples. Since "This is my body" is a paradigmatic utterance, it provides an articulation of time itself as it pertains to any proposition.

7.1. Arnauld and Nicole conclude chapter 12 as follows: "Moreover, we do not here purport to decide the important issue of whether the words 'This is my body' should be understood in a figurative or literal sense" (Arnauld and Nicole [1683] 1970, 197). This question will be the topic of chapter 14 of the second section, "Of the Propositions in which Signs Are Named after Things." Chapter 14 announces an important truth that is part of the conclusion to chapter 4 of the first section, which dealt with the differences between natural and institutional signs. Standing before a portrait of Caesar or a map of Italy, one can "offhandedly blurt out": "That is Caesar, that is Italy." "The visible relation" that exists between Caesar and his portrait, or between Italy and a map of Italy, "clearly indicates that when one asserts that the sign [the portrait, the map] is the signified thing [Caesar, Italy] one does not mean to say that the sign in question really is the thing that it signifies [that the portrait of Caesar really is Caesar, the map of Italy really Italy]. What is meant is that the sign is the thing in a figurative sense" (Arnauld and Nicole [1683] 1970, 205). Moreover, the utterance "That is Caesar," spoken in front of a portrait of Caesar, is triply or quadruply figurative. The phrase involves three different tropes: It is like a metaphor because there exists a real or supposed resemblance between the portrait and its model. The phrase is metonymic as a result of the manifest relation between the existence of a certain kind of portrait and the person of whom it is a portrait. It also involves an individualizing synecdoche (*autonomasis*); the utterance allows the spectator of a portrait (a generic noun) to designate it with the proper name pertaining to the individual whom it represents (Caesar).

7.2. In chapter 14, unlike some earlier chapters, the Port-Royal logicians show little interest in providing a linguistic description of semantic and syntaxical usage. They concentrate instead on articulating a rule, or rather a norm that would specify when one can rightfully bestow the names of things on signs. This is a natural right when confronted with a natural sign, such as a portrait or a map. To say the name "Caesar" upon seeing his portrait is to say that the portrait looks like him. Moreover, this utterance specifies that the portrait owes its existence to its model and that, in some sense, the latter's name is inscribed within it. On the other hand, in the case of institutional signs, it is necessary to establish a norm that regulates their usage. In the case under consideration, what must be regulated are the words which themselves "do not display a visible relation to the meaning that is intended by these propositions" (Arnauld and Nicole [1683] 1970, 205). For the Port-Royal logicians, the rule in question is a common-sense maxim: "Signs should only be given the names of things under the following conditions: when it can be rightfully assumed that the former already are considered to be signs, and when it is evident that the minds of other people are at a loss as to what the signs mean" (Arnauld and Nicole [1683] 1970, 208).

7.3 The conditions specified by the above maxim typically obtain in the case of dreams, oniric fantasies, figurative stories, and visions. More precisely, those who hear the words that are part of these experiences consider them not only to be representations of things, but also to be signs or figures of other things. Hence, Nebuchadnezzar's question to Daniel: "What is the meaning of the statue with the golden head which appeared in my dream?" To which Daniel quite reasonably responds: "You are the head of gold." "What do these bones mean?" says Ezekiel to God, who replies: "These bones are the house of Israel." The representation pertaining to the system of language—the word that is a sign—is perceived as a twofold sign. The words *head of gold* refer to a head of gold; yet this sign has two dimensions, for it is both what is referred to figuratively and the vehicle by which this figurative reference is achieved. As a result, the head of gold is a figure for Nebuchadnezzar. This figurative meaning is acquired in the context of a story about a dream, as well as a request from the human agent who experiences the dream that it be interpreted. This can be a kind of supplementary meaning but not an accessory idea in the way the Port-Royal logicians employ the term. In fact, the case more closely resembles one in which one thing reveals a second thing as a sign, while concealing it as a thing. The only difference is that, in this case, the whole transaction takes place at the level of signs themselves. One sign hides another first-level sign that it then reveals in the form of a second-level sign or figure. The problem raised by this chapter is that of figurative speech itself. It concerns metaphor, metonymy, synecdoche, all the tropes that do not give themselves away by any tidy little sign indicating a comparison (Nebuchadnezzar is like a head of gold). Nor do these tropes employ any of the ancient and enduring practices that would neatly disclose their presence, such as the laurel leaf as a figure of victory or the olive as one of peace. It is equally remarkable that in the *Art of Thinking* the Port-Royal logicians consider the problem of figurative speech exclusively from the point of view of a linguistic exchange. The tropes figure within various dialogic structures, which justify their use or non-use. It is these structures, and the way in which they function, that provide the rules specifying normative usage. A partner in conversation may already consider certain words to be figures for something else, without knowing exactly what. If the person speaking knows or can reasonably guess what they stand for, then he or she is in the position to give "the names of things to these signs." In other words, when it is a question of speaking, the poet is the interpreter of language.

7.4. "It is with the aid of these principles that we must decide the important issue of whether a figurative meaning can be attributed to the words 'This is my body'" (Arnauld and Nicole [1683] 1970, 209). The response is brief. "Since the Apostles did not consider the bread to be a sign and since they were not at a loss as to what it meant, Jesus Christ could not have attributed the names of things to signs without speaking in a manner contrary to the usage of all persons and without deceiving them" (Arnauld and Nicole [1683] 1970, 209). Jesus addresses a proposition to his disciples, beginning with the word *this*. As far as the disciples are concerned, this word indicates bread and nothing else at the moment it is uttered. By the end of the utterance, the bread—having been essentially destroyed as bread at the moment when the word *is* is spoken—has become the body of the person who utters the words *this is*. The sense is therefore literal; otherwise, Jesus Christ would have to be included among those fools and madmen who "without having given anyone notice of it, take the liberty of attributing to these imagined signs the name of signified things, for example, by calling a stone a horse, and a donkey the king of Persia" (Arnauld and Nicole [1683] 1970, 206). This is the horrible blasphemy of the Protestants, and it must be condemned in the name of the universal and natural rationality of speech and by means of the criteria of linguistic reason. One might even say that the universal rule of linguistic usage, the "catholic" norm governing everyday speech, is at once the mark of the greatest miracle in the world, as well as the rational proof of its truth and reality: the sign of an incarnated God who lives in the Eucharist among humanity and until the end of time. "As a result of these principles the whole Earth, all the nations in the world, became naturally disposed to understand the words "This is my body" literally and to rule out their figurative interpretation" (Arnauld and Nicole [1683] 1970, 209).

7.5. No doubt. By the end of the utterance, the bread indicated by the word *this* has been essentially destroyed as bread, and the divine body of Jesus is really present on the communion table and ready to be eaten at the banquet of the universal ecclesiastical community. It is no less true that there is still bread and wine on this table upon the completion of the eucharistic utterance. However, this bread and wine are no longer things, but signs instead. They are a kind of sign-thing that hides the body of Jesus Christ as a thing and reveals it as a symbol. More precisely, the bread and wine belong to those signs that are nothing more than the appearances or mere images of things. Thus the image of bread "helps us to conceive of the way in which the body of Jesus Christ is the food of our souls and of how the faithful are united among themselves" (Arnauld and Nicole [1683] 1970, 82). The act of uttering the eucharistic formula, words, and institutional signs has the power to make truly present on the altar a new and miraculous thing—the body of Jesus. Once this has occurred the thing indicated by the word *this*—the bread—becomes a sign or image, a natural sign that no longer depends on human imagination. This transformation is a kind of retroactive effect of the word *body*.

8. Thus the eucharistic body turns out to be the matrix of all signs, be they *phusei* or *thesei*—but only as a result of the uttering of the proposition that integrates signs into the unity of a sentence. We have seen in what sense the theological body can be said to be the semiotic function itself. Moreover, we have clarified how it was possible in 1683 for the Port-Royal logicians to believe that there existed a perfect adequation between the Catholic dogma of consubstantiation on the one hand and a semiotic theory of meaningful representation on the other.

Two

Eat,
Speak,
and
Write

2 "Donkey-Skin," or Orality

At the end of his narrative poem, "Donkey-Skin," Charles Perrault makes the following ambiguous declaration:

> The Tale of Donkey-Skin is hard to Believe,
> But as long as the World has its Children,
> Mothers, and Grandmothers,
> The Tale will be Recalled.

On the one hand, Perrault presumptuously attributes immortality to his own creation, since he expects generation upon generation of mothers and grandmothers to read it to their children. On the other hand, his statement also refers to the oral tale that readers already know, since they have heard it told again and again by their own mothers and grandmothers. Even before they read Perrault's poem, the tale is indelibly engraved in their memory.

This ambiguity is that of the paradox characterizing oral tales and written poems or stories. Writing down an oral tale ensures its recollection at a future moment, when it will again be repeated orally. The memory of the tale is preserved in the infrangible monument of signs which the writer erects through writing. Yet this monument can be erected only because its written signs repeat what was already inscribed in a memory far more ancient than the signs themselves. In other words, the tale that Perrault commits to paper is the *terminus ad quem* of a narrative orality, which is based on the permanence of the inscription of the tale in memory. Without this inscription, the tale

could not be repeated. In this sense, Perrault's version of the story
is but one among many, just one re-writing of the inscription.

In addition, however, Perrault's tale is also the *terminus a quo*
constituting the basis for a narrative orality. The guarantor of the
latter is the poem that Perrault has finished writing, for it functions as the condition for the tale's inscription within his own
future memory.

*There is the tale called "Donkey-Skin," which I was told as a
child. There is no written text, because I have not yet written
down any part of the text, even though I have begun to compose
it in my mind. It is a story that I have already told, a story that
itself is nothing more than the repetition of what I myself was
once told a long time ago, even though I cannot remember the
moment when I first heard it, nor where or when it happened. It
is as though I had always known this tale. There is no written
text to date because everything is always already written down;
there is no written text to date because nothing was ever nor is
ever really written down.*

*And if I today write down what I once told to others, it is only
because I have been able to situate myself in the unspecifiable
space that marks the indiscernible difference separating what is
oral from what is written.*

Perrault placed himself in that space toward the end of the seventeenth century when he began to write the story of "Donkey-
Skin." My aim in retelling and repeating the story of this tale is
twofold: I wish to demonstrate that Perrault occupied that site;
and I want to point out that he deposited certain signs within the
narrative which indicate that he was aware of occupying this particular space.

The following interpretation is part of a larger study that I dedicated to Perrault's verse rendition of "Donkey-Skin," which was
written in 1694 and published in 1695 in a thin little booklet. The
booklet included two other tales, "Griselda" and "Ridiculous
Wishes," and a very interesting preface. The present study is limited to the tale as it was written down and published in Perrault's
text, with a prologue and a moral that extracts the lessons of the
tale for the reader's benefit. In this sense, what follows is not a
comparative study, but simply a re-reading of a text. This discus-

sion will also be limited to those aspects of the earlier study that seem to me to have some bearing on the issue of orality. The reasons for this are both external and internal to the tale.

First, it should be pointed out that the name of the tale already figures in other literary texts written and published before 1694. Scarron mentions it in *Le Virgile travesti* and the *Roman comique*, Molière refers to it in *Le Malade imaginaire*, and La Fontaine writes in "The Power of Fables":

> Were I, as I draw this moral,
> To be told the story of "Donkey-Skin"
> I would experience a great pleasure.
> It is said that the world is old; yet I still believe
> That it should be amused just like a child.

This citation introduces the most crucial part of my thesis. I have shown elsewhere that it is not a coincidence that La Fontaine chose to cite this particular tale at the end of a fable dedicated to the power of fables and tales in general. Although the storehouse of potential tales available for citation was immense, La Fontaine settled on "Donkey-Skin."

Perrault repeatedly states, in his preface, that "Donkey-Skin" is an oral tale "told every day to Children by their Governesses and Grandmothers." There is further evidence for this point in other passages as well. At the end of the preface, "the witty young Lady," whom Perrault presents as the privileged reader of his tale, writes the following:

> The Tale of Donkey-Skin is here told
> With such simplicity
> That I derived no less pleasure from it
> Than when, around the fire, my Nurse or my Governess
> Would enchant my mind by telling it.

In the poem's last verse, which was cited above and makes up the moral of the tale, Perrault explicitly attributes the telling and reciting of the tale to certain persons occupying a very particular position within the seventeenth-century French family: to a young child's mother and, more frequently, his or her grandmother, governess, nurse, or godmother. The child to whom the story was told would typically be so young that it would not yet possess the right to speak or write.

It is even more noteworthy that Perrault and others should have implicitly underscored the fact that "Donkey-Skin" is not just one tale among others, but rather the very paradigm of the oral and popular tale in general. In those days, people spoke of "Donkey-Skin tales" or "Donkey-Hide tales" in the same way that we speak now, as they did then, of fairy tales. "Donkey-Skin" is a strange tale indeed, one that we are told is "hard to believe." As a kind of master tale, "Donkey-Skin" stands for the genre of oral tales as a whole, for we note that the title of this tale is employed as a generic term.

A fourth reason for focusing exclusively on "Donkey-Skin" has to do with the importance that I attach to the care with which Perrault seeks to justify the writing of this tale. In the preface to the little book of three tales, as well as in the prologue to "Donkey-Skin," Perrault tries to legitimate the writing down of oral tales in general, by way of reference to the particular case of "Donkey-Skin" (it should be noted that our author does not speak of the other two tales in these terms). Perrault's justifications invoke and square off against the norms and values pertaining to the learned literature of the age of Louis XIV. He emphasizes the educational value that arises from the pleasure such a tale can elicit. He insists on the universal and national value of the tale, in comparison to the then-prevalent norm of imitating ancient Greek and Latin texts. The controversy between the Ancients and the Moderns, which Perrault will help instigate at the end of the seventeenth century, is not far off. In 1694 there is already polemicizing along these lines: "Some persons who purport to be serious and who have enough intelligence to understand that these tales were designed for pleasure and do not treat of very important matters, look on them with contempt." This is not, however, the reaction of persons with good taste, for the latter were quick to point out that "these trifles were not as trifling as they might seem."

> They contained within them a useful moral, wrapped in a playful story which had been chosen to help it enter the mind all the more pleasantly, and in a manner conducive to the instruction and pleasure of all aspects of the person. . . . Yet since I am contending with people who will not be satisfied by reasons, and who are swayed only by authority and by example, I intend to accommodate them on that score. The Milesian fables, so famous among the Greeks, were no different in kind from the Fables in this collection. . . . Since I have before me such beautiful models from a wise and learned Antiquity, I do not believe that anybody has the right to level any reproach at me. I would even contend that my fables are more worthy of being told

than are most of the ancient Tales. . . . All that can be said is that most of the ancient fables in our possession were designed exclusively to please, irrespective of good morals, which were much neglected by the Ancients. The same is not true of the tales which our ancestors invented for their Children. . . .

The historical and social conditions that governed learned literary writing when Perrault wrote "Donkey-Skin"—a tale that is a paradigm of "popular" storytelling—was extensively regulated by constraints, rules, norms, and values. Perrault had a lengthy career as a man of power. From 1663 on, he was secretary to the "little Academy" and advisor to Colbert, the superintendent of the King's Buildings. For almost twenty years, Perrault was an administrator with political power in all areas of culture. In 1683, he was excluded from the center of power and forced to write from a position of marginality. Nonetheless, he continues to refer to the inner circle in occasional works (he dedicates an ode to the Dauphin on the fall of Philisburg in 1688, another to the king on the fall of Mons in 1691, and another to the king in 1693). At the same time his writings concern the limits of political power and the dominant culture.

The writing of an oral tale thus serves the dual function of reproducing the writing of political power as well as its limits. In writing down such a tale, the author (that is, the one who writes down the tale) takes the role and occupies the place that the tale traditionally (institutionally) reserves for a grandmother or nurse. At the same time, the author occupies the position of the father in relation to the child (the reader). In this way, the author becomes the transcendental instance of authority within the familial sphere.

Yet in the same gesture the author also substitutes for the King, who is a kind of originary author of all written cultural production. The author replaces the royal principle and provides a different principle of written textual production, since he is only transcribing oral tales that grandmothers and nurses have always already recounted "by the fireside." As "father," Perrault writes what grandmothers, governesses, and nurses have always already said to a child around the hearth in a maternal sphere. Yet as "substitute king," he rewrites or repeats in written form the oral stories told within this sphere, that which the maternal voice has told since time immemorial. This dual substitution establishes "Donkey-Skin" as a master or paradigmatic tale, because it tells the story of a King who is also a Father. It is a story about a Royal

Father's entanglements with his daughter, with his wife, who is the mother of his child, and with the child's godmother.

A twofold tension emerges. There is tension between the Father who is an author, and the maternal and oral narrative instance. There is also the tension between the absolute King, the originary author of all writing, and the substitute king who rewrites what the maternal voice already has always said. This dual tension manifests itself in the preface to the book of three tales in two cases where "Donkey-Skin" occupies a central place in the discussion.

In the first instance, Perrault emphasizes that the oral tale embodies an educational strategy vis-à-vis the child to be educated. The tale deploys a strategy of power pertaining to social morality and brings it to bear on "infantile" minds and imaginations: "Is it not praiseworthy that Fathers and Mothers, when their Children are still incapable of savoring the pure and unseasoned truth, make them swallow and even love this truth, by wrapping it up in pleasurable stories that suit their age. These stories are like seeds that one sows. At first, they only give rise to movements of joy and sadness, but they never fail in the end to blossom into good inclinations." Here, the metaphorical vocabulary serves as a cover for a discourse of power. The vocabulary concerns food and growth, but we clearly note the symbolic import of these words with respect to questions concerning orality and writing. These terms belong to a discourse of power and are typical of power as such. Moreover, the pleasure afforded by the tale is nothing other than an erotic trap laid by power, with the authority of the law, aimed at subjugating the tale's listeners, that is, of making them believe what they hear.

Then in the second instance, when he should be concluding his preface, and almost as a sign of the effectiveness of this strategy of power, Perrault hands over his writer's pen to a "young lady" who "writes a madrigal beneath the Tale that I had sent her about Donkey-Skin":

> The Tale of Donkey-Skin is here told
> With such simplicity
> That I derived no less pleasure from it
> Than when, around the fire, my Nurse or my Governess
> Would enchant my mind by telling it.
> Here and there one senses the traces of Satire,
> But they are without spleen or malice.
> For everyone alike it is a pleasure to read:

What also pleases me about its innocent sweetness,
Is that it entertains and gives rise to laughter,
Without anything to which Father, Husband, or Confessor
Could possibly take exception.

A twofold limit is inscribed within the dual margin of the written tale and the preface to the book, where Perrault justifies his writing. One limit pertains to the position of the writing author turned father, because a young girl writes in his stead and, without knowing it, demonstrates the efficacy or power of writing. We also witness the limits of different types of power, of power in general, since the perpetrators of power sense that they should take exception to something in "Donkey-Skin" but cannot pinpoint what compromises their power.

The writing down of the oral tale "Donkey-Skin" indicates the position occupied by the writing author, as the father substituting for the nurses and the maternal voice that tells the tale. The opposite, however, is also true. By virtue of the tale's orality, what was subversive in the oral tale with respect to power in general, is re-inscribed in the written text.

The hypothesis that will orient my re-reading of "Donkey-Skin" is as follows: Perrault's writing of a tale, "Donkey-Skin," which is paradigmatic of oral narrativity, amounts to a narrative staging of characters belonging to the realm of fiction. Through these characters, Perrault dramatizes what was potentially at stake in a writing of orality and in the orality of writing at a specific historical conjuncture, that is, at a given moment, during a certain century, and in a particular place. Nonetheless, before I undertake to demonstrate this hypothesis in a detailed re-reading of the written text of the tale, I need to formulate some general propositions on orality and on the relation of writing to orality.

The term "orality" operates in two semantic domains that share a common boundary constituted by a particular part of the body. The first domain is that of actual speech, of linguistic utterances—with the individual particularities of their occurrence. In actual speech, words function as phonic signs that give articulation to the voice, which itself is the resonant matter of expression, a kind of continuum that can be carved up and articulated and brought to exhibit all of its salient qualities, such as pitch, timbre, intensity, intonation, and so on. To speak of orality in this domain is to speak of the voice as it occurs in the words that make up speech. Now the voice is "a thing of the mouth," that is, a part of the body which consists of lips, teeth, a tongue, a palate, a glottis, and a throat. The mouth constitutes the site where a potentially articulate voice is made to produce or effect words. The mouth and its various parts may thus be said to designate metonymically the specificity of a speaking voice, ranging between the scream on the one hand, a discharge of almost raw sound, meaningful in spite of its near inarticulateness, and, on the other hand, an almost inarticulate whisper verging on silence. Thus it is possible to speak "between one's teeth," "in a forced manner," "through one's nose," or "from the depths of the throat," and so on.

The mouth is also an ambivalent part of the body, since it is the site of eating and drinking, the place where lips, teeth, tongue, palate, and throat engage in their specific labor of biting, savoring, triturating, masticating, and swallowing. At this point we enter the second sphere of orality where the term designates everything that bears any relation to the ingestion of food, the need for food and drink, or the instinct for self-preservation. In the original scenario of the drama of need and satiation, the child plays the leading role, since the child does not speak, but only sucks the maternal breast in order to drink its nourishing milk. The second sphere of orality exists from the moment that the first cry of want and hunger is released. It exists in the smacking sounds accompanying manducation, in the satisfied belch of sleepy satiety, and, at the other end of the cycle, in the excretion of the waste products resulting from the nutritious meal.

The language and social ritual, the ambivalent locus of the mouth joins two spheres of orality. Its ambivalence is marked by rules that articulate the difference between the two kinds of orality, as well as the danger of their possible conflation. Thus one should not speak with a full mouth, since the noisy chewing might hamper the articulation of vocal signs and the exhalation needed for vocalizing could lead to the expulsion from the mouth of bits of edible matter. Thus one ought not to speak and eat at the same time, for fear that an always possible short-circuiting might occur. For fear that the two functions, both of which take place between the lips and the throat, might suddenly be inverted. Speaking consists of expelling breath and giving it an articulate form as it passes through the mouth. Eating involves an inward movement, the ingestion of food, as well as a process of decomposition which is effected by grinding and chewing the edible substance in the very place where words are articulated.

Whence the specific secondary prescriptions that sometimes reinforce the law governing the basic activities of eating and speaking: to be properly heard, a voice must be carefully articulated in the words that it expresses; to be properly nourished, it is necessary to chew one's food meticulously before swallowing it. The inchoate words of a person who does not master the art of regulating his breath signal the absence of culture. Similarly, to swallow food without savoring and chewing it is to mark oneself as a barbarous glutton. Yet a banquet or meal can be, and is frequently, a special place and time for the exchange of words, for edifying or informative stories and discourses. Thus it is possible to speak metonymically about what is being eaten, while alternating between speaking and eating. Speaking metaphorically, one could say that, at a certain moment, what is being said will come to be eaten, an attentive ear will lap up the words of one of the other table companions or, wholly fascinated, will devour what is being recounted. According to Perrault, the children listening to a tale devour the pure truths of a morality that has been wrapped in pleasurable stories appropriate to their young age. We are reminded of the story which Aesop, the Master of Tales, acted out. This story was nothing more than a meal of language-like food twice repeated, to the point of nausea for Agathopus and the other guests. Aesop's enactment proved language and speech to be at once the best and worst of things.

Ambivalent, though privileged, as a site of speech and manducation, the mouth is also ambivalent in a second sense, which is closely linked to the first. The mouth is the locus of need, as well as the means by which this need is satisfied. As a result, the mouth is the place where a drive is inscribed. Through the need that finds an oral satisfaction, this drive comes to be anaclitically related to an erogenous, pleasure-giving zone where desire seeks its realization. Orality designates this anaclitic relation, which is nothing more than an inscription, the marking of an already marked trace, a bodily writing that inscribes itself as bodily desire within bodily need. Consequently, linguistic orality is the repetition, through the voice's symbolic articulation in the words of speech, of this relationship between an erotic drive and an instinct for self-preservation. It repeats the process by which a drive is inscribed as a re-marking of need in the body and mouth of the child clutching and nursing at the mother's breast, where he or she satisfies a need to eat, as well as realizing his or her desire.

Is the voice that is heard through speech the repetition of an archaic bodily inscription or writing? Does writing repeat an anterior voice when it inscribes itself upon a subjective medium? We have seen that orality is a matter of some ambivalence, stemming from the very nature of its locus. Moreover, the place in question cannot be properly accounted for in terms of a thing and should be thought of as a relational space—the mouth and the breast, which are alternately conjoined and disjoined. The ambivalence characterizing orality introduces us to the structure that governs articulation, as well as to its signs and marks. Is it not clear that this structure resolves the opposition between the oral and the written, between the vocal and the inscribed? It reveals a voice that is already a form of inscription, the re-marking of a trace with no origin. The structure shows this inscription to be constitutive of the body in its capacity as a desiring body. It also discloses a voice or phonic continuum that has already been dissected, cut apart, and re-marked by the law of the code. Has this voice, dual in its conjunction of infant and mother, not already been re-inscribed with the trace of their separation? Is it not clear that this is what "Donkey-Skin" is all about? The tale never ceases to talk about the disappearance of the opposition between the oral and the written, a displacement said to occur at the level of the structure and effect of signs.

Let me, then, restate the hypothesis that has been guiding my rereading of "Donkey-Skin": As a paradigmatic tale of narrative orality, this unique tale, written by Perrault, is the narrative representation of the structure of signification in general. It also represents the anaclitic relation between this structure and the need that has been re-marked in the form of desire and pleasure. Thus the anaclitic nature of the symbolic structure is represented by a metaphorical and narrative staging of what this symbolic structure relies on, of what it inscribes itself upon, and of what it re-marks as the trace of an origin, a trace that only appears to be originary in the context of this very repetition. "Donkey-Skin," a written and re-written oral tale is thus the narrative and fictive, that is, imaginary, representation of a symbolic regression to the "origin."

3 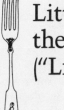 Little Butterpot, or the Spell of the Voice ("Little Red Riding Hood")

In "Sleeping Beauty" a Queen Mother Ogress is made aware of the presence of her habitual food when she hears voices. She hears the crying of a child whose mother is about to spank it because it has been naughty, and she hears another one talking. The ogress recognizes these voices as those of her daughter-in-law and grandchildren, all of whom she intends to consume. As a result she is overtaken by a terrible omophagous and cannibalistic appetite, the sign of which is a horrendous voice. This story suggests an essential, though more or less hidden, relationship between the voice, though not language or words, and food, though not cooking, dishes, or courses. The same issues arise in "Little Red Riding Hood."

The unfolding of the story in "Little Red Riding Hood" is punctuated by the almost ritual recurrence of a formula, which designates a griddle cake and butter, an ingredient and a culinary seasoning, though not a food in its own right. The butter is kept in a little pot, and Perrault's French expression for this offers to the attentive ear a savory cascade of labial and dental sounds: *petit pot de beurre* lines up in rhythmic succession three short *es* against the background of which erupts the brief stridence of a single short *i*.

This griddle cake and little butter pot recur no less than five times after their initial appearance at the outset of the story. The first mention is in "Take her a griddle cake and this little butter pot," and the last occurs in the scene immediately preceding the story's dénouement: "Put the griddle cake and the little butter pot on the kneading-trough."

The formula appears in each of the story's stages and is articulated in the mouth of each of the story's characters. In the beginning it is mouthed by the mother; the child mouthes it in the forest; the wolf "as child" utters it on the doorstep of the grandmother's house, as does the child; and then the wolf utters it dressed "as grandmother."

The formula occurs no fewer than five times, even though the tale has only three protagonists. Yet the wolf never utters it as part of his own specific wolf discourse. In his mouth, the formula always falsely represents another "speaker," little Red Riding Hood in the first instance, and the grandmother in the second. In other words, the griddle cake and little butter pot make the wolf speak as either little Red Riding Hood or the grandmother. Or to be more precise, these two figures both speak the formula through the wolf's mouth, or should we say his muzzle?

Little Red Riding Hood, on the other hand, utters the formula twice in her own name. First, she is the wolf's interlocutor, and the expression "a griddle cake and little butter pot" is simply part of an assertive utterance that expresses a plan of action in the narrative. The second time, the little girl is the interlocutor of the grandmother, or rather of the "wolf as grandmother." This time, the phrase figures within a context of conversational interaction where it serves as a form of self-identification.

The difference between the two utterances is readily detected. On the one hand, the wolf asks her where she is going. The poor child replies, "I am going to see my grandmother to take her a griddle cake and little butter pot from my mother." On the other hand, there is the phrase, "Knock, knock, Who's there?" Little Red Riding Hood answers, "It is your granddaughter, Little Red Riding Hood, who has brought you a griddle cake and little butter pot from my mother." In the first case, the child describes what she is doing and what she will do; in the second, she tells who she is by attributing to herself the predicates that define her person.

It is no surprise, however, that the wolf is her interlocutor in both cases. The first time, she speaks with the wolf-as-wolf, but "she did not know that it was dangerous to stop to *listen* to a wolf." The second time, she talks to the wolf-as-grandmother, yet when she hears the gruff voice of the wild animal she assumes that her grandmother "has a cold." In both cases, everything hinges on the voice. The voice of the wolf in the forest is as dangerous to listen to, as it is terrifying to hear it coming from the depths of a throat suffering from a bad cold.

During the rituals of its utterance, the formula "a griddle cake and little butter pot" has the power of beginning, of opening up a space where actions can take place. Mouthed by the mother, it begins the story's unfolding and initiates the telling of how a given terrain, the forest, is traversed. In the case of the wolf, the formula twice provides him with access to a socialized and human space, a space that is also one where food is to be had. Initially, in the forest, the formula results in his being shown a path which leads to the grandmother's house. Subsequently, the formula, more so than the latch, opens the door and gives him access to the grandmother's house. The formula also provides Little Red Riding Hood with her introduction and entry to the house. Finally, it makes the wolf's bed seem inviting to the little girl. The formula is like the aperitif that precedes a number of different courses: in this case, the story's consummation, the consumption of food, and sexual devouring.

As a result of its ritual aspects, the formula is precisely a matter of the voice, and not just of music, rhythm, or articulated words. It unites all these elements into a complex whole that is both greater than and different from its parts. It is greater than them because, in Perrault's French, phonic alliterations are at play in the words that create meaning. It is different from them by virtue of the performative power and magical efficacy which is exhibited at all levels of enunciation by the formula when it is uttered. This play of phonemes within the terms of the expression, as well as its performative force, make of the expression a formula in the sense of those sacraments of tridentine theology which hold *ex opere operato* both in the story and in its narration.

To speak precisely, the voice is a thing of the mouth, almost independent of the cavity where it is formed and uttered. Yet the voice is constituted only in this empty space that grants it resonance and amplification, allowing it to carry to the outside. The mouth is also the site where food, whether raw or fully cooked and prepared, is pulverized, mixed, and transformed for its incorporation. The formula "a griddle cake and little butter pot" thus pertains to the voice. It is a "thing of the mouth and voice" that names food, a cake and an alimentary ingredient, and identifies things for the mouth to eat.

In each case, the formula is connected with a devouring, as in the woods where Br'er Wolf, "who would have liked to eat" Little Red Riding Hood, only listens to her. The same holds for the moment at the grandmother's house when the wolf, having uttered the formula, pounces on the poor woman and devours her in no time at all, since he had not eaten for more than three days. Similarly, when Little Red Riding Hood subsequently utters the formula outside the door of the same house, the formula gives her access to the place where the wolf will repeat the ritual formula one more time. As a result of this final repetition, the innocent child is served up for the wolf's consumption.

Three manifestations of the formula are properly speaking a matter of the voice. In the first case, the formula comes from the mouth of the mother who sends her little girl to convey the formula, and the food that it signifies, to her grandmother, who lies ill on the far side of the forest. The second manifestation is in the mouth of the granddaughter who, in advance, conveys the expression to the wolf when he surprises her in the forest. In response to a voice heavy with a cold, she again utters the formula when she arrives at her destination. A voice is twice imitated in the muzzle of the wolf. The wolf impersonates the voice of a little girl so as to be able to answer the grandmother's question, penetrate her house, and devour its inhabitant. He then imitates a grandmother, orders the little girl to leave aside words and put aside the things they signify, and then invites this girl, who has also just uttered the formula, to join him in bed. The voice is eminently malleable, since it is conveyed by all the mouths in the story, whether real or counterfeit, and it spans the whole scale of tones, stresses, intensities, and pitches, running from youth to old age. It is as though the preparation and metamorphoses of cooked food bear no relation to words or sounds. Rather, they are related to the voice that articulates words and modulates sounds, and, in so doing, authorizes the wild animal to satisfy his hunger by simply devouring raw meat, whether as the tough hide of a grandmother, or the succulent flesh of a child.

I cannot help but think that the last avatar of the griddle cake and its accompanying butter pot, the ultimate vocal transformation of the formulaic and ritualistic expression concerning food, can be heard in the dialogue that takes place in bed between the wolf-as-grandmother and the little girl. The dual voice of Eros sings a duet consisting of the little girl's exclamations, which are implicitly questions about the unusual features of the "grandmother's" body, and the wolf's answers to these implicit questions.

Thanks to this voice, the beastly body is able, through antiphony and response, to elevate itself bit by bit to the site of the voice, to the mouth that has been metaphorically changed into the instrument of another sort of consumption:

"Grandmother, what long arms you have!"
"The better to embrace you with, my dear."
"Grandmother, what long legs you have!"
"The better to run with, my dear."
"Grandmother, what big ears you have!"
"The better to hear with, my dear."
"Grandmother, what big eyes you have!"
"The better to see with, my dear."
"Grandmother, what long teeth you have!"
"To eat you with, my dear."

The same dialogic structure of question and answer is repeated five times, as was the magical formula concerning food. In Perrault's French, the exchange involves ten repetitions of the same quality, "big" or "grand." It alternately names the name of the grandmother *(Mère-grand)* and qualifies a part of her body, from limbs to teeth. The echo of the erotic counting rhyme is broken by the small difference contained in the last response, in which the wolf's mouth designates the object to be eaten. Thus the response immediately gives way to manducation rather than to another question and response. Moreover, the manducation brings about the wolf's gratification as he devours the embodiment of the list of bodily parts. Thus manducation occurs in the all-or-nothing of an erotic pleasure, in which the list is summarized and made total.

Perrault seems to have worried that the vocal effects of the Little Red Riding Hood tale could go unnoticed, for in the fifteen lines in which he gives the moral of the story, he makes sure to dot the *i*s. Sounding a final echo of the voice, the name of the wolf recurs no less than five times. It is almost as though the tale possessed a musical score, the wolf's name being equally distributed on each of its five lines.

4   The Fabulous Animal

What is the meaning of the talking animal in fabulous discourse? One response is that we are dealing with an allegory of man. Indeed, but what might this allegory imply? We can begin to answer this question by saying that it points to the fiction of the *clinamen*, to the point of contact between a number of terms: between talking and eating, verbality and orality, the instinct for self-preservation and the linguistic drive. My thesis is as follows: the fabulous talking animal is a figure of this fiction of the infinitesimal swerve, of the *clinamen* imagined to be the origin. The animal figuring in fables is properly animal in that it is presented as a body that both eats and is eaten. Yet this animal also speaks. In the fable, the animal simulates a symbolic regression to the level of instinct: we have here a fiction that locates the origin of discourse in Eros and destruction, and which would serve the function of depriving the rulers of their power over discourse.

Right at the beginning of La Fontaine's "Life of Aesop," which dates from 1668, we find a short story presented in the guise of an introduction to the *First Collection of Selected Fables*, while (by chance?) describing the origins of the fabulator, the fable also tells a story about the origin of the fable. This rather odd story narrates and reveals, then, the way in which a story is produced: in a wholly self-reflexive manner, the fable describes itself in the process of telling a fable. What we have here is the story's endless referral to the act of narration that produces it, as well as the inverse—the endless referring of an act of narration to the story that does the narrating.

Yet the referring taking place in this short fable is interrupted as a result of the simple fact that the story being told involves a series of gestures, a silent story that is mute before language. The narrator in this short introduction is hardly a disembodied voice. Rather, he is a body, that is to say, a fabulous animal. The animal in the fable is a body that both devours and is devoured. In addition, however, this animal also speaks. In the case of the "Life of Aesop," however, man the fabulator is a beast, a body (devoured and devouring) which has not yet received the power of speech. At the end of the fable, as its moral, this body comes into language, with the advent of gestures that, as a conclusion or supplement, are made into a story. This supplemental acquisition of language functions as the moral of the tale. At stake throughout the fable are relations of mastery and slavery, of violence and justice, of claims and counterclaims; what is at stake is power and language.

> Aesop was a Phrygian, from a town called Amorium. He was born sometime around the fifty-seventh olympiad, some two hundred years after the founding of Rome. It is hard to say whether he had reason to be grateful to nature or reason to complain about her; for while she bestowed upon him a very good mind, he was born with a deformed and ugly face and hardly even looked like a member of the human race. Nature even went so far as virtually to deny him the use of language. With all of these defects it was inevitable that he should become a slave, even if he was not born one. In any case, his soul always stayed free, and independent of the whims of fortune.

From the very beginning of the story, we are struck by the irreparably ambivalent nature of the Phrygian: a good mind imprisoned in a deformed body, human intelligence cast in the form of a brute beast. Let us look ahead in the story. Aesop does not have, or barely has, the face of a man, for he cannot speak: he is an animal, or almost one. He grunts and stammers, much like Rousseau's original man: "he is nothing . . . he is stupid."

> His first master sent him out into the fields to work the land, perhaps because he thought him incapable of any other task, perhaps because he simply wanted to remove this unsightly object from his field of vision. Now it so happened that one day this master paid a visit to his country house where he was given some figs by a peasant: the master thought them very lovely and had them very carefully stored away. He

ordered his butler, called Agathopus, to bring them to him once he was through bathing. Now chance had it that Aesop had some business in the dwelling. As soon as Aesop stepped inside it, Agathopus availed himself of the opportunity to eat the figs together with some of his friends. He subsequently cast the aspersion of theft on Aesop, thinking that he would be unable to defend himself, since he seemed so clumsy and idiotic! The punishments typically employed by the ancients against their slaves were very cruel, and theft was a transgression that warranted severe punishment. Poor Aesop threw himself at the feet of his master; and making himself understood as best he could, he begged for grace and enjoined his master to postpone briefly his punishment.

It is at this point that the story really starts and, with it, the first fable—a silent and purely gestural story. The first gesture in this story is one of supplication, which introduces a temporal deferral and spatial difference: his punishment is momentarily stayed. Here we have perhaps one of the key points in the history of the origin: delay or *"distansion,"* as Saint Augustine would say; the apostasy of the now, as Aristotle would say. The spatialization of the punctual *now* is the condition of possibility of the story. In the story about Aesop, the originating gesture is not defined as in the first chapter of the *Phenomenology of Spirit*, where it figures as a kind of *stigmé*, a pointing, a finger pointed toward something, or as the *deixis* of a gestural instance. Quite the contrary, the originating gesture in the fable is that of a hand staying the imminence of a blow, delaying "a single blow." The gesture is characterized by its suddenness, and it opens up, within time and space, a place or stage where a game can be played out. The same point can be made slightly differently: the gesture effecting delay, spatialization, and divergence is something like the beginnings of a *clinamen*, like the tangential point of a curve. It is a minuscule angle, the tiny rift that constitutes a moment of delay within what is wholly urgent.* Or to say the same thing quite trivially: instead of confronting the urgent issue at hand, Aesop, somewhat duplicitously, goes off on a tangent.

After the gesture comes the body. We witness the complex pro-

---

Ecart poses some problems, particularly since its specific meaning tends to be context-sensitive. I translate *geste d'écart* as "deferring gesture" and *écart* as "difference," "distance," "scission," "split," "gap," or "rift," depending on the context. In "The King's Glorious Body and Its Portrait," *écart critique* is translated as "critical difference."—*Trans.*

cess that constitutes both the narrative body and the body of the narrator. To recall the beginning of the story, the slave master wanted to eat some figs once he was through with his bath. Together with some friends, Agathopus the butler—he who is good-looking, the *Kaloskagathos*—eats the figs in the master's stead, out of sheer greediness and gluttony. The result is that the figs have disappeared. These delicious things are introjected, incorporated, assimilated, consumed, and thus they lose the externality that characterizes the things of the real world. Agathopus and his friends cast the blame onto Aesop. They speak, and their speech is one of lies. They are all the more confident about being able to lie verbally with impunity because they, quite rightly, assume that Aesop will be incapable of responding verbally.

There is, then, an absolute divide separating the words that are good to say from those things that are good to eat. It should be noted that the arrangement of the words making up the discourse of those who are strong serves a dual function. On the one hand, their discourse is representational, and, on the other, it is mono-logic. Let us first look at its representational dimension: the discourse of the strong articulates being, the condition and state of things. It is true that this articulation is false, but it does, none-theless, articulate being. By virtue of its describing a situation in the past, Agathopus's discourse is able to constitute itself as a nar-rative discourse: Agathopus tells about what happened, he talks about past events. In this sense, his story is the trace of a situa-tion, of a certain kind of behavior: Aesop entered the dwelling, the figs have disappeared, and so Aesop must have eaten the figs. This narrative discourse falsely constitutes the archival record of a situation in the past. It is the trace of this situation, its only trace. Thus the story that Agathopus tells is more than just the narrative representation of the past. For there is almost no need to point out that this narrative representation discursively effects an explanation: by virtue of its representational aspects, the his-torical story is able to provide an explanation for the absence, the disappearance of the figs.

Agathopus's narrative representation is also monologic: since he does not speak, Aesop does not, will not, and cannot possibly respond. An animal cannot provide a counter-story or a counter-explanation. But what if such a response were possible? Let us for a moment attribute language to Aesop. What could Aesop pos-sibly have said? "I did not eat the figs. It is true that I entered the house but this was only by chance. Moreover, I do not like figs, etc." "Prove it," the master would say in return. At that point, it would be impossible for any such proof to be furnished, for the body of the crime has already disappeared. What we have here is a good fictive example of double discourse, in the sense of ancient sophistry: between the pro and the con, there exists an undecidable truth, an undecidability based on the disappearance of an object. The thing has been eaten. It is true that it is recovered, but only as a representation in a story. "It was Aesop who ate the figs," says Agathopus. Had he been able to speak, Aesop would have responded with "No, I did not, Agathopus did." Thus, we see an adversarial Agathopus who constitutes the narrative body "Aesop" as an eater of figs, an assimilating stomach; this is how a body of speech and words is constituted. It is all too well known that beasts are voracious. In Agathopus's story, this accusation takes a bodily form. Moreover, the story's ineluctable conclusion is punishment. The master, who is in the position of the arbiter, passes sentence on Aesop. Aesop is to be killed: this is the urgent and immediate implication of the story, of the narrative and monologic representation proffered by Agathopus.

Aesop, however, does respond to the accusation. As we have seen, his first gesture of response is one of deferral, serving to open up a space of possibility within the moment of urgency. His gesture sets the stage for a counter-discourse, for a discourse which will not, however, be spoken. Here I want to emphasize the opposition between Agathopus's accusatory story, which is both representational and monologic, and Aesop's discourse. The latter does not resuscitate the past in a story, for Aesop does not tell a verbal story. His response belongs to the present moment and consists of its deferral. To the body of verbal narration, to the archival record or representation of the past, Aesop opposes a different kind of body. This oppositional body is against neither speech nor myth. It is an anti-body which has as its salient characteristic a temporality that is of the present, that is of a punctual *now* implanted in an apostasy. This counter-discourse defers the present moment and sets the stage for a gesture involving supplication and distanciation.

Of what, then, does this fabulous anti-body consist? Aesop drinks lukewarm water, puts his fingers down his throat, and throws up the water that he has just ingested. This gesture involves the staging of two bodily functions that characterize the rhythm of the body: the moment of replenishment and ingestion, and that of excretion and expulsion. I say "staging" because Aesop drinks without being thirsty and vomits on purpose. The anti-body in question is a "produced body," not at all a natural body. That Aesop drinks warm and not cool water shows that his motive is not one of thirst. In putting his fingers down his throat, Aesop employs the classic gesture or technique designed to produce vomiting. The vomit that results can hardly be said to be the natural outcome of indigestion. Perhaps I was being a little imprecise when I said that Aesop does not tell a story. In producing his body as the rhythm of repletion and excretion, in staging his body, Aesop does narrativize it; on this score, we might do well to recall *Plato's Symposium*. La Fontaine's fable is all about this narrativization: "He went looking for warm water which he then drank in his master's presence. He put his fingers in his mouth, and vomited only water." Aesop's anti-myth is a bodily game in the sense that the body is made to perform a play. This anti-myth is Aesop's response to Agathopus's story, and it contains the following notion: repletion and excretion, ingestion and expulsion are all connected to one another. To assimilate is to reject; to incorporate is to exclude; to eat is to expel. The body has a rhythm oscillating between a yes and a no, between Eros and destruction.

We have seen that the body of language that belongs to Agathopus, the accuser, has a number of specific features: it is a lying body, it is monologic, and it consists of a narrative, of language. Aesop's response has the effect of replacing this accusing body with a body pro-duced by the accused party. The latter is a rhythmic body involving an oscillation between interiorization and exteriorization, the staging of which reveals a kind of play of *"Fort-Da"*: the water disappears, reappears, is lost, and then refound. Moreover, the *clinamen*, the swerve evoked above is accentuated here. In a sense, Aesop reproduces the past scene of the crime recounted by Agathopus; he reconstitutes it. Also, with his own body, he reinscribes the scene within the difference, the divergence, the swerve of the *clinamen*. He repeats its difference through a playful body. If Aesop truly has a story, then it is important to note that it consists not of a narrative body, but of a bodily narration. Words do not substitute for things by representing them in their absence; this is the role ostensibly played by Agathopus's words. Rather, in this point of origin, things substitute for words.

After having justified himself in this manner, he [Aesop] indicated that the others should be obligated to do the same thing. Everyone was taken aback: they could not believe that Aesop was capable of inventing such a strategy. Agathopus and his companions did not seem at all surprised. They drank the water in the manner of the Phrygian and put their fingers down their throats; but they were careful not to put them down too far. The water, however, did not fail to work and to bring forth the figs which were still quite raw and the color of vermilion. In this way, Aesop vouched for himself: his accusers were doubly punished, for their greediness and for their wickedness.

The anti-body of the confabulator is a dialogic body. Aesop signals that it is the turn of the others to repeat the scene that he enacted with his own body. They are to repeat his pro-duced body, the rhythmic functions that it brought into play. After the originating gesture of deferral comes that of pointing, the finger pointed at Agathopus and his friends. This pointing is hardly, however, one of accusation. Rather, it signals the moment in which a reversal takes place, it announces a rejoinder, a *méta-bolē*. It is not a question of saying something that runs contrary to what someone else has said, which would be a kind of anti-logos, but of doing the same thing they did *(omopoiesis)*, and in so doing, producing the opposite result.

One might go so far, however, as to say that the rejoinder required of Agathopus is situated in the pro-duced body that has been staged by Aesop. This would be the case because the rejoinder is demanded by a pointing gesture. Aesop is in control of the game. His staged body in turn becomes the stage upon which the bodies of others have to perform. He absorbs them. The slave has become his master's master. The water brings about the return of the consumed object, and thus the past event that left no traces is revealed. The act of eating figs once more appears on the scene, but in an inverted form, in the act of vomiting the figs which "still were quite raw and the color of vermilion." The manner in which these figs reappear or are returned is wholly improbable, unless we assume that Agathopus was so greedy he simply gulped down the figs without chewing them. Thus Agathopus is the beastly one, although this does not mean that Aesop is already fully human. The lost object is retrieved as such and bears precisely the same form as before; what we have here is homeostasis. In the meantime, the fable has been born.

We have seen that the story told by Agathopus, "the man with the good looks," refers to an event that is other and different; a story that re-produces, in inverted form, the event of the past that is lost to the present. The story focuses on the death and disappearance of the thing. As such, Agathopus's story has a certain truth value. It is a story told with language, the narrative representation of the voracious beast. The coincidence of a homeostatic situation with the birth of the fable suggests that the representational story comes to be replaced by a narrative fictional body. Moreover, this substitution occurs between two gestures, that of deferral and that of pointing. This narrative and fictional body is neither true nor false. It is a performative and dialogic body, a body of narration which produces, in the here and now, a past and lost event. This bodily event quite literally effects an analysis of the historical account that is presented in the story told with language. Yet the fact that this dialogic body assumes an analytic role does not mean that it functions as a meta-discourse about the story in which past events are recounted. Rather, it is the production of a body that tells a story, and in so doing, the body inverts the effects of the representational discourse. Let us recall Agathopus's story: "While the master was taking his bath, Aesop entered the house and ate the figs." Let us contrast it to the confabulator's bodily narration: "I drink water, I put my fingers down my throat, I vomit water. Agathopus drinks water, he puts his fingers down his throat, he vomits the figs." This is what the adversary's narrative body and the confabulator's bodily narration look like. The bodily narration involves a fictional eating, *hic et nunc*, the effect of which is the body's expulsion of the savory thing. By the same token, this bodily narration deconstructs the verbal story that explicitly claims to be true. It is a doing in the moment of the present, a bodily action, an "action-fiction" that brings truth into being in the form of an effect of the interlocutor's discourse.

We might then imagine that the master would speak the following words as a pragmatic consequence of Aesop's gesticulation: "While I was asleep after my bath, Agathopus entered the house and ate the figs." We are told that this is the truth. Whence the punishment of Agathopus for both greediness and wickedness, for having eaten the figs and told a story. The position in which Aesop finds himself also follows from this truth: having drunk the water and vomited, having made others drink and vomit, Aesop arrives at a condition that cannot yet be characterized as one of full verbal articulation, although it no longer fits the category of orality either. Between the two moments of a deferring and a pointing gesture, Aesop attains what I call "bodily and fictional narration." Another way of putting this is to speak of the simulation of a body by means of a body. What I am trying to bring to the fore is the idea that two gestures, that of deferral and that of pointing, form the basis for the constitution of a simulacrum, its very conditions of possibility.

At the moment of urgency and imminence, the temporal deferral of a *now* opens up a space of possibilities in the present. The spatial pointing brings with it the obligation of a repetition. What it requires is hardly the repetition of the "same" past event, but rather, that of a present or instantaneous difference. The idea is to make the master's discourse true, to introduce truth into it. Whence the idea of using a simulacrum and a fiction, a bodily simulation, as a defensive as well as retaliatory tactic. With his bodily gestures, Aesop silently repeats the narrative representation of his accusers. Yet he does this in such a way that his body inverts and displaces the syntagmatic relations governing the utterances of his adversaries. Thus the rhetorical abnegation of the accused party—his "No, it is not true, I did not eat the figs"—is transformed into the bodily reaction of expulsion, of vomiting.* Here we might refer to Freud's famous text on (ab)negation, for it could be said that there is a regress from the symbolic negation to the archaic reaction of vomiting. Yet the latter retains a symbolic dimension, since it is intentional, willed, enacted. This dimension is, however, retained in the presence and immediacy of a *now*. In other words, the act of vomiting implies "neither a yes nor a no," but simply a fiction or simulation, which would have the following perlocutionary force within the master's discourse: "Agathopus ate the figs and not Aesop."

I have already pointed out that Aesop does not engage in an act of accusation. He does not point to his accusers in order to accuse them, nor does he try to express a negation with this gesture. Rather, his pointing is a request that they silently repeat the fiction and simulacrum that he just enacted with his body and gestures. In granting his request, Aesop's accusers repeat his gesticulations, yet during the process of repetition, they produce a

---

*Although I have followed Anthony Wilden's translation of several psychoanalytic terms, I have chosen to render *dénégation* as "abnegation" rather than "denegation," just as I have opted for "death drives" rather than "death instincts" as a translation for Freud's *Todestrieb.—Trans.*

supplement, which effects the truth that will be asserted in the master's discourse when he says, "Yes, they ate the figs." Thus the power of accusation is inscribed within, and returned to, the very body that was given over to enactment and play. This aggressive capacity is articulated in the signs that tell the story of Aesop's life, in the language of the strongest. It could very well be that the fable, the story of the weak and marginal, generally constitutes a particular kind of apparatus within the medium of discourse itself. The function of this apparatus is to allow the weak to displace and reverse the power contained in the discourse of the strong.

> The next day, after their master had left and once the Phrygian had gone back to his work, some lost travellers (some said they were priests of Diana) asked him, in the name of a hospitable Jupiter, to show them the road leading into town. Aesop first of all made them rest in the shade; then, having presented them with a light meal, he wanted to be their guide and left them only once he had set them on the proper path. These good folk raised their hands to the heavens and begged Jupiter not to allow this charitable deed to go unrewarded. Almost immediately after having left them, Aesop was overtaken by the heat and, exhausted, he fell asleep. During his sleep, he dreamt that he saw Fortune standing in front of him and that she loosened his tongue. By the same token she made him a present of the very art of which one might say he is the author. Delighted by this experience, he awoke with a start; and upon waking he says: "What is this? My voice has been freed; I can pronounce properly the word *rake, plough,* anything I want."

The moral of this story is to be found in the episode that comes immediately after it: in Aesop's acquisition of full verbal articulation. I shall not analyze this episode, but am content to point out that it contains, albeit at a different level, all of the elements that I have been trying to bring to the fore in my discussion of Aesop's silent gesticulations before his accusers. The priests of Diana want to know the direction or the road leading into town. There is no accusation here: the priests ask for information; they, the very learned, ask to be taught the way. The slave has mastered a certain knowledge, that is, he knows a route, a trajectory, a way. Once again, he first performs a gesture of deferral involving the spatialization of urgency: this time the deferral takes the form of a rest in the shade of a tree to eat a light meal. This food and rest will restore the strength of the travelers and allow them to recover from their weariness. Once again, Aesop performs a pointing gesture, although this time he does so with his whole body: he accompanies the travelers on the right path. He makes them do what he knows and thus transmits his knowledge to them, not by a mediation by signs, but by simulating a journey in their company; he makes them do what he does and knows. The priests of Diana pray to Jupiter on Aesop's behalf.

Once they leave, Aesop falls asleep. Thus the process of spatialization is reiterated, but this time in the form of an opening up of a space of oneiric possibilities. Aesop dreams. Yet in his dream it is not Jupiter, the all-powerful Master, the Master of all masters, who unties his tongue, but Fortune. The advent of language, and of the fable that comes with it, is realized by force of chance and is a fortuitous event. Language, then, will be the supplement of gestures and of the body. It will be the story that supplements the fiction of the pro-duced body, even as it stimulates simulation itself. Aesop awakes: "What is this? This is a rake, that is a plough; I can pronounce anything I want." Aesop has become a logothete. The word "this" is a deictic term that redoubles the gesture of pointing through language. Thus it silently opens onto a field of nominal definitions, a field of signs, the domain of the symbolic. It makes way for the will, for the desire of the founding slave of language. The beast talks. The fables are told.

"The Reason of the Strongest Is Always the Best"

Furetière's *Dictionnaire Universel* (1690) provides the following definitions:

> *Moral*, adj. Pertaining to mores, conduct in life. There exist intellectual virtues, like faith, and others which are moral virtues, such as justice, temperance. . . . One speaks of the *moral* sense of the Scriptures, an interpretation of these writings that allows us to derive certain instructions pertinent to mores. The same is said of the instruction that is derived from fables under the veil of which are permitted the criticism of the faults of mankind, especially those of the powerful.

> *Morality*. The doctrine that concerns morals, the science that teaches the proper way to conduct one's life and actions. Christian morality is the most perfect of all moralities.

> *Morally*. In accordance with good morals. This proposition is morally true, that is, from a moral point of view and not from the perspective of physics.

> *Moralize*. To speak about morality, give moral lessons, or comment morally. . . . Some people make themselves unwelcome by moralizing, by finding something to criticize everywhere.

> *Moralist*. Author who writes about or treats of morality.

One of the issues raised by the *Logic of Port-Royal* concerns the possibility of articulating a propositional logic of judgment together with a discursive ethics that would aim to regulate "those erroneous reasonings that occur in civil life and ordinary speech." This issue is raised first by the manner in which the *Logic* was constructed, since it was written continually between 1662 and 1683, and second, by its explicit content. The "anonymous" authors of the *Art of Thinking* unfailingly define themselves as both logicians and moralists. Thus it is inevitable, if for no other reason than the authors' self-definition, that the *Logic* should deal with the fundamental problem concerning the relation between a series of coupled terms: a science of truth and a science of morals, theory and practice, speculation and morality. Suffice it on this score to point out that the whole grammatical and logical enterprise of the gentlemen of Port-Royal finds its historical point of departure in two different intellectual projects: in Augustine's powerful theory of the sign and discourse on the one hand, and in Descartes's epistemological project on the other. Let us begin with the former.

The semiological, semantic, and pragmatic analyses that make up Augustine's theory are all based on a religious ethics that deals with the good, with desire, and with love. It is based on a theory of value that studies the ends proper to the will and to desire. This theory is organized around a radical opposition between an evil and diabolical concupiscence, born of man's original sin, and a divine charity that results from grace, God's redemption of mankind. The other point of departure for the Port-Royal project is in the no less powerful Cartesian theory of the idea and judgment. This logical and epistemological theory of knowledge is based on a clear and distinct knowledge of speculative truth and on the methodological procedures for ruling out error. Thus the articulation of the connection between theory and practice will be provided by Descartes's positing of the cogito, a gesture that marks one of the philosophical foundations of scientific modernity and which the Port-Royal logicians find explicitly formulated, in terms of religious faith and morality, in the writings of Saint Augustine. Historically and theoretically, then, the *Logic of Port-Royal* is a strategic text, the purpose of which is an analysis of the relationship between two semiotic systems: a semiotics of the discourse of speculative knowledge and a semiotics of the discourse of "a doctrine of morals teaching the proper conduct of life and actions." Between 1662 and 1683, the dates of its first and fifth editions, the *Logic* expands as a result of the addition of discussions pertaining to morality and rhetoric. It is, however, striking that none of these additions seems to be extraneous to the initial project. In this context, I do not intend to analyze the *Logic* as a whole, but will simply suggest the broad strokes of a reading, which, in keeping with the letter and spirit of the work, does not consider its epistemological and moral elements to be two different and disconnected domains. Thus the interpreter's task is not a matter of relating two alien elements. What I want to suggest is an internal reading involving an analysis of the homogeneous and unified theoretical space to which both of these domains belong. The two domains are internally connected by a relation of reciprocity. Moreover, they both pertain to the historical site that witnesses the creation of a grammar and a logical system that is simultaneously an ethics and, vice versa, an ethics that is simultaneously a logical system and a grammar.

I shall take as my starting point two chapters from the second section of the *General Grammar*, the thirteenth, entitled "Of Verbs and Their Particular and Essential Features," and the fourteenth, "Of the Moods and Manners of Verbs." By chapter 13, the grammarians have already distinguished between two large groups of words, between those that signify the objects of our thoughts (nouns, adjectives, pronouns, adverbs, participles, prepositions) and those that signify the manner of our thoughts (verbs, conjunctions, interjections). The grammarians subsequently go on to define "the nature of the verb" in chapter 13:

> When we judge things (for example, when I say, "The earth is round"), our judgment necessarily includes two terms, the one called the subject, that is, the thing of which something is asserted ... and the other ... the attribute that is asserted; our judgment also includes the relation established between these two terms by virtue of an activity that is proper to our mind and which asserts the attribute of the subject. Thus mankind has had no less need of words that mark the assertions that constitute our principal way of thinking, than it has needed to invent words to mark the objects of our thoughts (Arnauld and Lancelot [1660] 1969, 66).

The Port-Royal grammarians articulated a famous definition of the verb that follows from the above, a definition that will be taken up once again in one of the editions of the *Logic:*

> A word, the main purpose of which is to signify an assertion, that is, to indicate that the speech in which this word is employed is the speech of a human being who not only conceives of things, but who also judges and asserts them (Arnauld and Lancelot [1660] 1969, 66).

These citations invite two remarks. First of all, every utterance confounds a mode of thinking with the expression of its object; a dual semantic function involving a modality and a thing has a simultaneous impact on precisely the same part of speech. Secondly, a triple reduction is effected by the way in which the Port-Royal grammarians and logicians rewrite a given elementary proposition, such as "Peter lives," a rewriting which is supposed to elucidate the way in which thought functions in the use of language: 1) a reduction of all verbs to the verb *to be,* a verb which is called substantive because it is thought to be the only one to have retained the exclusive function of indicating the relation between two terms (an example is "Peter is alive"); 2) a reduction of the verb *to be* to the present tense of the indicative, which is where we discover the signs that indicate that an assertion of the relation between two terms has been effected. Here we have, then, the speech of an individual, of a thinking and speaking subject (an example being [I say that] "Peter is alive"); 3) a reduction of the indicative tense to the third person singular, which is where we discover concurrent and contrary signs to the effect of the priority given to the objectival pole (the thing uttered) over the pole of manner (the utterance of the subject): (an example being [he is] "living Peter"). We might go so far as to say that this triple reduction effects the semantic deduction of the grammatical objectivity characterizing a proposition. Moreover, this deduction has the effect of redoubling the transcendental deduction of the objective value belonging to the judgment that takes place in thought.

In chapter 16, the grammarians bring their analysis of the verb to a close. It is probably true that the main purpose of the verb is to signify an assertion, but "Mankind also needed the verb in order to make their desires as well as their thoughts understood" (Arnauld and Lancelot [1660] 1969, 78). Thus we use the verb in order to signify "other movements of our soul" (Arnauld and Lancelot [1660] 1969, 67), such as desiring, commanding, questioning (section two, chapter 1), or such as desiring, commanding, requesting (section two, chapter 13). In chapter 16, these movements of the soul are systematically defined in terms of three main modalities that can be adopted by the will in addition to the modality of asserting. First of all, there is the modality of the wish by which we desire things that are independent of us. The second modality is that of acceptance. This involves coming to terms with the idea of concurring with something, even though we absolutely do not want to do so. Finally, we have the order and the request: what we want depends upon someone from whom we are in a position to obtain it. By means of an order or request, we indicate to this person our desire that he or she do what we want. Thus the moods of ethical discourse are inscribed within the general semantic structure of language by means of the optative, concessive, and imperative moods.

Let us assume that morality is understood to be "the doctrine that concerns morals, the science which teaches the proper way to conduct one's life and actions," in other words, the regulation of the will, of desire, and passion by means of values and obligations, by means of a series of *oughts* pertaining to what should be the case as well as to what should be done. It could then be said that the reasoned and general analysis of language proffered by the *Grammar* and by the *Logic of Port-Royal,* the kernel of which is the grammar and logic of judgment, introduces morality into language through a process that involves both the distinguishing and the confounding of two elements. In all acts of speech, the manner of thought is distinguished from and confounded with the expression of its object; this moral dimension is introduced as a result of the drawing of a distinction between the principal mode of thinking and its operations of conjunction and disjunction on the one hand and, on the other, the secondary modes of thinking, such as wishing, concurring, ordering, and requesting, all of which result from the movements of the soul, movements which simply involve a change in the inflexion and mood of the principal mode of thinking. Finally, the moral dimension is introduced by virtue of an ever more careful and elaborate articulation of the distinction between the act of asserting, along with its particular modalities, on the one hand, and the modalities of willing and desiring on the other. At stake in the articulation of this distinction is the regulation of the will and desire by assertions. Thus the assertion is the point of reference by which all modal divergences from the principal mode of thinking would be at once identified, measured, and regulated. The cognitive judgment, the objective proposition, the assertion are indeed all part of the same crucial kernel of Port-Royal semantics. Yet for their semantics to satisfy the criteria of their own theory, and for it to be valid for the whole theoretical domain that has been staked out, it must embrace an ethical or moral system.

In his article on "Port-Royal and the Geometry of Subjective Modalities," Claude Imbert shows how and in what way the logic

and grammar of Port-Royal could be said to embody both progress
at the theoretical level and a moral critique. Imbert claims that,
by virtue of its theory of subjective modalities, the Port-Royal
logic and grammar constituted a significant advance beyond
Greek, stoical, and Alexandrian logic, and he insists that this theory, ipso facto, also effected a radical critique of the morals and
doctrines of ancient wisdom:

> The very invention of a new semantic axis allowed Port-Royal to artic-
> ulate a relation between the main section of the *Art of Thinking* . . .
> and the *Grammar,* as well as between these two and the methodolog-
> ical section of Book Four. And thus Port-Royal established the prem-
> ises for a new regulation of the passions (Imbert 1982,
> 309) . . . revealing their concern with being able to think about sci-
> entific knowledge and moral knowledge within the same rational
> economy and with the same method. (Imbert 1982, 324, n. 28)

> Causes and effects
>
> . . . .
>
> Being thus unable to make right into might, we have made
> might into right.
>
> (Pascal 1966, 56 [no. 103])

Following these historical and theoretical points about the semiotic and semantic theory of Port-Royal, I want now to illustrate
them by analyzing a text that, throughout its successive re-
editions, is contemporaneous with the *General Grammar* and
the *Art of Thinking.* The text I have in mind is a fable by La Fontaine, fable 10 of book 1, "The Wolf and the Lamb." There are two
crucial reasons for the importance of this fable in the present context. The first has to do with its genre. As we know, the fable is a
story which employs a modality of speech derived from assertions. As such, it accentuates the objectival pole in a process
involving the disconnecting of the narrative instance from the
propositional contents of what is being narrated. What is more,
beneath the narrative veil (to use the words of Furetière), this
story also implicitly or explicitly includes a moral. That is, it contains educational maxims by means of which "the faults of mankind are corrected" in the name of values (what should be the
case and what should be done). These maxims "aim at turning
people away from their vices and thus at making them better."
How then does this transformation from a story to its moral take

place? How is the moralizing of a story effected? These questions raise the same problem that was introduced by our theoretical texts, the *Grammar* and the *Logic*, in which the Port-Royal logicians also propose a possible solution.

The other reason for attributing such importance to fable 10 has to do with the specific nature of "The Wolf and the Lamb." Its theme is the conflict between fact and value, between an objectively established given and an ethical and ideal teleology. This is a conflict encountered by a moral subject, acting within the sphere of practical reason. It is a conflict that has to be worked out and resolved within the context of the conduct of life. "The Wolf and the Lamb" raises a number of questions. For example, how can the assertive modality characterizing a factual judgment (such as "the sky is blue") be dialectically transformed into one of the other subjective verbal modalities, into that of desiring, concurring, ordering, or requesting? How can the assertion's transformation be effected by the very story in which it figures, at the level of both form and content? How can this story change the objective and assertive modality into one of the modalities characterizing judgments of value, where what is emphasized is the "intersubjective pole"? Among the utterances of the fable, we find certain narrative assertions that pertain to the domain of physical or mechanical necessity. The issue raised by the fable is, then, as follows: how do these narrative assertions, which the fable's utterances formulate in terms of conjunctions and disjunctions, come to be wrapped in a cloak of moral obligation? How do they come to take on the dimension of obligation that manifests the demands of ethical virtue within the sphere pertaining to those actions that ought to be performed? In short, how is a story about power moralized as a discourse of justice? Or contrariwise, how is justice factualized as power? This is what is at stake in the fable and its moral.

"The Wolf and the Lamb" is explicitly presented both as a story and as a moral lesson. More precisely, it is, on the one hand, a moral lesson and an explicit contract of utterance and, on the other, a narrative staging of this moral lesson and the realization of the contract: "The reason of the strongest is always the best. / We shall show this in a little while. / A lamb was drinking. . . . " The reader will have noted that the moral precedes its tale rather than being derived from it. Instead of witnessing the moralizing of the story, we see the narrativizing of the moral lesson. By the same token, before the story is actually read, it is proposed not

LE LOUP ET L'AGNEAU . Fable X .

Illustration of La Fontaine's "The Lamb and the Wolf," by M. Oudry

only as proof of the utterance that constitutes its moral, but also as the reader's acceptance of a sort of command that the fabulator issues. For the reader does precisely what the fabulator says: when the latter begins to speak, his words are announced as an act of discursive strength, as quite definitely the best. This show of strength is partly a result of the modalities affected by the fabulator's speech and partly a consequence of the privileged position that he occupies within the syntagmatic of the fable. The fabulator's words—"The reason of the strongest is always the best"—will be fully borne out by the rest of the fable. The person listening to the fable will be left with absolutely no possibility of contesting its message. From the start, the reader can do nothing other than content himself with granting something even if he absolutely does not want to. This is so quite simply because the fabulator has signified his desire that the reader grant his will.

"The strongest is always the best" is an equation established by definition and having universal validity. Thus it is uttered as the truth, as a proposition that will always be true: the strongest of the strong is the best of the best. A factual assertion concerning a maximal strength is posited as being the equivalent of an evaluation concerning a moral quality, as well as of an optimum of goodness. This equation will be proved shortly, in an argument that will then be presented as apodictically true—as necessary and universal. Yet, having read the moral that precedes the tale, we know that the fabulator does not quite say this: it is not the strongest who always is the best, but his or her reason. How are we to understand this additional clause? Let us assume that reason is understanding, that it is the soul's most important faculty since it provides us with a capacity for distinguishing between what is true and what is false. In this respect, reason is opposed to imagination and to sensibility, for both of these are capacities for error. With these clauses in mind, the reader will understand the fable's moral as follows: when those who are strong distinguish between what is true and false, they simultaneously distinguish between what is good and bad. We have, then, a new apodictic equation: the true is the good; the false is the bad. This is the traditional philosopheme of all intellectualism: every fault is an error, and the wicked person is necessarily ignorant.

This new equation involves a series of reductions: of value to being, of theory to practice, of deontics to cognition. However, our second reading effaces an important fact, just as, a moment ago, we forgot about "reason" in reading the fable's moral. We have failed to note that equating the distinguishing of true from false on the one hand and the distinguishing of good from bad on the other requires further qualification. The equation holds true only in the case of a subject who is endowed with a quality that does not stem from what is true or false, nor from what is good or bad. This subject possesses power, the most striking characteristic of which is that it does not derive from reason—the principal capacity of the soul—nor from imagination or sensibility. It originates in the body. Power is a palpable and very visible feature which "governs external actions" (Pascal 1966, 45 [no. 58]). The scandalous conclusion to which our first reading gave rise, that maximum power is always an optimal practical good, is transformed into a theoretical contradiction by our second reading.

This contradiction may be the result, however, of our having misunderstood the word *reason:* perhaps the term does not actually refer to the faculty that distinguishes between what is true and false; it may instead designate the motive or cause that makes somebody act. Following this view, the interpretation of the fable's moral would be as follows: the motive that the strongest has for exercising power is always the best. Yet what would it mean to speak of a power that is not exercised? Moreover, how can a power be qualified as the strongest or greatest if it does not exert itself against other powers, in a manner that brings about their annihilation or subjugation? At that point, the motive underlying the action of a given power would seem to coincide with power itself: its goal would be to be the strongest power by virtue of the actual annihilation of other powers. In other words, the strongest is always the best, which brings us back to our first outrageous conclusion, the only difference being that, previously, we sinned by omission and read poorly, whereas this time we have read all too well. In fact, the second time around, we read all aspects of the fable's moral.

Yet it could be that *reason* means argumentation or a discourse of truth, a process aimed at convincing others by means of the furnishing of evidence or proof. This definition does not really advance our interpretive cause, because we inevitably end up with the results of our second and contradictory reading. Indeed, the discourse of the strongest does not owe its persuasive power to a chain of reasoning with a self-evident fact at its base, from which a conclusive proposition can be securely derived, a proposition that unfailingly compels the rational assent of the interlocutor. The power of the discourse that belongs to the strongest would be nothing other than strength itself, and the latter is not a matter of discourse or of reasoning. Might is wholly different from discourse or syllogistic reasoning. Pascal calls it a tyrannical force, "the desire to dominate everything regardless of

order . . . wanting by one means what can only be had by another" (Pascal 1966, 45 [no. 58]). We should fear might and have an
absolute fear, which is the definition of terror, for what is most
mighty of all. This is a fear that is not dictated by moral obligation or rational necessity, but by a factual and mechanical relation between quantities of physical power. I spoke above of a
scandal of practical reason and of a scandal of theoretical reason.
It is now clear that these two types of scandals can be avoided if
and only if we give a very precise interpretation to what is supposed to be best about the reason characterizing the strongest.
"Best" should not be understood in a moral sense, as the superlative of "good." Rather, it should be taken in the sense of a
supreme efficacy, as the superlative term that designates that
which is capable of having an ultimate impact on something
else. It should be understood in terms of a description of what
cannot be resisted, of what might be said to have the irresistibil-
ity of a brute fact. In short, "the best" is to be taken in the sense
of "the strongest." The reason of the strongest is the strongest,
that is, the strongest is the strongest. Here we have a tautology: in
the case of sheer strength, there is nothing to be said or thought,
no evaluation to be undertaken, for he who is mighty does not
talk, think, or evaluate; the strongest is the strongest without
further qualification, a kind of pure violence, a dumb power that
acts. To this muteness corresponds the terrified silence of the person who is subjected to an absolute power. Our interpretive trajectory has come full circle: the attempt to move from a factual to a
normative level, from mere observation to evaluation, repeatedly
founders: norms irresistibly and inevitably point us in the direction of the brute facts that uphold them, and evaluation takes us
toward an unquestionable statement of fact. All that remains for
us to do now is keep silent. We are, in a word, to accept silently
the mute dictates of power.

   Yet the fabulator does speak and even insists that he will show
the truth of the moral statement that introduces the fable: "We
shall show this in a little while." It is almost as if the fabulator
were addressing the reader directly: if you will just momentarily
accept this scandalous utterance as a hypothesis or proposition,
you will find proof of it in what follows, in the story. A certain
motive (or reason) incited the fabulator to formulate the scandalous utterance in the first place, just as a certain argumentation
(or reason) guides him in the process of transforming this hypothesis into a thesis, his proposition into a theorem. These two

reasons will clearly be the most effective or best at achieving the following perlocutionary effects: making the listener concur with what the fabulator presents as true, making the listener agree with his convictions, and making the listener believe that the fabulator's truths are binding. These effects are all the more important given that, strictly speaking, the fabulator did not say that he would demonstrate his hypothetical "The reason of the strongest is always the best." All he said was that he, in a little while, would show this to be the case. He does not say that he will argue for his statement, but merely that he will point out the truth of the utterance by telling a fable. It is almost as though we shall be made to read the fable with the index finger of the fabulist carefully tracing the lines of the fable's text, the finger calling special attention to those textual moments that reveal the truth of the scandalous utterance.

Yet if the argumentation in question is a matter of demonstration, before the story has even been told, the hypothesis already proves to be a thesis, and the proposition an intellectual position. This is all the more striking, given that this story was supposed to show the truth of the already formulated moral lesson. Right from the start, and as an absolute prerequisite to the fable, we are told that the proof of the statement will be ostensive. Thus the argumentative reason that has barely been articulated is already the most convincing, since it involves ostension. The reader can and should do nothing but take note of a single fact: this fact, this given, is nothing other than the fact that the story asserts what is factual and given. The utterance "We shall show this in a little while" suggests that the narrative apparatus is being geared up for something that is to follow. This gearing up, however, occurs simultaneously with a gearing down that is equivalent to a deictic, to a demonstrative term that effects the exact inverse of a proof. It is for this reason that the phrase "We shall show this in a little while" can be said to be an anaphora (what will be demonstrated is that "The reason of the strongest always is the best), as well as a cataphora (what is to be shown is what follows, the story). It is this combination of tropes that allows the fabulator simultaneously to be silent and to speak. His silence (what we called a gearing down) allows the fable to speak itself in the form of a pure story (gearing down, silence on the part of what is most forceful—language). His speaking (what we called a gearing up) informs us that the fable will demonstrate the initial hypothesis, that it will transform the proposition into a theorem (the proposition is that the de facto violence of an absolute power is the equivalent de jure of an ultimate good). Thus we witness something like a complex *chassé-croisé* between the propositional content of an utterance and the utterance itself; between an objective assertive modality of speech on the one hand, and concessive modalities and subjective imperatives on the other; between factual observations on the one hand, and true proofs and deontic evaluations on the other. This play of lexical and discursive semantic ambiguities allows the narrative apparatus to make present what is theoretically unrepresentable—an absolute power and the practical scandal of a supreme value that would be its equivalent.

So the story begins. Actually the story is *stricto sensu* the staging and theatrical construction, the scenography for a confrontational dialogue between protagonists. The characters make only the briefest of appearances in the first four stanzas before they are replaced by actors whose actions are reduced to a set of quickly exchanged utterances. Moreover, it will not escape us that the wolf has an advantage over the lamb, since he has the first and the last "word": "Who made you so bold as to disturb my beverage? . . . I was told as much: I must avenge myself." At which point an inverse substitution causes the actors, who act exclusively with language, to become characters once again. Thus a brief dénouement occurs without any other form of narrative legal process.

"A lamb was drinking / Pristine water from a stream. / A fasting wolf unexpectedly arrives, looking for adventure, / Hunger having drawn him to these regions." The story introduces us to two characters, the lamb and the wolf, through whom the story is immediately situated on an ethical plane. From the outset, the characters function as univocal allegories of contradictory moral notions. The lamb stands for what is good and the wolf for evil. What is more, they are allegories of these notions at their absolute extremes. The lamb represents an absolute good, innocence. The pristine water from which he drinks is no more pure than the lamb who has just been born ("I still suckle my mother," says the lamb). In the wolf, we find the incarnation of absolute evil or of rage. The confabulating director of the confrontational dialogue fleetingly tells us as much in an ambiguous expression that hesitates between two different functions: as a dramaturgical didascaly, the expression makes rage the salient feature of the tone with which the wolf addresses his words to the lamb; as the description of an ontological trait, the expression defines the very being of the wolf. Yet upon closer consideration, it becomes clear that the lamb and the wolf are the epitome of goodness and of evil, respectively. Moreover, these features are precisely what makes it possible for both of them to transcend the ethical order in which the reader automatically situates them by virtue of their names. As a result of its innocence, the lamb is in some sense situated at the origin or beginning of its own life story ("it had just been born"), a peculiar story that will consist of a series of thoughts and actions.

The moral evaluation of this story will determine whether the lamb's character is axiologically positive or negative and will thereby signal either a feature meriting praise or one indicative of guilt. Neither praiseworthy nor guilty, the lamb is beyond good and evil by virtue of an actual purity and a natural innocence. The same holds for the wolf, as a result of the rage that characterizes its animal nature. In the world of human agents, "rage" is the very illness that drives away reason and stirs up fury; the term designates an extreme passion or a desperate need. It would seem, then, that the very nature of the tale's "raging animal" serves to situate the wolf beyond good and evil. The wolf is a fortiori beyond all culpability as well as all ethical merit. As a result of the notions that attach to the fable's protagonists, we are immediately inclined to interpret the encounter between the wolf and the lamb within a moral framework. Yet the very reasons that incline us toward such a reading are also responsible for establishing the locations and moment of this meeting in the state of nature prior to individual or collective history, in a time and place where good and bad do not yet exist. It is as though, through a strange paradox requiring elucidation, the excess of evil and the excess of goodness situate those whom they characterize beyond the moral categories which made it possible for us to evaluate them as either excessively evil or good. It is true that what we read is a story about animals, who are first and foremost animals, prior to being the allegories of humankind that typify the creatures of fables. It is a story about animals who remain oblivious to the history and ethical evaluation of actions and decisions, as well as to the motives and drives that govern responsible, voluntary, and free agents. It is a story about animals that describes what happens in the state of nature at the moment

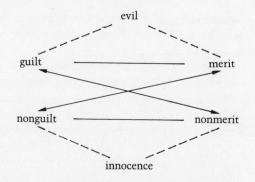

The elementary structure of ethical signification

when the strong and the weak, the strongest and the weakest, "accidentally" meet: the physical and mechanical sanction governing this meeting specifies that the former will devour the latter. This amounts to a natural equilibrium, a law of necessity: wolves eat lambs, and lambs are eaten by wolves.

The fact, however, that things are not quite as straightforward as they appear is revealed by the difficulty that we have in situating the wolf, by nature the epitome of evil, within the schema of "the elementary structure of ethical signification." Indeed, the lamb is naturally the epitome of goodness and, as a domestic animal, belongs to the society of domestic animals. More precisely, it is part of the flock that is herded by a shepherd and guarded by his dogs. This situation is quite the contrary of that of the wolf who, by definition, is a solitary creature, a savage and inhuman animal, a wild beast. In spite of its being an animal, the lamb, in a sense, figures as the delegate or epitome of "culture" within the story and maybe even outside of it. The lamb is more than the allegorical representative of a civil society governed by legal contracts. It makes manifest the dimension of community, of an affective and ethical communion from which it cannot be separated ("I still suckle my mother"). The wolf's case, on the other hand, is quite different. Within the story, and perhaps outside of it, the wolf figures as an "animal filled with rage" and thus designates himself as a kind of natural excess. He is apparently without companions, a solitary individual, free from all natural ties, subject to no necessities other than that of his own voracity.

It is appropriate, then, to introduce into the first diagram of the elementary structure of ethical signification a second one that develops further the category of nature and of culture. In this respect, the lamb—the representative of the class of devoured beings, of those who are weak by nature—is brought into relation with, or displaced into, the world of culture, where it acquires its innocence by virtue of its excessively weak physical nature. The wolf, on the other hand, figures as an allegory of what culture construes as evil. Thus the wolf is displaced into the world of nature, where a paradoxical process determines his being: the very excessiveness of the moral and cultural evil that surrounds the wolf is itself responsible for situating him in a sphere that is beyond all guilt, beyond all negative value. "Full of rage," the wolf is just naturally evil.

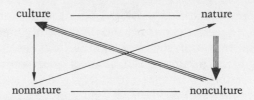

By virtue of the way in which his cultural and moral badness is displaced into the sphere of nature, the wolf appears to be naturally evil, notions of guilt and merit simply being inapplicable to his being. The lamb's being is determined by a similar, yet inverse, transformational process: as a result of the way in which his natural weakness is displaced into the sphere of morality and culture, the lamb is culturally innocent, this side of both guilt and merit.

The construction of the tale's protagonists reveals that "he who is strongest" exists in a sphere beyond all morality, since a moral category has been transported into the state of nature. On the other hand, "he who is weakest" exists squarely in the domain where moral notions apply, a situation brought about by transferring a natural category into the sphere of culture. Thus we witness a dual transformation, the symmetrical inversion of strength and weakness, of evil and goodness. The tale's moral, which we have already read, points to the existence of a fundamental disymmetry: it tells us that the strongest is always best, but it does not designate the weakest as the most evil.

Let us assume that the tale is to demonstrate a hypothetical morality by means of an enunciative contract. In that case, the tale must effect a transformation of the initial state of affairs, which derives its salient features from the event that makes up the encounter between the tale's two protagonists. This transformation must bring about a nonsymmetrical inversion; it must produce the two notions of an existence beyond or this side of the sphere of morality. These two categories are diametrically opposed to each other and result from an inverse and symmetrical transformation of something natural into something cultural, and of the cultural into the natural, of a fact into a value and vice versa. In other words, the tale is supposed to provide the kind of evidence that will constitute a justification of power ("The reason of the strongest is always the best"). Yet this demonstration must be such that it does not hold for the contrary case, which would amount to a condemnation of weakness. The proof in question must, however, establish what is indirectly contrary to the fable's axiom—"The reason of the strongest is always the best"—for it is to bolster justice. If weakness is not condemned by the end of the tale, then power will have to be justified, which means that justice cannot be made strong. Weakness is explicitly a matter of guilt. At least, this is the message of the sociopolitical cynicism that is implicitly the hidden backside of the moral discourse generated within actual civic society. The idea that morality should be bolstered, that is, explicitly declared to be the strongest, is itself a form of ethico-utopic idealism. As such, it is the ideological backdrop for the type of political discourse that privileges an abstract cultural community. In short, what is weak is not morally condemned, although what is strong is morally justified. Here we witness the asymmetry that gives rise to the abyss that proves to be unfathomable for both a theoretical and practical reason: the idea that a sin lies at the origin of reality and history. Because of this asymmetry, the tale cannot provide a proof of its initial hypothesis, but merely presents it as a statement of fact.

"A lamb was drinking / Pristine water from a stream." This sentence is written in the imperfect tense and thus stages a temporal chunk of some duration that takes place in a stable past. The sentence's grammatical features suggest the immediate and effortless satiation typical of the state of nature. "A fasting wolf unexpectedly arrives, looking for adventure, / Hunger having drawn him to these regions." Here the use of the present tense to express the occurrence of an unexpected event allows us to experience or witness something like a "punctual now." Here is a

schema of events, which pertains to a pure narrative and which
has been pushed to the absolute extreme with the sudden emergence of the present tense. Semantic and syntaxical features are
once more intertwined, and thus the present tense suggests a vol-
atile process of need, a voracious quest. It should be noted that
the wolf is not simply said to be hungry. Instead, the wolf is said
to be seized by hunger as if by a natural destiny. In a sense, this
hunger moves or motivates the wolf from the outside in the manner of an absolute passion. The taste for adventure that animates
and motivates the wolf is nothing other than the fortuitous and
organic dimension of this factual necessity: it designates the
potential prey that might be available in one of the sites constituted by the desire and need for food. Thus the predator's action
involves a twofold movement: first, the wolf engages in a wandering search, then his attention is focalized on the edible object. In
La Fontaine's French, this two-step process is imitated by the
disymmetry of the long Alexandrine and the short decasyllabic
verses. The metric rhythm overturns the articulation of narrative
syntax, and the sphere of prosodical signifiers pertaining to the
wolf englobes the diagram of the incidence.

To be more precise, the dual space sketched by the form of
poetic expression also sketches the site where the encounter
between the two protagonists will take place in the narrative representation. The lamb has left the domestic cultural space
within which he belongs, to drink from a stream of natural water;
similarly, the wolf, overcome by hunger, has left the forest, a wild
and natural sphere, in search of adventure. The encounter between the satiated yet weak lamb and the famished yet strong
wolf thus takes place in the no-man's-land between the sphere of
nature and that of culture. The site of their encounter is a limit
or boundary that will be doubly and inversely transgressed by the
protagonists in the drama. One might say that this space, in its
lack of definition, nonetheless is more natural than cultural. The
lamb's distance from the cultivated and domestic sphere is
greater than the wolf's distance from the world of nature. The
lamb leaves culture behind him in favor of nature, while the wolf
turns his back on a natural excess (pertaining to the savagery of
the forest) in favor of nature, the banks of the stream. The lamb is
entirely surrounded by the space of the wolf.

Yet the scansion that governs the confabulator's poem in
French also authorizes one of the narrative figures to begin to
speak, the one to whom the greatest quantity of speech has been

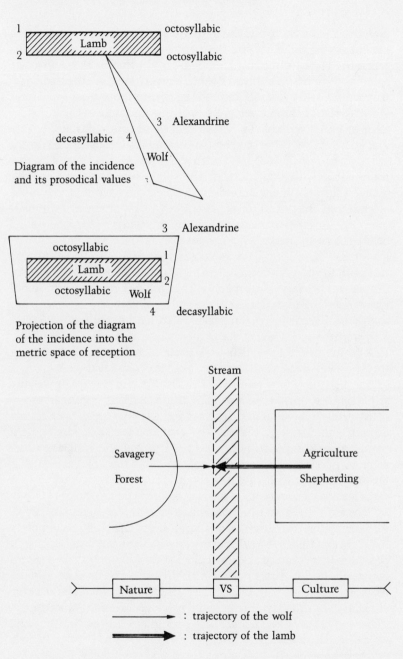

Diagram of the incidence
and its prosodical values

Projection of the diagram
of the incidence into the
metric space of reception

assigned. Thus the wolf, the animal filled with rage, speaks first. He speaks in order to put into words the intrusion that occurs when the lamb enters the sphere of nature, that is, the wolf's own sphere: "Who makes you so bold as to disturb my beverage? / Says this animal full of rage, / You will be punished for your temerity."

By virtue of the conventions of fables, the will of the confabulator makes it possible for the animal to attain language. The animal achieves a level of quasi-culture and is thus positioned on the border between nature and culture, in the no-man's-land that is more natural than cultural. At the same time, language and discourse establish a new boundary between the need that drives the animal and the act of devouring. They bring about a distance, a temporal difference that defers the immediate satisfaction of desire. In speaking, the wolf begins the return from nature, or at least from his notion of it, to culture. Similarly, in responding to the wolf, in the very act of speaking, the lamb begins to lose some degree of the natural innocence that his notion of nature originally had introduced into the sphere of culture. In becoming agents of discourse, the animals realize and make explicit a certain transformation: the fact of power and of natural weakness is transformed into the cultural power and weakness that pertains to discourse. Discursive power and weakness take the form of either a success or a failure at the level of proving an argument, one designed with an eye to persuasion or the bringing about of conviction. The question is whether the strongest will be the best or the worst at playing the cultural game of language, it being understood, however, that the rewards and sanctions contingent upon success or failure remain those of the state of nature, that is, eating or being eaten. Will the reason of the weakest necessarily assert itself against that of the strongest?

To return, then, to the moment when the wolf begins to speak: we witness an immediate translation into language of the powerful position that the wolf occupies within the animal sphere, a position immediately acknowledged without explanation and recognized without further ado. From this unchallenged and powerful position, the wolf accosts the lamb with a declaration that allegedly establishes the latter's presence on the banks of the stream. The wolf's words are also articulated in the interrogative mode, for he poses a rhetorical question. We know that the salient feature of such questions is neither "to express a doubt nor provoke a response but, on the contrary, to articulate the greatest degree of conviction and to challenge the interlocutor's ability to produce a denial or even a response" (Fontanier [1827] 1968, 368). Normally, a question takes the form of one of several subjective modalities that characterize wishes or desire: "the movement of our soul by means of which we both hope to acquire knowledge about something and ask to be informed about it" (Fontanier [1827] 1968, 368). In the case of a rhetorical question, however, the interrogative form is at some remove from the ordinary functioning of the question. The question becomes a figure that aims at "making the expression penetrate the very heart of the interlocutor, in the manner of a piercing arrow that tears, overwhelms, and confounds him. To put it bluntly, the interlocutor is placed in a position that admits of neither a reply nor an excuse" (Fontanier [1827] 1968, 369). Thus, for example, the wolf does not ask the lamb: "What are you doing here (instead of being in your domestico-cultural sheepfold)?" Instead, the wolf says: "You should not be where you are right now. Moreover, the very idea that you might be able to justify your presence in some manner is ruled out in advance." Here we have the rhetorical formulation of a de jure interdiction.

One other dimension of the rhetorical question deserves mention in this context. A figurative question is, in fact, the expression of an underlying threat, of the ostensible figure of thought known as a commination," defined as "a threat (or the announcement of a more or less horrible misfortune), the image of which is evoked in order to transmit anguish and fear into the soul of whomever it is that has mobilized our hatred, anger, indignation or desire for revenge" (Fontanier [1827] 1968, 434). In its figurative and interrogative form, the juridical interdiction is an expression that pertains to the passions. Thus the confabulator is anything but wrong when he qualifies the wolf as "an animal filled with rage."

The principle of right that grounds the wolf's peremptory questioning is that of property rights: the wolf refers to his beverage. The lamb then, is, construed as a thief who violates the wolf's rights by drinking from a stream of pristine water. The lamb's gesture amounts to an illegal crossing of the border that separates culture from nature. We might ask ourselves whether there can be such a thing as property in a state of nature, given that the concept of property is one of the salient features of culture, one of the institutions of civil society. It is precisely by usurping a right that can only belong to culture that the wolf manages to "denaturalize" a natural element—the water. How will the wolf legitimate this usurpation? How will he transform his discursive appropriation of the water into a property title?

We shall see that the wolf will provide grounds for his appropriative gesture, yet they will be purely de facto. His grounds amount to an assertive statement about a physical, empirical, and natural situation. In short, the legitimacy of the wolf's gestures is found simply in the existence of a natural element and in the situation provoked by the lamb's presence. Thus the wolf utters the following question: "Who makes you so bold as to disturb my beverage?" As we saw above, the act of uttering a juridical interdiction in a rhetorical manner is, in fact, an expression of certain passions, and we referred to this utterance in terms of a figurative comminatory question. We now note that a juridical utterance, as well as the interdiction that follows from it, has purely de facto bases. These bases are simply a matter of what is and can be stated: in the case of the fable, it can be asserted that the lamb disturbs the wolf's pristine water. To justify the assertion of his rights, the strongest provides grounds for his appropriative gesture. Yet the modality characterizing these grounds is not continuous with the appropriative utterance and thus severely weakens the discursive efficacy of the latter. The production of rights and titles is, in fact, a matter of simply submitting grounds that are wholly de facto to an empirical test that aims at either confirmation or falsification. Thus deontics is grounded in alethics. It should be noted, however, that the wolf returns in the conclusion to his speech to a discursive level concerned with rights and with justice: "You will be punished for your temerity." The future tense announces the ongoing set of legal proceedings that the wolf intends to conduct against the lamb.

Perfectly expert at recognizing discursive modalities, the lamb has an unfailing understanding of the situation. Thus he does not justify his presence on the banks of the stream nor does he try to legitimate it by invoking an alternative set of rights. Instead, he discusses the fact itself of disturbing the water. We saw above that a comminatory question does not solicit a response, and that it, in fact, even rules out the possibility of a reply. How, then, does the lamb react to the wolf's question? His response takes the form of a demonstration or proof: "Sire, replies the lamb, would that Your Majesty / Might refrain from anger; / Instead let Him consider that I drink / From the stream / at more than twenty feet below His Majesty. / As a consequence I can in no way / Disturb His drink." The lamb, who is physically weak, takes up a position of no mean discursive strength. Yet the price paid for the development of his alethic and epistemic argument is the definitive loss of his natural innocence. Thus he renounces his former status, which was characterized by its externality in relation to all matters concerning guilt and merit. This loss results from the lamb's reply to the wolf. There is also a further reason behind the lamb's altered state. The lamb deftly employs what he believes to be a tactical rhetorical ruse involving the manipulation of discursive games. His response is thus compromised in two related respects: first, the chances of its being successful qua response is severely endangered; second, the lamb's response opens the door to a compromise in the sense of arbitration. As a result of his having compromised with the discourse of the wolf and with the latter's presuppositions, the lamb compromises the alethic and epistemic force of his response. This compromise finds a dual expression in the lamb's response: the lamb first accords his interlocutor a title, and then accepts the fact that he was disturbing the water in order to propose an amicable arrangement that might be acceptable to the wolf.

Indeed, the lamb's gratuitous act of bestowing a title on the wolf indicates the former's willingness to recognize the wolf's right to appropriate not only the water, but also all of nature. It should be noted that the lamb does not just employ any arbitrary title, but invokes that of the King. The lamb's speech act has the effect of immediately transforming the natural universe into the world of a civil society. It also institutes the wolf as the authorized sovereign of this society. One might say that the wolf had limited himself to merely denaturalizing the water ("my beverage"); the lamb, on the other hand, engages in a process of generalization for he culturalizes the entire natural domain and presents it as a terrain that legitimately belongs to his interlocutor. Thus the lamb accepts the juridical presupposition that underwrites the wolf's peremptory questioning: *modus concessivus*, the lamb contents himself with granting the presupposition even if he absolutely does not want to, even if he absolutely disagrees with it. In so doing, however, the lamb takes the conciliatory process one step too far, something that the wolf does not fail to note. The lamb's excessive concession cannot be anything but distasteful to the wolf, for it is clear that his absolute sovereignty over nature derives from the lamb's gracious speech act, from his linguistic move. The title that he bestows on or concedes to the wolf basically suggests that absolute power is legitimate, and thus the lamb actually provides the sovereign with a ground or basis for his power: the lamb recognizes the wolf as sovereign in the very act of authorizing his power. The lamb's strength is his weakness. The potency of his discourse turns out to be his greatest failing.

The lamb does more than simply accept the wolf's discourse. With a single word, he dismantles the juridical validity of the form in which the wolf had cast his utterance, that of the comminatory question: the wolf did not express a passionate indignation at seeing one of his ostensible rights flouted, at witnessing the transgression of an interdiction. Instead, the wolf expressed anger, rage, "an illness that drives away reason and stirs up fury." So the question becomes one of how to bring the wolf back to a state of reason, to a reasonableness that would be best even though it pertains to the figure who is strongest. In accepting that he might be disturbing the water by occupying a site alongside the banks of the stream, the lamb articulates a concession that simultaneously takes the form of an implicit refusal of the wolf's claim: he grants the idea that he might be disturbing the water. This is clear from his suggestion that he move some twenty feet and drink downstream from his Majesty the Wolf. The lamb resolves the problem rationally: the resolution relies on a theorem that specifies the dynamics of fluids and abides by the rules of politesse, that is, by the norms that make up etiquette. The lamb proposes to situate himself below the wolf, which, according to the physics of flux, means that he will drink further downstream. According to the rules of hierarchy, this means that the lamb will occupy an inferior position, second to that of the King. The lamb's words implicitly suggest that rational and reasonable considerations might take the place of anger. Ideally, a careful consideration of the issues would be justice incarnate and would embrace both the moment of a cognitive utterance as well as that pertaining to a social rule. The lamb casts his phrase in an implicit future tense—"That I drink . . ."—and thus projects a temporality of decisions and actions that involve obligations pertaining to politesse as well as the laws of physics.

It is within this projected temporal framework that the lamb contests and denies that which he has just accepted. He does not say the following: "Let His Majesty consider the idea that I could go and drink downstream from Him. If I were to be twenty feet downstream from His Majesty I would no longer be able, at that moment, to disturb his drink." Although the lamb's proposed action is to take place in the future, he presents the consequence of this action, the clarity of the water, in the present. The consequence of his future action takes place in the very moment of his utterance: "As a consequence I can in no way / Disturb His drink." In other words, "I accept your statement that I am disturbing your drinking right now. I propose to go and drink further downstream. Yet this future action is useless and absurd, for I am not, in fact, disturbing your drink right now."

The emphasis placed on the total efficacy of the lamb's future action and on its outcome, "as a consequence I can in no way," is a way of concealing the lamb's withdrawal of the very concession that he so readily had granted. If we clean up the lamb's response and remove all of the modal superstructures that give it its tactical thrust, we are left with the following: "Even if we accept that you are the legitimate proprietor of these waters, it will become quite clear to you, once you look closely, that I am not, in fact, disturbing them." The lamb's argument takes the form of an ostensive. Yet his argument is not reducible to an indicating gesture, and his chain of modalized reasons serves neither alethic nor epistemic purposes. Indeed, his reasons do not even have a deontic thrust, for they are mobilized with the aim of achieving a pragmatic effect in relation to a particular set of circumstances and matters of fact: "How am I, the weakest, going to escape right here and now from the clutches of the strongest?"

Let us consider the wolf's second response: "You are disturbing it [the water]." His reply involves a statement of fact in the present tense; the utterance refers to exactly the same moment and place in time as the assertion made by the lamb: "I cannot be disturbing it." Who is to say who is right? This is the point when the strongest takes up action against the weakest: the future punishment with which the strongest threatens the weakest is motivated by the sense of duty that accompanies the rights belonging to a legitimate proprietor. This threat is almost temporally conjoined to the observation of the lamb's error, and thus the commination resolves into imminence. Yet in his desire to justify his power, the wolf goes one step further: a new respite is thus introduced into the situation of imminence and, as a result, the pending danger is slightly lessened: "And I know that you slandered me last year." In granting a proposition that he actually contests, the lamb had suggested a "good" action that was to take place at some future moment, and that would resolve the conflictual statement pertaining to the present state of affairs. The wolf, in his desire to justify what he wants, dogmatically insists on speaking about a "bad" discourse that (ostensibly) took place in the past. Thus he hopes to obtain legitimately what he presently possesses by virtue of a de facto state of affairs. At this moment in the fable, a new displacement, a new transformation takes place. The lamb has committed a serious mistake with respect to the wolf, since, at some moment in the past, the former maligned the latter. Moreover, the wolf claims to have knowledge of this particular speech act. The error in question no longer concerns the things or goods that the master of the natural universe possesses legitimately; instead, the crime refers to words and discourses. What is involved here is quite simply high treason, because His Majesty the Wolf is also the legitimate proprietor of language. The presence of the lamb in the here and now disturbs a natural element, the water, just as he at some moment in the past muddied and perverted the rules governing the authorized usage of discourse. Once again the lamb's response is both factual and conclusive. He proves the nonsensical nature of the wolf's statement by reducing the argument to the absurd: "How could I have done that given that I was not yet born / . . . I still suckle my mother." The lamb does not reprimand his interlocutor for his error: "I did not malign Your Majesty." The juridical proceedings would at that point have to involve the convoking of witnesses for both the defense and the prosecution, and their respective arguments would have to be made subject to evaluation. For the lamb to have been the speaker of an utterance, be it good or bad, one would have to be able to show—indeed, it would have been sufficient to prove—that the lamb existed at the moment when the speech act in question was uttered. The lamb was not yet born at the time the crime referred to by the wolf was committed; the proof of this is furnished by the lamb's response, which is articulated in the present tense: "I still suckle my mother."

"Well, if it was not you then it was your brother. / —I do not have one. —In that case it was one of your kind: / For you and yours hardly spare me / You, your shepherds and your dogs." The wolf develops his juridical argument by displacing the responsibility for the crime away from the individual subject and by attributing it instead to the nearest of kin. Ultimately, he even goes so far as to blame society at large. The crime is of a collective nature; as a result, the lamb ceases to be a subject in rebellion against his sovereign. He has at this point become the sovereign's enemy. It is not within the sphere of civil society that the lamb is considered to have transgressed the laws of property and of correct linguistic usage. Rather, he is construed as the delegate from another society that exists within the sphere over which the wolf is master. Moreover, the lamb's society is at war with everything in the wolf's sphere of influence. Now, universal warfare is the salient and fundamental feature of the state of nature. It is a de facto war, since nobody can legally claim the right to possess a good or to say (or not say) what must be said: this kind of war is governed by brute facts and sheer power relations. In other words, by displacing responsibility from the individual de jure subject onto the collectivity as a whole, the wolf reinstates the very border between nature and culture which he had effaced when he claimed to be the legitimate proprietor of the water, the lamb having tacitly accepted this effacement.

At this point, the entire ethico-juridical superstructure erected by the two interlocutors during their negotiation and acceptance of their respective rights and duties collapses. There then emerges with startling clarity a pure state of nature unrestricted by sanctions or obligations, a realm governed by the physical necessities of sheer power relations. The wolf takes this transformation into consideration when he insists that his being generally slandered ("You, your brother, one of your own") is related to the general warfare to which culture subjects him in the manner of a cause and an effect, a motive and a consequence: "For you and yours hardly spare me / You, your shepherds, and your dogs." The domestic society of sheep, lambs, and ewes is itself but a part of human society, which defends the herd from a natural savagery. The war between culture and nature spares nothing, is ruthless, and without mercy: it is a matter of submission or destruction. Caught in this universal life-and-death struggle of culture against nature, the lamb—who is a delegate and representative of culture, although he has strayed into the domain of nature—can be only a victim. By the same token, however, thanks to the wolf, the lamb's notion is returned to nature, where it recovers an innocence beyond all considerations of good and evil, that is, this side of guilt and merit. As the weakest is devoured by the strongest, the lamb retrieves the innocence that had been momentarily lost in his appropriation of language, in his dialogue with the wolf. Unlike the lamb, however, the wolf discovers his true being during the exchange with his weaker partner in dialogue. Instead of simply consuming his opponent without further ado, the wolf transfers the moral and social notion of evil, as well as the guilt that ensues from it, from its original site in society and culture into the sphere of nature, where it loses all meaning. Thus the notions in question travel along two diametrically opposed trajectories, one moving from nature to culture, and the other from culture to nature, from morality and law to power and sheer necessity. Moreover, these trajectories intersect at the exact boundary separating nature from culture, a boundary that is momentarily blurred and transgressed. It is this intersecting that produces the story of the meeting between the two notions. Their meeting also produces the exchange of two incommunicable discourses: the speakers of these respective languages both adopt the language of the other for strategic and pragmatic purposes; the wolf adopts the language of law and the lamb that of brute facts. The scission between nature and culture, fact and law, can only be surmounted by means of a violent war in which the one is destroyed by the other: the resolution is to be found in relations of power. That nature or power should destroy culture and law makes perfect sense for the means are suited to the end in question. That culture or law should destroy nature or power is, however, both incomprehensible and absurd, for the means are incompatible with the goal guiding the act of annihilation. That does happen, however, and this means that violence will always lie at the origin of law; power will always be the basis of morality; and law and morality will never be anything but justifications of power. Unable to make justice strong, mankind ensured that power was made just. This is essentially the meaning of the wolf's discourse. The discourse of the shepherds and their dogs, of the keepers of the social group, would surely have conveyed the same message, had the confabulator allowed them to speak. The reason of the strongest is always the best. The discourses of the wolf and the lamb prove the truth of these words, while the story simply shows the saying's veracity. The wolf's last words are perhaps to be understood in this light.

"I was told as much: I must avenge myself." What are we to make of this anonymous utterance that overshadows the wolf's behavior with a mysterious dictate? What is the nature and status of this categorical imperative that prescribes revenge? It is the linguistic expression, not of an ethical or juridical obligation, but of natural necessity. Aggression is the only way to respond to the warlike behavior of a given group, and the ensuing conflict will necessarily be perpetuated until one of the two parties is totally destroyed; the greatest power will determine the outcome of the conflict, and peace is an impossibility from the outset. What we have here is something like an inexorable Iron-Age law: the instinct of preservation requires the satiation of hunger (since one must eat to live), as well as the annihilation of any wild animal that might endanger the multiplication of goods and riches. The confrontation that involves a struggle until death cannot possibly be just a matter of legitimate or rightful punishment. It is always wholly a question of revenge. So be it. Yet we are left with a remainder: the speakerless, subjectless discourse for which the wolf has since forever been the receiver: "I was told as much." The phrase is inextricably linked to an instinct for self-preservation (mediated through death), to a natural destiny, and to the violence pertaining to the sphere of necessity. At this point, the wolf still speaks, although he soon will revert to the silence that characterizes the actions that reveal the strength of those who are strongest. By effacing the name that the beastly wolf would be incapable of uttering, the confabulator gives voice to an ultimate justification, to a transcendent power, to God or Nature. This strategy amounts to another way of saying that the wolf is without guilt, that he is just as innocent as the lamb he is about to consume. We are led to believe that the wolf is moved by the mysterious power that issues the order dictating revenge: "I must avenge myself." This phrase articulates a metaphysical avatar of the subjective imperative mood, which resembles those analyzed by the *General Grammar of Port-Royal,* the only difference being that, in this case, the avatar does not concern a verbal form and cannot be attributed to a subject: rather, it manifests all the irreparable unhappiness in the world.

It is worth taking note of the examples that the Jansenist grammarians employ to illustrate the *modus imperativus:* the commandment "*non occides,* you shall not kill, do not kill." One paragraph later, the grammarians invoke another commandment: "you (plur.) must love, we must love, you (sing.) must love." The commandments are those of the Old and New Testaments respectively. It is true that the grammarians had two figures in mind while articulating the grammar that governs the verb and its moods: the lamb of God, killed in order to efface the sins of the world, and the divine shepherd whose task it is to lead back into the fold of the Church the sheep that has strayed into the midst of predatory wolves. Once again, the thrust of my discussion concerning the encounter between the lamb and the wolf is best summed up by one of Pascal's *pensées:*

If it had been possible, men would have put might into the hands of right, but we cannot handle might as we like. Since it is a palpable quality, whereas right is a spiritual quality which we manipulate at will, and so right has been put into the hands of might. Thus the name of right goes to the dictates of might.

Hence the right of the sword, because the sword confers a genuine right.

Otherwise we should see violence on one side and justice on the other (end of the twelfth *Provincial Letter*).

Hence the injustice of the Fronde, which sets up its alleged right against might. It is not the same thing with the Church, because there genuine justice exists without any violence (Pascal 1966, 52 [no. 85]).

6   Utopic Rabelaisian Bodies

    This discussion is motivated by dual and untenable ambitions and may be seen as one utopic site among many others.[1] On the one hand, I wish to speak about utopia and to elaborate a discourse about texts that prove very difficult to classify and which seem to be exceptions to the typology of genre that they presuppose. On the other hand, I want to show that this critical discourse about utopia is an untenable one. It is not that such a discourse cannot be developed, for it is always possible to speak and to write on the subject of a text. Instead, the problem is as follows: this critical discourse cannot capture what is indicated by the utopic gesture; indeed, it neutralizes its referent. This is so, no matter how hard one tries to make the discourse exact and rigorous; in fact, the problem is perhaps proportionate to the exactitude and rigor achieved. In order to circumvent this problem, one would somehow have to keep intact the activity and efficacy of the untenable contradiction within the discussion that seeks to come to terms with the utopic gesture.

    In other words, in proposing yet another set of reflections on utopia, I am not simply extending the study that I devoted to this

---

1. For a general discussion of the utopic genre see Dubois (1968), Messac (1962), and Versins (1972). See also Trousson's appropriate remark: "At this point the boundaries of the genre burst apart and ultimately this would make any systematic study of utopia impossible" (1974), p. 368. For a discussion of the theoretical issues pertaining to the notion of genre see Granger (1968) and Guillén (1971).

topic elsewhere, nor am I applying the theses that underwrote it.[2] What is at stake here is the difference and the distance between this and the earlier discussion; it is a matter of developing a critique of the earlier work, critique being understood less as the establishing of a judicial instance, which would measure it by the yardstick of truth and falsehood, than as a digression, as the diverting of the trajectories of analysis previously followed. Thus this return to utopia is also a detour of my discourse on utopia: here and now, then, and in this present discussion, the earlier text is reactivated and destabilized.

The discourse about utopia is an untenable discourse: the topographical, political, and economic spaces of utopia play in the way that we say that "there is play" when the pieces of a mechanism, the elements of a system, or the parts of a whole are not perfectly adjusted to one another. At times, there is empty space between the spaces that are full; at certain points, the mechanism becomes jammed or stuck as a result of an excessive concentration of elements. In its reading of a text, the discourse about utopia consists of making the spaces signified by the utopic text cohere. It does this by replacing the empty spaces between them with its own signifying substance or by explaining the textual sites where they are implicated. By revealing, articulating, or explaining these points of play, by speaking about what is liminal or in between, the discourse about utopia puts a ban on them. This discourse makes the quasi-system of the utopic construction into a real system, into a structured totality where there is no play. My purpose in this text, the dual ambition or intention abruptly referred to above, is to restore the play of the utopic text, to allow it to play, and thus to displace the play of the utopic quasi-system, its consequences, its incoherences, its absences and excesses, to displace them all in the direction of pure fantasy, of the lucidity of the text. The idea is to derive from this play, without imposing any speculative or practical interest, all the pleasurable advantages that it proffers. In the final analysis, we shall be able to ask ourselves what is instantaneously manifested in this play.[3]

I shall focus on the Rabelaisian utopia: by virtue of a kind of doxic self-evidence, which I have simply accepted, I shall discuss

---

2. See Marin (1973), pp. 15-50, 249-56.
3. I have developed these remarks in Marin (1976).

Thélème. And for purely calculated reasons, I shall take up a chapter from *The Inestimable Life of the Great Gargantua, Father of Pantagruel*.[4] I shall accept the received idea of Thélème as a utopic representation. My aim will be to discern the fiction that produces this representation. The representational process can be seen to reorient the free play of this fiction toward the image. Thus I shall be concerned with discovering the particular traits or marks that are deposited by this fiction within the image, as well as with what they indicate. The idea, then, is to introduce play into the text, a play that is detrimental to the representational process and representations that it signifies. In the final analysis, we shall discover that the text of Rabelais is, quite happily, utopia itself, an immense body of pleasure.

Structure

That Thélème exhibits many of the features characteristic of the utopic genre is a matter of some self-evidence. Some of these characteristics are the dialogic structure of the voices (Gargantua, Friar John); the use of a mode of expression that places both the story and the description within a frame; the founding of an institution by delimiting a place or site; and the construction of an architectural form that organizes this place according to the principle, if not the mechanism, by which it is inverted into its historical and social contrary.

Let us take up these different points and quickly indicate the syntagmatic structure of the passage that we have in mind:

1. First of all, we have a narrative layer, a story involving two sequences of events: how Gargantua had the abbey of Thélème built for the monk, and how the abbey was built and came to be inhabited by Thelemites. Central to the first sequence is an architectural plan and its result, while the second is the story of an origin and the manner in which this place of origin was occupied by a representation. A characteristic of the two sequences is that they are inextricably intertwined. The story about the building project functions as a frame for the description of the result of its execution. However, this frame is somewhat blurred, since the

---

4. Citations are from Rabelais (1973). For discussions of Renaissance utopias, see Dermenghem (1927) and *Les utopies à la Renaissance* (1963). [The translations of the Rabelais passages are, on the whole, drawn from Rabelais (1952).]

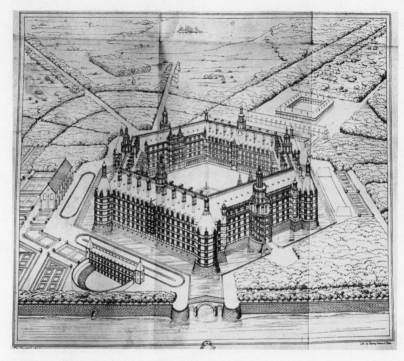

Reconstruction of the Abbey of Thélème, by Charles Lenormant

contents of the chapters exceed what is indicated by their titles. The narrative frame does not contain the descriptive image in any precise way; indeed, the image is displaced. Thus the title of chapter 52 only designates the first part of the chapter, for the second part presents some of the rules of the order of Friar John, that is, the principles governing the institution. These same points apply to chapter 53, where they can be discerned in an even more complex form. The means of construction (the various endowments) have been provided. On the other hand, the story of the construction is, properly speaking, absent: there is not a trace of the process of building itself. Yet the result of this process is described at great length and, from this point of view, the interruption of this description by the poem of the inscription that will be placed upon the gate of Thélème proves not really to be an interruption after all. The inscription is part of the discourse that will be developed in subsequent chapters. It does, however, have the effect of introducing a break or rupture into the text. After its inscription, the abbey becomes a manor.

2. Subsequently, we encounter a descriptive layer that begins by developing the description, already started in the story, of "what manner of dwelling the Thelemites had" and continues with a detailing of the clothes of the monks and nuns of Thélème and of the rules governing their daily existence. As for the riddle that takes the form of a prophecy, it is noteworthy that it points to the process of construction that was forgotten in chapter 53, since it is in excavating the foundations for the abbey that this enigma is discovered "engraven on a copper plate." This second inscription contains a story, but as an inscription, it is also part of the description. Lastly, while the final dialogue between Gargantua and Friar John displaces the inaugural dialogue between the two protagonists, in which the project for the creation of order was decided upon, it also refers back to this dialogue.

Desire-Law

This rough sketch of the general features of the text's structure reveals a kind of generalized erosion of the story as a result of the stubborn presence of the image that is mediated by the description: the decor moves into the foreground; the story frames the image, but in an uncertain way, since the representation constantly displays a tendency to transgress its borders. Yet is the inaugural story really what it seems to be?[5] It is true that it grounds itself in a series of verbs conjugated in the past tense. Yet most of these verbs do not assert a fact or an event; instead, they qualify an assertion. The story concerns the modality of desire or the will.[6] It derives less from history than from discourse, a discourse of desire and the law. Much more than in history, it finds its origin in a performative utterance that creates the space and place, the institution and its architecture, by virtue of simply proffering itself. And yet, this performative is uttered as a constative, since it is presented in the historic and narrative past tense. This conflation of a performative and constative function is noteworthy for two reasons: it reveals the Founder of the law, of the law of desire, to be a solitary figure; and it also seems to reveal the rift that separates desire and the law, a rift inscribed within the very name "Thélème," where the will of God and human

---

5. For a more detailed discussion of this issue, see Marin (1973), pp. 53–86, 87–114.
6. For a discussion of this issue, see Benveniste (1974), pp. 187–89.

desire are harmonized."[7] Yet nowhere is the aporia entailed by
the advent of human desire really problematized. As is frequently the case, the name Utopia manifests a scission within its
learned unity. Thélème is neither the will of the divinity nor
human desire, for it is both the one and the other. In the very distance that is instrumental in producing both the law and desire,
representation brings about the synthesis of the two. The play on
the name opens up a distance, it establishes a difference. By virtue of the fact that it brings what it names into being, the act of
naming conceals this difference in the unity of its utterance.

Now we find the same duality inscribed within the text at all
of its discursive levels. The fundamental principle underlying the
construction of the abbey is that of contradiction: what is at
stake is the institution of an order that is the logical opposite of
all the others, an order that is not so much an anti-order as simply a non-order. It is less a matter of contraries than of a negation
internal to the act of speaking; a negation that, through the act of
naming, simulates the indefinite sphere of possibilities, which
connects with historical and social reality only at the precise
point constituted by the "no/name."[8] It is not surprising to discover that the new institution is first accorded a spatial characteristic: "First then, said Gargantua, you must not build a wall about
your convent, for all other abbeys are strongly walled and mured
about." The Monk's possible abbey is situated in the land of
Thélème: this place already involves the circumscribing of space
by the means of a name that at once unifies and creates a distance between the transcendental will (the law) and natural appetite (impulse and desire). The site of the abbey is an unenclosed
space: it is not open, since it is already a place, a named place
bearing a name that designates it in its specificity; nor is it
enclosed, for no walls will be built about it to circumscribe its
boundaries.[9] This same analysis could be repeated with respect

---

7. For an analysis of the name Thélème, see, in particular, Nykrog (1965). For
another toponymic reference, see Rabelais (1949), p. 1, and Lefranc (1905), pp. 4–5.
The same tensions between geography and etymology exist in the name of the
island Utopia in Thomas More's work. On this issue see Marin (1973), pp. 115–31.

8. The basic texts on this topic are Aristotle (1963), 16a 2, 30, Kant's discussion
of the category of negation and of indefinite judgments in the "Transcendental
Analytic" (1934) and Husserl (1931), part 3, chap. 10.

9. For a discussion of the manner in which the category of the neuter functions, see Greimas (1970), pp. 141–45.

to the other features characterizing the new order. Other examples would be the regulations concerning the use of time in the abbey-manor or those specifying the manner in which residents are to be recruited. Through repetition, the timetable brings time to a halt in the regular return of the same, symbolized by the ringing of the bell, "the moving symbol of eternity." This closure of Thélème will be neutralized, not by this bad atemporality, but by the aleatory distribution of the content of time" . . . according to the opportunities and incident occasions." However, the intervention of Gargantua's voice brings about an equivalence between, on the one hand, the free disposition of activities according to available circumstances and, on the other, the rules dictated by common sense and reason. By the same token, the "Do as you wish" will amount to the same over the hours and the days: "If some man or woman said 'let us drink,' then everybody would drink; if they said 'let us play,' everyone would play." The same situation obtains with respect to sexual segregation or wishes. Through a contradiction, the word of the Law-Desire (of) Thélème dictates the rule of the nonrule. Yet such a dictate is itself a contradiction. Indeed, it is the very contradiction that characterizes all utopias, the double bind by which desire is always bound and determined: in a single stroke, utopia opens up the neutral (or other) space that is the difference between yes and no, the place that is nowhere; and this same gesture fills the place with an image, a representation in which contraries that have already been neutralized are harmoniously reconciled in what is, however, the imaginary.[10]

The same duality is found at the level of the act of uttering and of those who perform the act in the text. The "plan" of the abbey is the doing of the Monk: "Gargantua wanted to make [him] the abbott of Seuillé. . . . He wanted to give him the abbey of Bourgueil. . . . Give me leave to found an abbey after my own mind and fancy." Yet it is Gargantua who, in a fundamental gesture, promulgates the first rule of the order: there will be no walls. The same holds for the regulation of time: "For the counting of time was the biggest waste of time that he knew of, said Gargantua." It is true that Gargantua and Friar John engage in dialogue, but it is Gargantua who speaks, dictates, promulgates, orders, and decrees,

---

10. On this issue, see first of all the basic texts of Freud (1922) and (1950). See also Lyotard (1971), pp. 269–70, 354.

while Friar John is silent. Once the gift of the land and site has been made, the ambiguity of this false dialogue becomes apparent in the very principle that underwrites the founding of the abbey: Friar John asks "that he institute the religious order contrary to all others." To whom does this *he* refer? Does Friar John, the monk, ask Gargantua to be allowed to institute his order in a manner contrary to all the others, or does he require of Gargantua that he, Gargantua, institute the order in a manner contrary to all the others? Quite aside from the juridical and legal connotations of the use of the impersonal form—"was ordered, was decreed"—we are inclined to ask a much more general question: Who founds the laws? Who is the nomothete? Is it the word of the donating King in all of the impersonality attendant upon the "Self of the State"? Are Gargantua and Friar John responsible for these laws? Does the impersonal form refer to the *they* of those comrades in arms, the feudal overlord and vassal? Another hypothesis, perhaps somewhat scandalous, may come closer to the truth: maybe what is manifested in the duality of the dialogue is neither Friar John nor Gargantua, but Thelema—Desire-Law. The dialogue is an equivocal or ambivalent site with respect to this Desire-Law, since it is where the scission inscribed within the latter is enlarged, as well as where the two terms achieve their synthesis.

Wordplay

Nonetheless, there is something even more surprising: it is not entirely true that Friar John falls silent after the initial request. In fact, he intervenes twice. He twice breaks into the founding discourse, through which the Law is promulgated and Desire satisfied (in the Law, desire; in Desire, the law). Although these interruptions are incongruous, impertinent, and untimely breaks, they are both presented as justifications for the utterances voiced by the Sender-Narrator: "—Yea—said the Monk and not without reason. . . . By the way, said the Monk . . . " The interruptions legitimate the two laws of the nonconstitution of the abbey, that of its nonclosure (or of its noncontainment) and that of its noncontent (the women to be admitted will not be nuns). The two justifications are puns, plays on words. Play, the play of the signifier literally founds the discourse of the signified in all of its coherence and intelligibility, even though this play is responsible for breaking this very coherence.

The inversion has a crucial impact on the text itself: at the

level of its signifying organization, it introduces the principle that
governs the constitution of that about which the text speaks, of
the creation of a new religion or order, which is to be the contrary
of all those already in existence. The first pun is perhaps the most
perfect and the simplest as far as its power of disruption and creation are concerned: "Where there is *mur* before, and *mur* behind,
there is store of murmur, envy and mutual conspiracy" (*"où mur y
a et d'avant et derrière, y a force murmur"*). The pun constitutes
itself by describing its own literal and graphic organization; by the
same token, it constitutes the signified, by which I mean the word
that makes sense, and thus justifies or legitimates the first non-
law dictated by Gargantua. *Mur devant* comes first; *mur derrière*
comes second. Thus we have a double *mur* that encloses within its
circular phonic relation (the walls circumscribing the circumference) a silence of the voice, a typographical blank, the con-spiring
(the shared breath, con-spiring) that at once moves and kills, in a
silent movement of the one toward the other. We witness the displacement and the condensation of the signifiers *mur* (1) and *mur*
(2), which, through metonymy and metaphor, are made to constitute a word that is the result of their lateral and reciprocal conflation. The word produced in this manner resembles its component
parts, since they are repeated within it. It is also, however, different
from or other than these elements, an ambiguous mixture of
voices, "a murmur," that really is a con-spiring, a movement that
also involves ex-piring. This means that if there is no wall designat-
ing the boundaries of the abbey, then there will be no murmur and
no mutual conspiring. If the "other" to this con-spiring were to
establish itself, then there would be a spontaneous harmony of
desires in an upright will, that is, quite precisely, a conspiracy that
mutually moves and kills.

   Ample evidence for this statement can be found in chapter 57,
which discusses "How the Thelemites were governed, and of
their manner of living." The wordplay, which is also a form of
literal play, breaks the narrative discourse of Desire-Law at the
moment of its utterance. By means of the break it constitutes the
utopic text in all its textual reality. How does this take place?
The play on words, through the break, introduces pleasure into
the utterance, makes the text erotic for the brief moment of a
playful reply.[11] By letting the signifier go, by leaving it to its own

---

11. The crucial reference here is Freud (1963).

devices, at the levels of both writing and hearing, the type of meaning that is determined by its relationship to representation is extirpated and replaced, although it is also, in the final analysis, produced in this manner. The discursive economy that is produced in this way—that of a laborious theoretical justification of the absence of walls—is replaced by a free phonic and graphic expenditure, *mur/mur*. This free expenditure creates precisely what the discourse never ceases to discourse about in the form of edicts, decrees, and powers (although the creation takes the form of a text, of an ephemeral object-text). Thus "Thélème" is indicated in the place of the text: utopia is in the play and in the pleasure of the play of the signifier.

Yet utopia is only to be found in this site if a certain condition is satisfied: first, representation through (narrative and descriptive) discourse must laboriously have occupied the scene. Utopia manifests itself as the pleasure of the text, but only if the establishing of the text involves breaks and tears in the narrative thread: the sensuous thrill is to be found in the contiguities of the discourse of representation.[12] Through word-play, the image of utopia, Thélème, tears away from its position within a referential discourse, within an utterance. The image is momentarily interrupted as representation and establishes itself as the pleasure of the signifier, as text: pleasure that is like the resolution and the climax of the thrill of the break. In other words, the Monk's wordplay twice interrupts the edict of the nonrule, the discourse of Desire-Law. His interruptions are among the most futile and ridiculous, and his propositions are but a game—the worst kind, puns. Yet these words assume a certain value precisely because they take the form of an interruption. Within the linearity of discourse and at the surface of its signification, this interruption is the mark of the most utopic and profound gesture: the "word" that is spoken most lightly points to what is most thick, to what is not verbal. The game played out at the surface level frustrates what we, following Bateson, called the double bind of the rule of the nonrule. Whence the following suggestion, which is anything but a full-fledged concept: utopia is a kind of principle that, at a certain point in the space of its own discourse, instantaneously unravels, or frustrates, or downplays (*déjoue*) the

---

12. The text that develops this point of view most cogently is Paris (1970). See also the admirable study by Rigolot (1972).

order of the image, the order of representation. Thus it also appears to be the site where desire surrenders in a moment of satisfaction, in the instant flash of the word, which is like the most absolute nonsynthesis. It is this unraveling of the ties of desire that lends a flavor of incongruity and incoherence to the reading of utopic discourse. Inspired by Nietzsche, I would even go so far as to say that this kind of reading seems untimely. It is a playfulness that frustrates. For the Monk's two words are at once incongruous and yet situated in the discourse: as a result of these words, by virtue of the fact that the signifier has been freed from its congruity and connection with the signified, the nonclosure of Thélème is justified and realized as the pleasure of the text; the same is true for the delightful free time, the nonwork, that is the lot of the Thelemites.

Representation: The Geometrical

We must now enter into the representation: as noted above, the meeting point between narration and description, between the story and the image in its discursive form, is a confused and uncertain site. The initial utterance pertaining to the description is that of a totalizing and planimetric sketch: it is the geometrical part of the architectural plans. The verb that articulates this utterance corresponds to the temporal framework characteristic of pure storytelling; the verb is in the past tense and relates bygone events. "The building was in a hexagonal figure." The general task of a synoptic description is to inscribe or transcribe an image, something visible, onto or into something that is legible: does not the linearity of the linguistic signifier imply that the written space is traversed by a temporal reading trajectory that dissolves the spatial order into that of the duration of time? With the announcement of the global plan in the first sentence, a process of enunciative memory is unleashed, a sort of feedback of reading that allows the subsequent traits of the description to be inscribed within the initial and totalizing sketch.[13] This is how the hexagon of Thélème is drawn, the space being enclosed by a mental and geometrical line that reinforces the similarities between the towers. The towers are all similar, only their names are different. As they situate Thélème within a geographical cos-

---

13. On this issue, see Marin (1973), pp. 76–82, 257–65.

mos, they in turn introduce a circular movement of enclosure and centralization. The map of the abbey-manor unfolds quite regularly when the principle of symmetry is systematically applied to it; a series of duplications through binary oppositions are generated by the rotation of an axis that turns around the center north/south, east/west, masculine/feminine, water/land, hot-and-dry/cold-and-humid, etc. Thélème is a paradigmatic town, a productive center, an omphalos of structures from which the surrounding, external, and geographic space can be organized and similarly detailed in terms of the play of the masculine and the feminine.

Two basic types of utopic space compete with each other within the structure of the plans: the square and the circle. The axes north/south and east/west define a square; the introduction of Calaer and Arctic creates a disequilibrium that can be compensated in one of two ways: by adopting an octagonal structure or by making the plans themselves more dynamic—the dynamics in question being those of the reading of the description—or by regularly rotating the organizing axes.[14]

The paradigm of the architectural site is the spatial matrix. Yet we note that only a half-space is generated by the deep structure of the manor-abbey: the Western space, the feminine part. Hence the white part on a map which is otherwise well filled; hence the terra incognita that is the masculine space. Is this unknown territory the site of agriculture, of the geography of work? As far as the building itself is concerned, no mention is made of the places of nourishment. Where are the kitchens? Where are the dining rooms? Given that we are dealing with the writings of Rabelais, this absence is surprising, to say the least. Thus the sites of play and of culture are overdetermined, while those pertaining to work and food are censured; what is high is magnified, and what is low is simply left unspoken.[15] In its exclusion of work and food,

---

14. For discussions concerning the layout of the abbey, see Blunt (1958), pp. 8–14, Heulhard (1891), p. 5, and especially Lenormant (1840). For more general issues relating to utopic urbanism, see Klein (1970), part 2, chap. 8, p. 312, and Choay (1965), (1973), and (1974). The bibliography on this topic is immense, so we refer the reader to only one other interesting discussion: Mollé (1971).

15. See Bakhtin (1984).

this discourse signifies Theleme as a place of free time and culture, although we shall see that food in all of its possible functions will be the play of the text itself.

Allegories of the Body, Mutilations, and Phantasms

In the center of Thélème, that is, in the center's center, there is a fountain decorated with the Three Graces carrying cornucopiae.[16] Water gushes from their breasts, mouths, ears, eyes, "and other openings in the body." Such modesty is surprising. Yet it also furnishes a negative indication: the body of the utopian town neither assimilates and incorporates, nor excretes. It is an abstract and asexual body, one that is not alive. The central fountain does indeed symbolize food and production, but, much like the plans for Thélème, it is only the allegory of these processes. It is an emblem of the human body, but of a certain kind of body:

> The design of a temple depends on symmetry, the principle of which must be most carefully observed by the architect. . . . Proportion is a correspondance among the measures of the members of an entire work, and of the whole to a certain part selected as standard. From this result the principles of symmetry. Without symmetry and proportion there can be no principles in the design of any temple; that is, if there is no precise relation between its members, as in the case of those of a well-shaped man. . . . Then again, in the human body the central point is naturally the navel. For if a man be placed flat on his back, with his hands and feet extended, and a pair of compasses centred at his navel, the fingers and toes of his two hands and feet will touch the circumference of a circle described therefrom. And just as the human body yields a circular outline, so too a square figure may be found from it (Vitruvius 1960, 73).

Thus, Vitruvius's architectural text allows humanity and the world to be reconciled by a system of analogies governed and organized by the circle and the square.[17] More precisely, the human body is integrated or inscribed within a geometric system that guarantees the correspondence and reconciliation. A beautiful harmony is thus achieved, but only at the cost of not considering

---

16. It seems that the model for this fountain is Francesco Colonna's *Le Songe de Poliphile*. On this issue, see Lote (1938), p. 203.

17. The most important book on this issue is Wittkower (1961), esp. 14 sqq.

the body in its essence as body, that is, as a body in the prime of its adult perfection, between infancy and birth on the one hand and the decrepitude of death on the other. Another price is paid for this harmony: between the extraordinary points of the square and the circle, between the four apexes and the center, the quartering must be performed on the body laid out on the plans; the point of a compass is planted in its navel in order to define the circumference of the circle and enclose the square within it. The body is seen from a vantage point that allows no particular perspective; the map of the body allows it to be grasped in its abstract universality.

Precisely because it involves the body, this inscription, in spite of its intelligible clarity, leaves some of its sites or places suspended, displaced, condensed, or effaced: the central point is the navel, the omphalos which, according to a certain tradition, attaches the dwelling to the focal point of its space and allows for communication between the earth and the heavens. Yet the center is also the head, the site of *nous*, of reason and logos: this remarkable point accommodates both the head and the navel. The head is to be put in the area of the navel and the center is to be overdetermined by both of them, in order to create a kind of two-headed monster, to experience the fantastic imaginings that allow a face to become visible in the area of the stomach, a cyclopean eye in that of the navel; unless, that is, we conceive of the head's position as being straight above the navel, outside of space, situated at a point that provides a perspective outside the point of view of the geometer, who reigns supreme and is free to manipulate his compass and construct his perfect figures.[18] Here we have the transcendental and universal head-eye of the perspector-dominator, Gargantua or the Law-Desire, names that are equivalent to a universal and abstract theory that legislates from above. This theory governs not only the ordinance of the traces of representation, but also the order of the Monk's new religion, as well as the narrative and descriptive discourse that provides this religion with its articulation.

The overdetermination of the center (the head/navel, the intersection of the square's diagonals and the generating point of the circle) finds its contrary in the effacement of the anti-head, in the

---

18. See Marin (1973), pp. 333–34.

site of what is base, the site of the genitals. To point out this blank on the map of the male's adult and well-built body, a blank mapped into the circle and the square, is to notice yet another absence pertaining to the head. The head has been reduced to a theoretical eye that telescopes the world's species and allows them to reproduce themselves, in an ordered and regulated manner within the space of representation; what is absent is the axis of orality. The mouth's hole suggests a quite different kind of disappearance, that of absorption and ingestion. And this absenting process refers us to yet another hole, that of excretion and rejection. Here is where we find the axis of orality. It is an axis intimately connected to that of the genitalia, as well as to the cavities of the matrix and vagina.[19] These statements may seem like the products of a purely phantasmic reading, and perhaps they are. Yet they take on a different light if we reread Panurge's project contrapuntally, a project that pertains to "a very new way to build the walls of Paris." It figures in the main chapters of the second book where the narrator explores the mouth of Pantagruel. Our statements also require that we construe the Rabelaisian text in all of its thickness as a body of text; our proposed reading differs from that involving the linear pursuit of discursive signs, and it is within this profound difference that the utopic text will be spun out. The vaginal holes, the opening of the female genitalia, enclose the town like a gigantic erotic body. This body is open, however, as long as the giant's gaping orifice and mouth, the site of ingestion as well as of vomiting, is in the process of absorbing the narrator of the discourse into the main body of his text and story.

In the final analysis, the representation of Thélème both raises and leaves unanswered the following question: How is the perceived or visible body, which functions as our most basic model for the body, to be reconciled with the lived body, with the living form of a given substance or matter? How are humanity and the world to be reconciled without sacrificing the harmony that goes by the name of happiness, without mutilating the body? Is it possible to fill the gap that separates life from logos without reducing the living body to a rational body that is operated upon and represented with the instruments of reason—the geometry of pro-

19. See Choay (1974) and Bakhtin (1984), pp. 303–67.

portions, of symmetries, of rule-governed repetitions of the same? The very goal of utopia lies in the elaboration of a proper and adequate answer to these questions.

The Living Body and the Text

The idea alluded to by the Monk's puns in the imperative discourse of Law-Desire is perhaps that the utopic body is nothing other than the text, the text as a living body. His play on words may suggest that the utopic is not to be sought in the representation that the discourse recounts and describes, but rather in the sites of intense pleasure where the discourse spreads itself thin, becomes punctuated with empty spaces, and, as a result, is constituted as a text of happiness. As we have seen, Thélème is the allegorical projection of the sleeping body of a well-formed man onto a background that may be a map or a plan. His navel was the fountain crowned by the Three Graces, itself an allegory for the eating and producing stomach and for the mouth, the vagina, and the anus which are present in the holes, orifices, and openings in the body that decorates the fountain. It is precisely this allegory of a building's architecture, this allegory of the body of the text, that we now must explore in an attempt to discover exactly where the sphincters and orifices of the text are located. In a certain sense, the Monk's two puns are the site of a perforation of the discourse. They strongly resemble the nostrils of that body which put us on the scent of strange, intoxicating, and repugnant odors; they are also much like the ears that suddenly alerted us to curious sounds, to surprising and unexpected meanings, to the vulgar rumblings and winds of the text. Other more important orifices can be discovered in the text, extending all the way to the level of typographical materials. Examples are the inscription on the huge door, the prophetic riddle found at the very base of the abbey; the mouth of the text by which one enters the abbey, the anus or vagina of the text by which one leaves it. What is represented in the discourse—"the big bronze plate" which the narrator describes to us in the guise of a conclusion—is, however, based upon these orifices. As in the above discussion of the Monk's puns, it is not the play on words that is the textual space of Utopia. Rather, this site is at once the moment and the place, in time and space, where discourse is ruptured by a difference and when silence appears on the surface of meaning and signification; it is in the pulsing back and forth between two linguistic instances that utopia is revealed. The inscription and the riddle open the discourse, conceal its isotopy and in the same gesture occupy its openings and notches with their own discursive form. This process is much like the one entailed by Friar John's puns when he interrupts Thélème's specifications of the rules governing nonrule; although the puns disrupt the discourse, they also serve as a means of connecting with it, since they create a link that is at once incongruous and logical, incongruous in that it involves free association or a play on a phonic and geographic signifier, logical in that it legitimates the nonclosure of the abbey as well as the regime of nonwork.

The Cry

It is easy to see that the main door's inscription takes up and develops the abbey's edicts of nonrule, as they were promulgated by the voice of the king, Thelema. At the same time, however, it displaces them by introducing the explicit contradiction of a religious, moral, juridical, economic, and sexual enclosure into what was proposed as the site of nonclosure: "Do not enter."[20] It is also important, however, to note that the poem written on the door is the exact counterpart to the cry, that is, to the "spiel" *(boniment)* used to convoke people to the popular representation of a mystery or farce: the edicts of Gargantua and Friar John are taken up once more and developed as the spiel of jugglers announcing the performance, the representation of Thélème. The inscription on Thélème's door effects the displacement of the utterance's content to the form and modality of the act of uttering. It is the mode and modality of the latter that parodies the content of the former by diverting the moods which, as we have shown, modalized the descriptive and narrative constatives of the discourse. This parody and diversion does not annul the content of the discourse. This content remains valid, and the enunciative modality is more than the simple and pleasing decoration attached to a serious content. By the same token, the entire representation of Thélème that is to follow takes place on the stage of a popular spectacle.[21] The representation becomes equivocal and this ambivalence is globally produced by the formal structure of the text;

---

20. We are drawing here on Beaujour (1969). See also Desonay (1953).
21. See Bakhtin (1984), pp. 156–57, 163.

yet the most important point is that an effect of displacement is produced, a diversion or difference that allows a space of play to emerge, a space that absorbs the reader who is ingested in and through the text. I shall call this difference the mouth of the text, the orifice that is its point of entry. We shall eat-read the text and we shall be consumed-read by it. As a result of having read the text as a body, we shall be constituted as an other-body, as a body of pleasurable sensations.

The Riddle

The riddle poses a single question in its form and content as well as in the so-called metalanguage of interpretive reading. This ambivalent question can be stated in two ways: How are we going to be expelled from the Thélème text? How is this text going to give birth to us, how will it engender or regenerate us? In my opinion, these questions are one and the same. First of all, they both play on the ambivalence of the double orifice of the vagina and anus. Second, the poem that we read at the end of the discourse of Thelema is at the foundations, at the basis of Thélème. In short, the peroration of the discourse, its noble part, its end, understood as its completion and perfection, is also its base, its anal foundation. If the cry was the spiel announcing the beginnings of a public performance, then the riddle, as we know, is the allegorical apocalypse of a game of pelota. Better still, in Rabelais's text, the riddle is the citation of another's poem, one by Mellin de Saint-Gelais. Yet Rabelais introduces the excerpt with two of his own lines of verse, noteworthy in that they point to happiness as the ultimate achievement of humanity: "Poor mortals, who wait for a happy day / Cheer up your hearts." Rabelais also provides a ten-line conclusion, which opens up a possible avenue of inquiry that may lead to the deciphering of the riddle. Although this line of interpretation is somewhat surprising, it reinforces the apocalyptic character of the poem by reiterating the statements encountered throughout Thélème that suggest the segregation between the elect, that is, the Utopians, and all others. In this respect, we are particularly reminded of the cry that accompanies admission to Thélème: "It resteth after those things to declare, / That those shall sit content, who chosen are, / With all good things, and with celestial manne, / And richly recompensed every man; / The others at the last all stripp'd shall be, / . . . / This is their lot."[22] We have suggested that the abbey-manor is a cosmic, architectural body that brings about happiness, a harmony between humanity and the world, by means of a geometry of proportions and symmetries. The discourse indicating that this abbey exists somewhere between the domains of story-telling and description also provides us with its representation, with an insistent image of an imaginary fulfillment that is the result of the harmony between Law and Desire, Thelema. If an apocalypse is at the basis of the architectural structure, then this would mean that the story of a historical and cosmic catastrophe founds the natural, social, political, and moral macrocosm at the level of or within the microcosm. The foundation is less of a basis than an inversion or advent: the new world of a perfect happiness is a world turned upside down. The great flash of lightning that, in the poem of Mellin de Saint-Gelais, "Licks up the water, and the enterprise," is the unique moment in which the return of the new world takes place. It is the return of the space of happiness that Rabelais announces in his introduction and refers to, although in a sketchy manner, in the conclusion that he appends to his borrowed materials by attaching the citation to his own discourse. Thélème has to be founded on an inversion if the advent of the new world is to take place. Thélème has to be destroyed if the world of happiness is to come about. In fact, the last statement is somewhat misleading, for it suggests that two temporalities and two moments are operative here: the temporality of history and that of parousia, along with the negative moment of revolution and that of a synthetic affirmation that will realize this negativity as the very end of history. However, by placing the apocalypse at the basis of the building, at the origin of the process whereby the utopic representation is constructed, Rabelais indicates that the new world, utopia, is not the synthesis that completes the movement of a historical and natural dialectic; this is true, even if Rabelais does present his reading at the end of the discourse describing the process of utopic construction. Instead, utopia is the other to reality and to history. The inversion is the foundation, the foundation is the inversion. It may be appropriate at this stage of the argument to push this point one step further: the new world is not the other of this world; the

---

22. For a religious interpretation, see Telle (1953). See also Bakhtin (1984), 232 sqq.

founding-inversion in question is effected and realized by the construction-representation of the abbey-manor. This founding inversion is the other or the opposite of the utopic representation. It points to the utopic gesture in the process of representation in which it realizes and neutralizes itself.

Interpretive Tricks

The analysis or interpretation suggested above is common to all discourses about utopia. As we said at the outset, this discourse transforms the various expressions of playfulness characteristic of utopia into a system and thus cancels them out. Such a metalanguage states the meaning of a more basic or first-level discourse and, without knowing it, restrains and constrains it. Thus a discourse of truth is made the complement of the utopic discourse, for the former provides the latter with self-awareness. Our interpretation is hardly any different from the one proposed by Gargantua, since, in both cases, a discourse that purports to speak the truth is superimposed upon the enigmatic poem. This is a straightforward interpretation of Gargantua's words, since he speaks of it as a religious prophecy of the Gospel of the Spirit; it is also an indirect interpretation of the metautopic discourse, which construes the poem as a kind of philosophical allegory of the utopia and of its most basic gesture. Yet the Monk's interpretation frustrates these others and even undermines the strategies underlying Rabelais's textual incorporation. For the Monk reverts to the enigma's first and last meaning, a meaning that it already carried outside of the discourse, before it was included in the book written by Rabelais: that of the game of pelota. With a simple signifier, which requires the most complex and learned of interpretive processes to be understood, the Monk not only reduces the meaning at stake here to a game, he also frustrates the game that involves the insertion of a citation within Rabelais's discourse. Thus he resituates the poem by Mellin de Saint-Gelais outside Rabelais's discourse.

The Monk's interpretation is the game of a game of a game. It consists of putting in question the discourse of Thélème, and the discourse about Thélème, the utopia, as well as the discourse about utopia. Although his tirade figures last in the passage and book in question, it is far from negligible, since it speaks the most basic truth about them both. Without further elaboration, it shows that the meaning proposed is not, in fact, beyond the religious one pertaining to a gargantuesque or metalinguistic evangelism as well as to a discourse on utopia. The meaning in question is, rather, on this side of Rabelais's discourse and book. In this sense, we can be said to leave both the discourse and the book behind, because they have been interrupted; in this sense, their disruption can be said to transform them into the text of happiness. Let us reread the Monk's tirade, as it appears in the first editions:

> I believe that it is the description of a set of tennis and that the round machine is the ball and that these guts from innocent animals are the rackets and that these heated and competing people are the players. In the end, and after having worked hard, they feast and make all good cheer.

The passage speaks of work that is a game, the very question at the heart of reading and writing. The game is work because its pure essence is subtle and almost elusive. The discourse that tries to grasp it may tire itself out completely before it realizes its goal, since the latter can be attained only if this discourse lets go, both of itself and of its object. Thus expulsed from discourse, we emerge within the text, which is like a blissful body, at the moment when it is time to say-read-write "Good cheer," for nothing more will be written: this is the moment when the blank page emerges, when discourse blanks out, the text comes to an end; the final word is absent in the place that is no-place, in utopia:

> Let difference surreptitiously replace conflict. . . . Difference is not what masks or sweetens conflict: it is achieved over and above conflict, it is *beyond and alongside* conflict . . . the text establishes a sort of islet within the human—the common—relation, manifests the asocial nature of pleasure . . . grants a glimpse of the scandalous truth about the sensuous thrill: that it may well be, once the image-reservoir of speech is abolished, *neuter*. (Barthes 1975, 15)

The Fantastic and Phantasmatic

At this point, by way of conclusion, I propose that we read chapter 32 from *Pantagruel*, entitled "How Pantagruel with his Tongue covered a whole Army, and what the Author saw in his Mouth." The chapter is doubly fantastic: it is part of what we today would call "fantastic literature," yet in this case the term "fantastic" also means "phantasmatic." This text brings the phan-

tasm into play by staging it as a story. As a result of this representation of representation, the text indicates what is phantasmatic
about all texts and in particular about the utopic text that we
have recognized Thélème to be. The term "utopic text" should
also be accorded a dual meaning: as utopic discourse and as the
discourse about utopia. This redoubling of the term's meaning
practically points to the theoretical phantasm of the desire for
truth and knowledge.

Writing-Reading

I shall present a number of themes that may usefully orient our
reading, although this is not the time or place to develop them in
minute detail.[23] A first issue concerns the arbitrary connection
between the intracorporeal voyage and visit, on the one hand, and
the utopic representation, Thélème, on the other. We know that
Book I was written after Book II, *Gargantua* after *Pantagruel*,
although the order of writing is inverted in the act of reading. At
the same time, the exploration of the giant's interior, the superimposition of the conclusion to *Gargantua*, of Thélème, onto that
of *Pantagruel*, is not just the artifact of an interpretation that
aspires to demonstrate a particular thesis. Instead, this superimposition is an analytic operation that tends to account for the reciprocity of writing and reading and to constitute the text "as the
constructed state of reading" (Meschonnic 1970, 204–301).[24]
Suffice it to say for the moment that chapter 32 of *Pantagruel* is
related to utopia and to the discourse about Thélème. In other
words, it remains for us to determine what the relationship is
between the journey to a land that is other (the new world) and
the stay in these regions that are construed as being elsewhere.
Our task is to make explicit the relationship between the story of
the journey and the construction and description of the No Place
of Utopia. Moreover, the historical connections between Utopia
and America have frequently been underscored. Much as in Thomas More's book, history becomes phantasmatic to the extent
that it is a historicization of a phantasm. The newly discovered

---

23. It would be interesting to reread Auerbach's analysis of this passage and to
confront it with Bakhtin's reading. Auerbach's analysis (1953), pp. 262–84, served as
the starting point for my own interpretation.

24. A very similar problem can be found in Books I and II of More (1972); as for
Rabelais, see (1970), preface.

continent harbors a utopic potential that will not be exhausted in the near future. Its inscription into the reality of geographic and historical space allows the utopic vision to slide continuously toward the political and social project of realizing utopia in this other land found on the other side of the Atlantic.

The Deep Body

The second theme of our reading is directly connected to the one just presented: on the drawings of Thélème, we discerned the image of a body in accordance with a tradition of ideal architecture that begins with Vitruvius and continues to the present day. This body is well defined. It is that of an abstract, adult man, lying down in a horizontal posture with his arms open, his legs spread and stretched. He is pinned to the ground by the point of a geometric compass planted in his navel. He is circumscribed by a circle and framed by a square. In chapter 32, we read the story of a journey inside a body or, rather, inside a mouth, inside an immense body that has been reduced to a mouth, to a tongue and teeth, a pharynx, a larynx, and a throat. What we have here is a deep, thick, and dark body-mouth, replete with slopes and inclines, in which one journeys and resides; this mouth defines the body in terms of orifices and cavities. Once again, our question is the following: what is the relationship between utopia and the body? The question is a matter of time and space: what is the relation between the paradigm or geometric diagram of the body, between this rational and intelligible extension, and the abysmal cavity, pit, and orifice of the living body? "Utopia, the Play(ings) of Space(s)" is the title that I gave to an essay on Thomas More. Yet what are the spaces referred to in this title? The body is also a space and an architectural construction of sites and places. Indeed, it is much like the writing that unfolds in an oral discourse, unwinding its thread along the lines of the tale, weaving a text that exceeds the linearity deployed in the very method of its creation. What we have here is the intelligible, geometric space of logos or the instantaneous, intense, and obscure sites of vibrant pulsation, the sites of *bios*.

Topic-Typology

Our third theme is derived from the preceding one: the geometric body of Thélème was nothing short of the projection onto the ground of cosmic space; by providing this space with names, the body articulated its geography, in a process involving both mapping and inscription. As an architectural body, Thélème was analogous to the cosmic body. It was its analogue and reduced model, the metaphor for a grand order that found its realization through a small order and was governed by a system of proportions. Pantagruel's body-mouth is also a world, indeed it is the world, but in a somewhat different sense from that attributed to this term by a rationalistic discourse. First of all, this body-mouth is part of the cosmos; it stands upright, vertical, head in the heavens and above the clouds.[25] What defines this body-mouth is not its relation to an astronomical geometry, nor its relation to the celestial constellations. Rather, what defines it is its practical, meteorological relation to the world's elements. It is in the heavens and part of the cosmos, but it also is a cosmos: the mouth is a world complete with its mountains, plains, fields, towns, forests, seas, desserts, vines, and orchards . . . and so on ad infinitum; in this world, there are Thélèmes as well as lands of Cokayne. Thus the relation between the microcosm and the macrocosm is displaced and turned around: the analogic correspondences, the metric proportions, are transformed into a diversified whole where differences proliferate endlessly, their totalization having been immediately detotalized by the game or play of reciprocal inclusions. A topological space is substituted for the projective and metric space: the mouth is part of the world and the world is part of the mouth, which means that the internal is the external, the inside the outside, and vice versa. It essentially means that the situation is one of undecidability. Once more, we are led to ask the following question: what is the relation between utopia (what is commonly meant by this word) and the topological space of the world-body-hole? It is true, utopia always appears as the organization and structuration of space by means of an idea or representation, with an eye to its perfect habitability. Yet the discourse about utopia is, in the final analysis, nothing short of the writing of this topic. As a result, it reduces the play of topical instances to a system that engulfs utopia itself. Yet this topic could very well be a topology of transitional spaces between the categories that organize space into a series of binary oppositions:

---

25. Marin (1973), pp. 325–42. Interesting connections can be made with Xénakis's emphasis on the vertical dimension in his cosmic city (1971), pp. 151–60.

big/little, inside/outside, container/content. It could very well be a fantastic and phantasmatic space where separations, breaks, and caesurae are the very possibilities proffered by conjunctions, relations, and connections.[26]

The Story of Narration

The fourth theme is the radicalization of the preceding one and involves an attempt to articulate, to the greatest extent possible, the topological relation characteristic of the sites of the body. In the case of Thélème, we suggested that the representation of the architectural body, its inhabitants, and their manner of living, was nothing other than the representation of utopia. We insisted that the former representation was the utopic imaginary caught in the illusory referent of discourse, a referent that was seen to be necessary, insofar as the body was to constitute itself as a body of happiness by virtue of the breaks and openings in the text that titillate us and arouse our desire: the Monk's wordplay, the ear with which we hear, the cry or spiel, the textual mouth that swallows our reading, apocalypse, the anus and vagina that expel us from discourse so that we are reborn to the real possibility of happiness. Thus the text is the utopic body, for it frustrates the very games that it displays: it is the text of climactic pleasure about which nothing is said, about which one does not speak, even though one speaks in it and through it. In chapter 32 of *Pantagruel*, we read that the narrator was swallowed by the giant's mouth: the narrator enters the giant and tells about his ingestion; here we have the incorporation of narration into what is being told about the journey through the transitional space that is neither inside nor outside; it is the story of the transitional space between narration and story. Is it not true, then, that in the content of what it utters, the utopia-text is the metaphor in representation (the metaphor-representation) of its own discursive space and its own act of enunciation? What does the chapter tell us? As in *Gargantua*, it tells about the end of a war, although, unlike *Gargantua*, the war is terminated outside the bounds of

---

26. On the topic of transitional spaces and phenomena, see the excellent study by Winnicott (1980). For discussions more directly concerned with the utopic structures of time and space, see the suggestive article by Starobinski (1974) and Sami-Ali (1974), particularly pp. 42–64.

the story. By absenting himself from the end of the war, the narrator introduces himself into the story as its narrator. Thus another story is substituted for the missing one: in the place of history is another story, its enunciative inversion. The initial space of the story is the one covered by Pantagruel's tongue when he shelters his army "as a hen doth her chickens." The "*I*, who relate to you these so veritable stories" is excluded from this sheltered place: the act of uttering the historical story, which is both tale and truth, is excluded from the story itself. Yet according to one of Benveniste's most noteworthy arguments, this excluded dimension resurfaces within the story by virtue of its inclusion within the utterance: "Then, as well as I could, I got upon it, and went along full two leagues upon his tongue, and so long marched, that at last I came into his mouth." The main task at hand here is to show how, at all levels of textual analysis, the reader will find him or herself in the presence of a new space. We must show that, together with the narrator, the reader will enter into what the discourse says, as well as into the manner in which it is said. What emerges is a new or other space. This other space is both regressive and phantasmatic, and it brings relations of reciprocal inclusions into play. Thus the inside reveals itself to be the outside, and the outside, the inside; the small contains the big, and the part, the whole; what encloses is enclosed by its own process of enclosing. In short, a process takes place in which substitution occurs: a textual body is substituted for the narrative-descriptive and imaginary representation of the body and space, of history and of the event. This substitution takes place in representation itself, for it is always a matter of a discourse and an image. Moreover, all of the operations effected by the textual body will consist of displacements, slippages, condensations, and overdeterminations. All of these operations serve to make the binary categories that structure the systems of signification both indeterminate and unstable. Thus they guarantee that being is represented, theorized, and appropriated.

The first sign-signal, the most primitive indication of the destabilizing process that puts in question discursive representation, is the emergence of the narrator in what he tells: the narrative utterance becomes the narration of the act of uttering; it becomes the story of the act in question. This transformation is brought about by the exploration of what is the very symbol of the instrument and site of story-telling: the mouth. The narrator's word turns inside out, like a glove. His speech will tell about its own site—the mouth, the tongue, the teeth of its "product," and the central character of its story, Pantagruel. The narrator is swallowed by his story, but this does not stop the story from being told: to be swallowed by the site of speech is still to produce the story of this ingestion, a story which simply takes the place of the history that ought to have been told at the conclusion of the war against the Dipsodes. The product is at once identified with its place of production and replaced by it. In other words, the story is no longer a representation produced by an internal narrative activity that assumes an external, historical referent during the act of enunciation: the referent, history, is the exploration of the site where the narrative activity takes place. It is the exploration of the mouth, of the interior of a body-world that has been reduced to a prodigious orifice, to an immense and resounding cavity. Without distance, the story produces its own site of narration. In this way, the text becomes the story of the body, and the body, a text.

Regression, Symbolics, and Play

This is not the appropriate place to develop an analysis of the entire episode. In conclusion, I simply want to point to one final characteristic: the space or sites of the utopic text could very well be characterized as the sites of a regression from discourse to the signifier; more precisely, of a regression to the pulsating signifier that frees itself from the signified within these sites. The signifier is freed from the phonic linearity that characterizes the signified and from the contiguous concatenation of words and phrases that takes place in its written translation. This liberating process feeds directly into the pleasure experienced in the interstices and fractures of discourse. In chapter 32, and at the level of semiotics, the symptom of this regression of "pulsating signifiers" takes on extraordinary proportions: the entire discourse is included and developed within the corporeal site of its utterance.[27] Thus a regressive equivalence between verbality and orality is surreptitiously and explicitly established. To speak is, by the same token, to be eaten (just as, elsewhere, eating will be equivalent to fucking and being fucked). This fusion is beyond the reach of all the extraneous impositions of *Bildung*, and thus

---

27. On this notion, see Kristeva (1974), part I.

the happy bestiality of language is returned to a primary narcissism, freed from the fetters of the pleasure principle. It is reunited with Eros. What do we expect Pantagruel to ask the narrator when he comes out of his creature's mouth? Will he ask the narrator to speak and tell a story about his inner journey? Not at all: "And wherewith didst thou live? What didst thou drink? I answered, my lord, of the same that you did, and of the daintiest morsels that passed through your throat I took toll. Yea, but, said he, where didst thou shite? In your throat, my lord, said I. Ha, ha, thou art a merry fellow, said he. . . . I will give thee the *Chastelleine*, or Lairdship of Salmigondin." The story ends where Thélème began, with the Master-Suzerain's gift to his vassal, in recompense for services rendered in a battle that he did not fight; instead of Thélème and the Law-Desire, we find Salmigondin and ragout. The story of the journey in the gigantic throat is not even evoked and does not take the place of the missing story about the end of the war against the Dipsodes. Rather, it is replaced by a narration that takes the form of eating, drinking, and shitting. In short, it takes the form of all those bodily functions that had hardly been referred to by the story itself. We witness a narcissistic regression to primitive impulses. Yet the text frees these impulses by an inverted symbolic order that makes mock of the law. We should not forget that we read this huge pornographic-erotic body, nor should we lose sight of the fact that we figure in it through the effects of writing and language. What we have here is a utopic text-body where the representation of utopia— Thelema, the Law-Desire—is at once neutralized and realized as a text. We have read the last word in the dialogue between Pantagruel and the narrator: " . . . where didst thou shite? In your throat, my lord, said I. Ha, ha, thou art a merry fellow. . . . " The last word is a pun, for in France it was the custom to respond to the insult "shit" with the phrase "in your throat." In this case, the insult simply becomes the description of the event. This change can similarly be observed in the contrary case, for we note that the discursive constative becomes the very expression of the performative in the act of language. The aggressive anger of "shit (where did you shit?)—in your throat" is transmuted into a kind of parasitical gift: "Ha, ha, thou art a merry fellow. . . . " This game of reconciliation has its rewards, for the absurd recompense witnessed in the story, the donation of the domain of *Ragout*, affords us pleasure. Yet in the language of the text there is the thrill that results from the overturning of the institutional norms of language, of discourse, and of society: "outside any imaginable finality . . . nothing is reconstituted, nothing recuperated. The text of bliss is absolutely intransitive . . . an extreme continually shifted, an empty, mobile, unpredictable extreme" (Barthes 1975, 52). This is what is utopic about utopia.

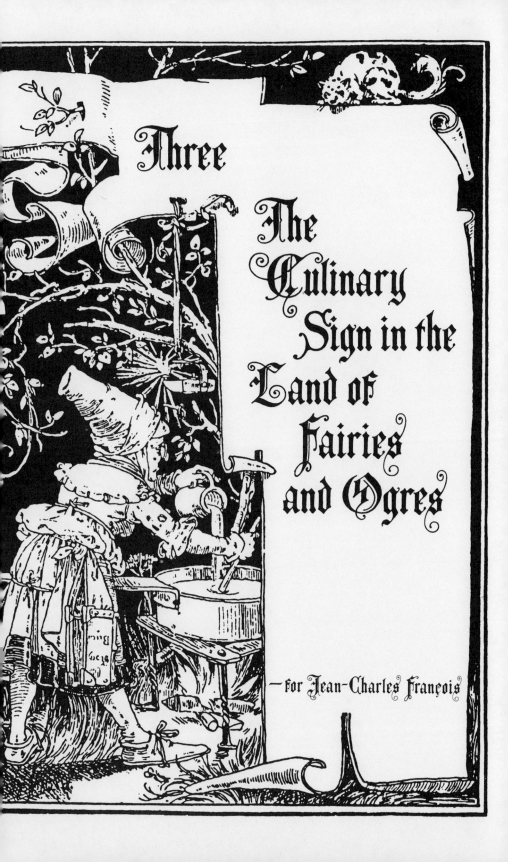

Three

The Culinary Sign in the Land of Fairies and Ogres

— for Jean-Charles François

7    Theoretical Aperitif

Cuisine (Latin *cocina, coquina, coquere,* "to cook"):
(1) A room where food is prepared and cooked.
(2) The preparation of food, the art of preparing food.
(3) The prepared food served at meals.
(4) By extension, those who work in the kitchen.

      The French term *cuisine* possesses an extraordinary semantic plasticity: its meanings range from the place where food is prepared and cooked, to the people whose task it is to undertake this preparation and cooking. Its meaning embraces those operations that constitute the art of cooking, as well as what this art produces. Indeed, one might even find, within this single term, not only an example of the theory of four causes, but also an instance of Aristotle's table of categories. The term is itself the site in which the metamorphoses that it designates take place; a site where human agents busy themselves with specific techniques and processes, inherited or of their own invention, which have the power to transform what is generally edible into culinary works of art that will be consumed within a social context. The same relations that obtain between the word *cuisine* and its various meanings also animate every dimension of the object that this word signifies. As it shifts and mutates across the range of its various meanings, the word *cuisine* echoes the way in which the various possible worlds pertaining to basic foods are constantly displaced and transformed into rigorously regulated systems of cookery: it is within these systems that human beings maintain the basic level of nutrition necessary for

---

Note: This text was originally translated into English by Marie Beatrice and Richard Macksey. See Marin (1983). I have consulted their translation. —*Trans.*

their preservation, establishing diets that are meaningful, since they are informed and governed by specific rationales, by logical processes that are both physical and tangible, economic and political, cultural and ideological. These logical processes set a limit to the choices by which edibles can be organized into limited paradigms of consumed signs. They also restrict the ways in which these signs can be arranged and connected to each other, and thus constitute a narrative syntax specifying the proper times and places of consumption. Examples of these logical processes are the cookbook, with its major sections (such as soups, sauces, eggs, fish, poultry, meats, game, vegetables, desserts and cakes), and the meal itself, with its various prescriptions and combinations (hors d'oeuvres, entrées and sidedishes, fish and roasts, salads, cheeses, and desserts). Both the cookbook and the meal can be said to illustrate and even symbolize the two major features of these culinary logics; on the one hand are terms and phrases, and on the other, discourse and its units. Thus we encounter the two dimensions characteristic of such systems, the syntagmatic and paradigmatic axes that are the poles of their realization and constitution. Along with language, the art of cooking defines humanity in its appropriation of itself and the world; moreover, it is one of the languages of human culture by which cultures are constituted, both in their differences and mutual oppositions; finally, the art of cooking is structured like language and obeys the same structural and functional constraints.

What then are the nature and structure of the culinary sign? Is it appropriate to speak of a culinary sign just as one speaks of the signs of language? Do culinary signs form a system? If so, what are its characteristics? In what way does the culinary system of a given society correspond to its economic, social, political, religious, and cosmological systems? What might these correspondences look like and what would their specific functions be? Some of the major scholarly works that have had a crucial impact on contemporary social science provide very competent answers to these questions. In what follows, I shall deal with a much more limited subject, limited in its nature and importance, as well as in its spatial and temporal framework. It is my aim to undertake a study of the very notion of the culinary sign as it appears in a corpus of marvelous fairy and ogre tales dating from the seventeenth century: the tales of Perrault entitled *Histories or Tales from Past Times with Moral Lessons* (1697) and his *Tales in Verse* ("Donkey-Skin," "Ridiculous Wishes," and "Patient Griselda"), which was published a few years before the tales in prose.* In spite of these restrictions, and perhaps because of them, this study will make a twofold, though modest, contribution. On the one hand, it will contribute to a better understanding of the questions raised by the idea that the art of cooking is a matter of a signifying system. On the other hand, this study will aim at improving our comprehension of the questions raised by the uncanniness of certain texts from former times.

From the Miraculous to the Marvelous within Classical Semiotics: From the Logic of Port-Royal to the Tales of Perrault

The first part of the *Logic of Port-Royal* elaborates a representational theory of the sign in general: the sign is the "thing" that represents the "idea of a thing." In this sense, every sign is a representation of a representation. Yet the process of representation constitutive of the idea of the sign must not be allowed to obscure the presence of the sign in its material dimension as a thing: a natural example of this dimension is provided by the famous example of the warm cinders; a supernatural case is that of the visible human forms adopted by angels when they pay humankind a visit. If the warm cinders are a sign of fire, they conceal as a thing what they disclose as a sign; this is shown to be the case by the very expression that signifies the thing in question: the noun "cinder" gives a name to the material component that does the concealing; the adjective "warm" designates a hidden fire, the heat of which is the indice within the thing itself. This materiality may persist or subsist in indexicals and even in icons, although to a lesser degree; for example, in the bodily symptoms of illness, in the bodily signs of the soul's passions, in exegetical figures, as well as in the signs of the sacrament. Symbols are, however, quite a different matter: for in these linguistic signs, the thing (or rather, the idea thereof) takes the place of a sign in an almost immediate manner and thus privileges what is represented by neutralizing both the thing itself and what does the representing. In the same way, the inverse substitution of the

---

*In French, Perrault's tales are designated as belonging to the genre known as "les contes merveilleux" (literally: "marvelous tales"); "le merveilleux" is an expression used to refer to the specific marvelous or supernatural quality associated with such fictions, and will be translated here as "the marvelous."—*Trans.*

sign for the thing, through the deceptive charms of mimesis, offers to our sight and hearing a world of signs that is a trompe l'oeil representation of the world of things.

Elsewhere, I have shown that there exists a singular example of the sign that cuts across the diverse classifications of signs elaborated by the logicians of Port-Royal. In its marginality, this example is at once the productive source of the representational model of the sign, as well as what throws the whole model into question. Indeed, the eucharistic sign tampers with all the boundaries of the systematic charts with which the logicians of Port-Royal categorize the different types of signs: probable and definite signs, connected and disconnected signs, natural and institutional signs. With eucharistic signs, an uttered phrase becomes a body that is eaten. The insurmountable distance, which is both natural and rational, between words and things is annulled in the realization of a miraculous identity between the spoken word and the body being eaten: a word offers itself up for eating; the spoken word is the body eaten. The bread and the wine are neither spoken nor signified, for they are shown by the utterance "this"; during the split second that it takes to pronounce "is," they become the signified body of the person who utters the formula "This is my body"—provided, that is, that the formula is said under appropriate conditions, by an appropriate person, and addressed to an appropriate audience. Beginning with the bread that is shown by the expression "this," the utterance brings into being, transforms, or, more precisely yet, transubstantiates the bread into an utterance, "my body." The edible thing becomes a spoken word, "my body," by virtue of the power of "is." Yet this spoken word miraculously preserves the features of the thing that is shown, for it has the quality of being edible and is indeed subsequently consumed. The spoken word is eaten as a body, as the body of the person who speaks. The edible thing is signified as a spoken word, as the word pronounced by the person speaking.

The eucharistic sign-body tampers with the boundary separating deixis from semiosis, and the act of showing something from the act of signifying it: it transforms what is edible into a signified and what is sayable into something eaten. This sign-body is eaten during the communal meal, a meal that plays a twofold role: it founds the universal social body of the Church and simultaneously maintains it through the recitation of a body of narrative telling of the Church's origin in a particular moment of past history. Thus it is fairly accurate to say that the utterance of a determinate formula, by an appropriate speaker, and addressed to an appropriate listener, brings into being the social (ecclesiastical) body. This creation is effected by the eating of a body of language during the meal that occurs at the appropriate time and place. What is at stake here is not only an important epistemological paradigm pertaining to the history of semiotic theory, but also a theological dogma, an ideological and a political apparatus. An edible thing becomes a signified term. Yet the term is signified only in order to become a body that is eaten. This process is only circular in appearance, for its end is not the same as its point of departure. What is eaten at the end of the formula is not the edible thing of the beginning; what is eaten is both a sign and a body, a body as sign and a sign as body. It is in this way that the bread shown in an act of deixis is sublimated *(aufgehoben)* into semiosis. The effective universal linguistic utterance both negates the bread as bread and preserves it as something eaten. What is eaten is no longer bread but the negation of this bread, a negation wrought by the person who, having uttered "This is my body," offers up his words for eating.

With no desire to be provocative, one might say that every culinary sign is eucharistic in some sense and to some extent; or, to pursue this vein of thought one step further, one might say that all cookery involves a theological, ideological, political, and economic operation by the means of which a nonsignified edible foodstuff is transformed into a sign/body that is eaten. In their own inimitable way, Perrault's fairy tales never stop telling a single story, and this story is the tale of the dialectical relations between a series of oppositions: the edible and the eaten, a thing and a body, what is shown and its sign, need and desire. While in the *Logic of Port-Royal*, the Catholic Church's universal and ceaselessly repeated miracle of eucharistic transubstantiation is presented as though the circumstances of its production were as natural and reasonable as those pertaining to any utterance governed by the rules of common sense and ordinary communication, in the tales of Mother Goose, this miracle is retold. In the retelling, however, the miracle becomes wholly marvelous, involving marvelous beings and actions, figures and processes, social ranks and kingdoms. In these tales transubstantiation becomes trans*signifiance*.* By this term, I understand the follow-

---

*Heath's account of why *signifiance* should not be translated as "signification"

ing: as in the *Logic of Port-Royal*, where the miraculous eucharistic sign tampered with the taxonomic boundaries separating the
various kinds of signs from each other, the marvelous cookery of
the Tales tampers with the full range of the practices of *signifiance;* it is this cookery that permits all the slippages, displacements, and transformations. The cookery takes on every different
valence that can be acquired by substances and symbols. In a manner that is anything but haphazard and that even obeys a certain
logic, this marvelous cookery goes so far as to take things for
words and words for things. Yet these marvelous processes are
neither a pure disorder nor a sheer chaos. Their apparently chao-
tic nature stems from the lack of correspondence between their
features and those of everyday language, life, and society. In
Perrault's tales, the means mobilized to attain certain ends may
be unfamiliar within an ordinary context; the same is true of the
sanctions that are sometimes brought to bear against misdeeds
and of the rewards won for good deeds. On the other hand, these
aspects will not be wholly different either; what makes the difference between a marvelous context and everyday life is that, in the
former, the means will not always be suited to their ends; rewards
and punishments do not always belong to the same isotopy as
errors or good deeds. It is in the following sense that I spoke of
trans*signifiance:* I did not mean to imply that a marvelous story
somehow represents processes or states of affairs that are transcendent in relation to those of everyday life; by trans*signifiance,* I
mean to suggest that, through their representation in a marvelous tale, everyday processes and states of affairs begin to slip
away and tear loose from the natural level on which they occur,
to switch to another level which is equally natural, although the
second level naturally proves to be without any connection to the
former. To take the most obvious example, what could be more
straightforward and normal than to pick a pumpkin in a vegetable garden? Similarly, what could be more simple than going to a
ball in a carriage? (Would one even be let in if one arrived any
other way?) On the other hand, when a pumpkin becomes a carriage, we witness something that at first sight really seems quite

---

makes sense to me (Barthes 1977, translator's note, iv). Although the translation of
Derrida's *Eperons: Les Styles de Nietzsche* simply uses "signifiance" as though it
were already an English word, I have chosen to leave it italicized in the
translation.—*Trans.*

strange and that seems to have required the intervention of super-human powers. Yet try to imagine, side by side, a beautiful yellow pumpkin, ripened perfectly in a fertile vegetable garden and hollowed out by the expert hand of a farmer, and the prince's wonderful golden carriage, brilliantly decorated by expert craftsmen. We quickly discover that the carriage is the exalted image of the pumpkin, and vice versa, and we suddenly realize that "Cinderella" is a tale about dual and inverse metaphorical movements between a series of terms: the pumpkin and the carriage, an elevated and a lowly style, burlesque and irony, dusk and midnight. In this modest example, the site of trans*signifiance* proves to be the boundary or distance separating vegetable plants—in this case, the cucurbitaceae called *cucurbita pepo*—from technically produced objects—in this case, a carriage, a four-wheeled vehicle, fully equipped with suspension and canopy, and drawn by magnificent horses. Trans*signifiance* takes place, then, on the border between a lowly domestic culture on the one hand and the social techniques of the nobility on the other. Moreover, the tangible and material qualities of the pumpkin and carriage make it possible to cross this border in either direction, to traverse the distance separating the two cultures. The key is that metaphor becomes metamorphosis: in other words, a metaphorical process pertaining to words must be realized in a metamorphic process pertaining to things. The result is a sudden change in the being of the natural product as well as in that of the crafted object. Within the story that is told, this change will represent the rise and fall of a cultural and stylistic regime, the movement from one regime into another. Thus we witness the twin spectacle of a ridiculous ascent and an ennobled lowliness, beyond which may be glimpsed the tale's social and political critique, a critique at once incisive and gentle.

I have been trying to illustrate what I mean by *signifiance* with reference to the pumpkin and carriage from "Cinderella." It seems to me that what was said on this score can be generalized to characterize all of the apparatuses of the marvelous genre.* Moreover, it is precisely within the framework of such a generalization that we come across cookery as a system of culinary signs. Here we encounter the functions and effects that cooking

---

*I have followed numerous other translators in rendering *dispositif* as "apparatus."—*Trans.*

exerts in relation to a number of different systems and apparatuses of communication and exchange: the exchange of goods within an economical system, the exchange of women within a marital system, the exchange of words within language. My working hypothesis in relation to Perrault's *Tales* is as follows: in the marvelous tale cookery in general and culinary signs in particular figure as one system of *signifiance* among others. This culinary system may be more fragmentary and more latent than the others. Moreover, cookery and culinary signs function as the privileged apparatus within which are inscribed the marks of trans*signifiance* so characteristic of the marvelous. To a certain extent, this apparatus can be held responsible for the marvelous way in which the tales shift between economic, matrimonial, and linguistic levels, these transitions being a matter of narrative slippages and leaps, of metonymy, synecdoche, and metaphor. It is not difficult to understand why cookery and culinary signs assume such a role.

I have been suggesting that the culinary sign results from a process by which an edible thing, food, is transformed into an artifact that is to be consumed, the dish. Inasmuch as this really is the case, the culinary sign must necessarily be such that it allows the thing that it signifies to subsist within the sign, just as the inverse must be the case. That is, the sign persists within the thing that is its vehicle and allows for its manifestation. Similarly, the culinary sign also necessarily allows a need to be satisfied. Hunger, the signal emitted by an instinct for self-preservation, is stilled by a nutriment, just as desire finds gratification in the pleasure afforded by the eating of a culinary dish. This does not, of course, mean that a culinary dish is separable from its nutritious content, just as it was determined that, in the case of a culinary sign, the sign and the thing cannot be separated. Thus the culinary sign or dish is revealed to be the extraordinary site and efficient apparatus of a marvelous trans*signifiance*. This is true insofar as the culinary sign vehicles, but also effects the formation of a dialectic between logos, eros, and *sitos*,[1] three terms that refer to the three salient poles

---

1. *Sitos*, in Greek, is a noun with the following meanings: (1) wheat (in its natural state); by derivation, ground wheat, flour, from which we get bread (as opposed to meat); (2) solid foods in general (as opposed to drink); by derivation, nourishment, what feeds humankind; (3) particularly in Athens, an allowance or

alluded to above: words within a system of language and communication, women within a kinship system, and goods within an economic order. The dish—a sign of culinary art, to be consumed during a meal—is at once the object and subject of love, a word belonging to language and a discursive entity, a material possession that can be transferred or exchanged. Yet the dish is also the locus of a trans*signifiance*: the processes of trans*signifiance* themselves give rise to metonymy, synecdoche, and metaphor, and these tropes effect the trans*signifiance* of words, of amorous bodies, of riches and economic goods. Is it not true that our admittedly cursory definition of the culinary sign lays bare the intimate relations between food, desire, and wealth? As a result of the sublimation effected by the culinary sign, what is edible is always to a certain extent a little bit of all three of the following: a desirable erotic body awaiting consummation, an economically appropriated possession, and a linguistic sign exchanged within a system of communication. It is not, then, the least bit surprising to witness a many-faceted process in which words become goods, bodies, or dishes; a process where dishes become words, bodies, or goods; a process where bodies become words, dishes, or goods; and finally, one where goods become dishes, bodies, or words. The culinary sign is at once the transformational process that turns edible food into dishes ready to be savored and the result of this process itself. Exactly like the elements belonging to the other systems of signification, the culinary sign will, in its own way, represent the economic transformation of a thing into a good, the erotic transformation of an object into a body, and the linguistic transformation of an entity into a sign. These transformations constantly play on the possibility of a shift in modalities: what is impossible becomes possible, that is to say, real; what is forbidden becomes permissible, indeed obligatory; and what is excluded becomes plausible, that is, certain. Thus we note that the transformational process that turns edible foods into savory dishes also turns need into desire. It transforms the organic complement of an absence into the value and psychic representation of a lack. Desire becomes pleasure, eros satiation, and finally, spatiotemporal or sociocultural disjunctions turn into happy and peaceable conjunctions.

---

stipend paying for one's board; (4) prepared food; (5) refuse from consumed foods, excrements.

8 Roast Blood Sausage, or the Gush of Performatives ("Ridiculous Wishes")

In the second of the three tales that Perrault published in verse, the story is preceded, much as in "Donkey-Skin," by a prologue in which the author begs the person to whom it is dedicated to forgive him for the subject matter of his "crazy and inelegant" fable: "an ell of blood sausage provides the story with its subject matter. / An ell of Blood sausage, my dear: / What a pity / It's monstrous, / Exclaimed a *précieuse.* . . . " Perrault goes on: "Yet you who better than any other . . . know how to charm people by telling them stories, / Your expressions always so natural, / That the listeners believe themselves to be seeing what they hear, / You who know that it is the way, / In which something is made up / Much more than the content itself, / Which makes for the beauty of every tale, / You will love my Fable and its moral." Thus Perrault rehearses in relation to his own tale what happens to potential edibles when the art of cooking is applied to them; this art not only transforms the tale into a food that is actually eaten, but also into a dish that is consumed and shared, both socially and aesthetically. The tale's subject is the story of a blood sausage, a wholly vulgar type of food, the very mention of which is enough to offend the taste of a *précieuse*'s delicate palate: black blood sausage or pork gut filled with pork blood and fat; white blood sausage or the same gut, filled this time with blood of capon, milk, and other ingredients. Nonetheless, the art of narrative cookery, the poetical recipe following which the story is prepared, makes an exquisite dish out of the blood sausage. Although the result remains a very popular story about a sausage, the delicate telling of the tale allows it to figure among the readings of Mademoiselle de la C***, who knows how to charm people in telling a story, since she knows how to conjure up what she talks about. When Perrault sends Mademoiselle M*** "Patient Griselda," the third of the versified tales, he accompanies it with a letter containing a little poem, throughout which he plays on the idea that accomplishing a critical reading may be a matter of eating, somewhat like a gourmet meal: "Is it reasonable / To deprive a meal of a good dish / Because there happens to be a guest / Who perchance does not like it? / Everyone must be allowed to live, / And for the dishes to be pleasing to all, / They must be as varied as taste itself." Moreover, the blood sausage that figures in the dedication of "Ridiculous Wishes" to Mademoiselle de la C*** is perhaps less of a sausage than vulgar people or a coterie of *précieuses* might think. Perrault's contemporaries often spoke of "sending someone a blood sausage" to refer to "making a present of some part of one's best work?" This expression originated in the custom of making a gift of blood sausage after having slaughtered a pig. Yet there is more at stake than might meet the eye in this playful oscillation between a reading and a meal, between the "what" of food and the "how" of cooking, between a common and an elevated style, etc. It is not simply a matter of providing the tale, "Ridiculous Wishes," with an introductory metaphor. Nor is it a matter of establishing a frame of reference for its reading, of providing the codes that should inform its interpretation. For the story told in the fable is not just about a common blood sausage. It is a story about what we now would call the semantico-pragmatic articulation of the relation between a certain use of discourse on the one hand and food, the prepared dish, on the other. In short, of the relation between language and cookery.

The general organization of the tale is straightforward: a poor woodcutter, tired of his miserable life, longs for death: "Expressing his deep grief / About the fact that from the day of his birth / The cruel heavens had not once been willing to fulfill a single one of his wishes." Jupiter, supreme ruler of the world, appears and promises "to grant him fully the first three wishes" that he cares to mention, no matter what they turn out to be: "Say what it is that would make you happy, / Say what would please you, / And since all your happiness depends on your wishes, / Think hard before you make them." Thus the fable will relate a marvelous story pertaining to the two performatives, wishing and promising. What constitutes the marvelous nature of this story is the coincidence of illocutionary and perlocutionary force of wishing and promising in an unequalled pragmatic happiness, all to the ultimate misfortune of our woodcutter. The blood sausage will thus appear on the scene, stay there, and disappear, all depending on the nature of the human, all too human wishes and on the divine, all too divine promises.

The next sequence begins with a discourse of reasonable calculation on the part of the woodcutter: the extraordinary importance of the divine promise, the boundless magnitude of the hoped-for gift, the obvious possibility of a divine trickery and human error — all these factors call for a rigorous calculation: "I must not, he says to himself as he runs along, / Undertake anything lightly here / The matter is important and I must, / Consult the opinion of my Missus." Yet the context of the calculation is optimistic and could hardly be anything other: "Well Fanny, he says upon entering his fern-roofed home / Let us build a big fire and have a big feast / From now on we are rich / And all we have to do is make our wishes." The salient feature of this context is the immediate and sumptuous depletion of the poor woodcutter's reserves in the form of a fire and a huge meal. This extravagant expenditure is diametrically opposed to the prudent considerations which ought to govern all calculation. Fanny, his wife, promptly and with great energy fashions "a million grand projects in her own mind." Yet she knows the essential difference between a rational project and a wish: a rational project is derived from a precise determination of means with an eye to a given end, and it relies on the modalities of the possible, the plausible, or the permissible; a wish, on the other hand, is by definition oriented toward the impossible itself, toward what is excluded or prohibited. Ordinarily, the projection of the impossible is ruled out and forbidden, and one of the charms of the wish resides in its power to project precisely what we know can never be fulfilled. Blaise and Fanny are faced with the problem that the jovial appearance connects a rational project to a wish or, more precisely, a wish to a project. What is impossible, excluded, or forbidden becomes possible, plausible, or permissible. Indeed, it even becomes necessary, certain, and obligatory.

"Blaise, my dearest, says she to her husband / Let us not allow our impatience to spoil anything, / The two of us should carefully consider, / What the situation calls for. / Let us postpone our first wish till tomorrow, / And sleep on it. I quite agree with you, says

Blaise good-naturedly, / But go pull out some wine from behind the firewood." This is how the dangers hidden within the absolute performative insidiously begin to take shape: because their human wishes will certainly find realization, combined with the concurrent obligation, on the part of the divinity, to fulfill his promise. The bottles of wine, hidden behind the firewood and brought out in order to consecrate certitude and obligation, will prove to be the unhappy occasion for the realization of these dangers. "Upon her return, he drank and / Next to the big fire, savored the sweetness of rest. / Leaning against the back of his chair he says, / Now that we have such glowing cinders, / An ell of blood sausage would really come in handy."

Did the woodcutter just express a wish, the first in the terrible series? This is how Jupiter interprets his words. I would be more inclined to think of them in terms of the saying out loud of a delightful culinary reverie. The uncorked wine beckons to be drunk, the evening fire crackles in the hearth — signs of a modest domestic happiness based a confidence in the future and a guaranteed divine benediction. Even so, it is nonetheless true that the words have been pronounced, the formula said, and nothing can undo or unsay them. Intention and connotations are hardly of any import here. The formula is much like the sacramental sign as it was construed by the Council of Trent: having been uttered by an appropriate person, under acceptable circumstances, and having been addressed to an appropriate listener, the sign produces its effects *ex opere operato*, simply by virtue of being uttered. Not only does the expression describe a certain action, its utterance also accomplishes the action. In saying "I wish," I not only articulate the verb "to wish," but in so doing, I actually do wish. What is marvelous about Blaise's case is the fact that in saying "I wish," not only does he wish simply by saying "wish," but at the same time the wish becomes reality: "Hardly had he finished saying the words, / When his wife noticed to her great astonishment, / A very long blood sausage which, from one of the corners of the chimney, / Came towards her like a snake. / She immediately let out a cry, / But thinking that this affair / Must have been caused by the wish / Which, quite stupidly / Her imprudent husband had made, / There was hardly a charge or an insult, / That she did not, in fury and resentment / Lay at her husband's feet." The blood sausage can certainly be considered as the object of Blaise's wish. Yet, in the utterance itself, the sausage is in fact the possible sign of a happy state of affairs — namely, that in which performatives do what they say. Jupiter, however, does not agree, bound as he is by his promise as the absolute ruler of the universe. Blaise's performative does what it says: it is the successful performative that characterizes a happy situation. Yet the utterance in question is of a superhuman nature. It is a divine utterance, and the blood sausage, since it is the precise length of an ell (1.18 meters) is no longer the meager daily fare of the unfortunate and starving woodcutter. Instead, it takes on the status of an object of desire and becomes a sign, part of language. Uttered in the modality of a wish, "an ell of blood sausage" realizes the object that it stands for as a sign. In so doing, it grants the possibility of satisfying desire through the pleasure of eating. In the vicinity of a blazing fire, and with freshly uncorked wine from behind the woodstack to drink, desire might be satisfied in the silence that accompanies the satiation offered by an ell's worth of grilled blood sausage.

But is this what will really happen? Had the poor fellow been single, the story, or at the very least its first act, might have drawn to a close here, leaving the other two wishes unsaid. There is something troublesome about this blood sausage, about this maleficent serpent that looms forth from the chimney the way that another serpent, at the beginning of all time, seduced womankind from the branches of an apple tree: one will wonder about the edibility of a sausage that appears under such circumstances. Can a linguistic sign be eaten once it has found its realization in a culinary sign? When formulated in this manner, the question is almost sacrilegious or heretical, if we bear the eucharistic sign in mind. In any event, the question does not arise: the performative sausage of language may be inedible, but its perlocutionary effect is to elicit multiple words, not from the mouth of the husband, but from that of his listener, the beautiful and prudent Fanny. First, it provokes her accusations and insults, then it elicits a lengthy discourse in which she develops an elaborate comparison, entirely to her advantage. The rational calculation pertaining to a project, which has been indefinitely postponed till some future moment, is followed by regrets about bygones, about what would have been desirable and preferable: "When, she says, one might obtain an Empire, / Of Gold, of Pearls, and Rubies, / Of Diamonds, and beautiful Clothes, / Is it then that one should desire Blood Sausage?" We might go so far as to say that the blood sausage speaks through her mouth, but only to be annulled in an exchange which has become impossible: the exchange of sausage for power, riches, and clothes. The blood sausage, which is henceforth inedible, proves to be overly productive in this respect, giving rise to a giddying process of autonegation: the sausage causes a verbal excess, just as it is the overgrown effect of a wish and a promise.

At this point, the second wish is articulated as a response to Fanny's tirade: it does not call for the death of the pestering chatterbox—Blaise just barely avoids that potential wish—but for her punishment by means of the very sausage that lends such fervor to her discourse. "Men, he says, were surely born to suffer. / A pox be on all Blood Sausage / So please it God, you damned creature, / Let Him hang some on the end of your nose! . . . The prayer was immediately heard in the heavens, / And as soon as the husband the word did give / To the nose of the irritated Wife, / An ell of blood sausage did attach itself." The culinary sign thus becomes a grotesque decoration, a ridiculous ornamentation of the face: a sign definitively bereft of its function, since it is now permanently inedible. Even if the sign does not actually become part of Fanny's body, it does turn into a nasal appendage. In an extraordinary process of inverted metonymy, the furious wife becomes blood sausage because of her nose! Once this has happened, a dual and noteworthy effect ensues, the first of which concerns eros, the second, logos. The already fantastical performative sausage of language has now found embodiment: the sausage is inedible, yet it occupies a new perlocutionary site, one that renders Fanny unpalatable as an erotic body. "The woman was pretty, and full of grace, / And to speak the naked truth of the matter, / This ornament in its place / Did not make for a good effect." The second effect of the Sausage-body (or nose), however, is to reduce the wife to silence. The sausage (of language) which incited her to speak when it was still edible, makes discourse impossible now that it has found embodiment. Indeed, it precludes and forbids discourse. The sausage certainly does not make for a good erotico-aesthetic effect. "As it dangled around the lower part of her face / It all the time stopped up her mouth / And hindered her from speaking with ease, / A splendid advantage for a Husband." At this point, the discourse about plans and projects resurfaces, although this time it does so in the mouth of the husband, rather than in that of the wife: how should the last wish be employed? He wonders how he should articulate the last linguistic effect while taking into account the first two wishes, the sausage too speedily brought to sight and too efficiently rendered a bodily blight. It is noteworthy that this time Blaise naively engages in a discourse of power which is, in fact, that of the king. Moreover, in this discourse, the unpalatable erotic body becomes like a portrait that is difficult to contemplate, even if it is that of the queen. Quite wisely, the woodcutter leaves the last wish to the choice of his wife: she can either have the signs of power—a throne, a scepter, a crown—all conjoined with this other nose-sausage sign, or she can retrieve her former body, favored with natural beauty, and find her gratification in being desired and in a love that may be presumed mutual. Let us allow the narrator to speak for himself: "Having examined the matter closely, / Although she was aware of a scepter's worth and effect, / And that when someone wears a crown, / Their nose is always shapely, / Yet since nothing is stronger than the desire to please, / She preferred her peasant's Bonnet,[1] / To being an ugly queen." And the last wish—"a fragile happiness and meager resource"—was used to "return his Wife to her former state."

Let us replace Perrault's moral of the tale with a pedantic one of our own: the culinary sign is the fantastical embodiment of a linguistic performative; that is, it is brought into reality in a wholly abstract manner involving no labor. Blaise's grilled blood sausage is a linguistic sign that has become reified as a result of performatives that perform all too perfectly. The sausage amounts to an insane course, to an inedible and unpalatable dish. It could only be assimilated by effacing it forever. Thus we come to understand that in reality a prepared dish always, in some sense, involves the symbolic sublimation of raw foods pertaining to basic needs *(Sitos)*; with the help of Logos, these foods are transformed into an erotic body (Eros). Moreover, the prepared dish resembles a narrative in this respect, for the tale itself is the aesthetic sublimation, by means of literature (the how), of a popular and lowly story (the what), which it transforms into an exquisite and agreeable poem.

---

1. The word in French is *Bavolet*. According to Furetière's dictionary, a *bavolet* was a "headgear worn by young peasant girls in the region of Paris. It was made from pieces of starched cloth and displayed a long shoulder-length ribbon." He adds that "the peasant girls were mighty touchy about having their *bavolet* rumpled. Moreover, sometimes one speaks of a peasant girl as a pretty little *bavolet*." Thus we realize that Fanny preferred the peasant *bavolet* that reached to the shoulders, to the royal blood sausage attached to her nose and dangling before her face.

9 Robert Sauce ("Sleeping Beauty in the Forest")

In which we learn that it is sometimes right and appropriate that an ogress should be deceived about what she eats—that she should think herself to be eating something quite different from what she actually consumes ("Sleeping Beauty in the Forest").

Histories or Tales from Past Times with Moral Lessons introduces its prose tales with a story about a "Sleeping Beauty in the Forest." Without any further ceremony than the ritual "Once upon a time," this story raises its curtain onto a feast being held in the palace of a king and queen on the occasion of the birth of their daughter. There is good reason for celebration, for the king and queen had longed for a child for many years. The huge feast is the last of the magnificent ceremonies celebrating the child's baptism, and it is supposed to fête the princess's seven fairy godmothers. Since food is a major component of any feast, the readers may be somewhat surprised to find that we are made privy to the way in which the table is laid, but not to the feast's menu. Although we remain ignorant of the dishes consumed during the feast, we do have some knowledge of the utensils which enable them to be eaten: "After the baptismal ritual, everyone returned to the king's palace, where a huge feast awaited the fairies. Each fairy was provided with a lavish place setting. A solid gold case was placed in front of each of them, and within it was a spoon, a fork, and a knife, all made from the finest gold and decorated with diamonds and rubies." We know how the story continues and are familiar with the incident involving the old fairy, "who had not been invited because for more than fifty years she had not been known to leave her tower and was presumed either dead or bewitched." Although uninvited, this aged fairy nonetheless enters the banquet hall and presumably installs herself at the

table. Her gesture is clearly a transgression of the rules of politesse that govern dinner parties and feasts: to show up without an
invitation is a breach of protocol that easily gives rise to a scene.
In the fairy tale, we note that the old fairy's behavior puts the
king and queen in a very uncomfortable position. The scene she
creates leads inevitably to another embarrassing scene that does
not concern the protocol of invitations and acceptances so much
as it does the rules that define good table manners, rules which
the king is destined to transgress, his intentions to the contrary
notwithstanding. Even if the king, in an attempt to treat the old
fairy like his other guests, were to give her a place setting, he
would not be able to present her with a solid gold case, "for they
had only had seven of these cases made for the seven fairies." The
old fairy is quite definitely a supplement, and this is evident to
all, even if the king politely attempts to conceal the fact. By being
one too many, she upsets the harmonious sacred totality which
her fellow fairies incarnate by numbering seven, and the absent
massive gold case is the mark, by default, of her superfluity, of
the surplus that she imposes.

Like all good godmothers in those days, as well as in our own
times, the fairies were supposed to make the newborn princess a
gift at the outset of the meal, the only difference being that the
fairy gifts consisted of personal qualities, rather than objects. The
paradoxical consequence of the undesired old fairy's supplementary presence is that the royal child only receives six gifts as
opposed to seven or eight: having heard the old hag mutter men-
aces under her breath, one of the young fairies "comes to the conclusion that she would be quite capable of inflicting some
troublesome gift on the little princess. When everybody gets up
from the table she hides behind the tapestry in order to speak last
and to rectify, to the greatest extent possible, whatever damage
the old hag might cause." To make sense of why the child only
receives six as opposed to seven or eight gifts, we must understand the astonishing arithmetical calculation that is performed
in the fairy tale. Beginning its calculation with the occasion provided by a meal, the marvelous tale proposes the following equation: $7 + 1 = 7 - 1$, or to be more exact, $7 + 1 = 7 + 1 - 1$. Thus
three bodily and spiritual qualities are bestowed upon the princess: she will grow up to be beautiful, cerebral, and gracious. She
also receives three gifts that are a matter of skill or know-how,
those of dance, song, and music. At this point, only the oldest
and the youngest fairy have yet to make their gifts known:

"Death," says the old fairy, to be administered by a spindle that, in the hands of the princess, becomes a fateful needle of death. A pernicious gift if ever there was one. "Life," responds the young fairy; she lacks the power to undo completely what her elder has ordained, so her countergift is that of a deathlike life, an eternal death converted into a sleep lasting one hundred years. Thus, a supplement and a lack—the old fairy is one too many, and the hosts are one table setting short—are behind the emergence of a drama or, in other words, time and events. The drama takes the form of a story and has the role of subverting and annihilating, or at least of suspending, the immobile disposition of perfections that would have been the happy princess's lot.

The old and the young fairies engage in a dialogue that is a successive confrontation, a testing of their respective and unequal strengths: each speech act done by the one is then undone by the other, because each speech act temporally follows upon and negates the previous one. A number of events are responsible for introducing history or temporality into the tale: two incidental events, involving the breach of politesse and the transgression of good table manners; a fortuitous or accidental event that occurs at the level of the meal's organization. The meal is strange indeed, since it includes not a single prepared dish and nobody eats during it; the manifestation of a sign or mark that signals a lack in the feast that has been reduced to a matter of the distribution of table settings. History is introduced in the form of an exchange of antagonistic words and sentences governed by an order of succession, the anticipated effects of which are retroactively cancelled. While the order, the time, and the place of the meal provoke an exchange of linguistic signs, this exchange also stands in for the nourishing dishes that are conspicuously absent. This is how, in the final analysis, $7 + 1$ comes to equal 6.

We shall not relate the events that immediately ensue. The predicted misfortune comes about after a period of fifteen or sixteen years, and we see the beautiful princess stretched out "on a bed of silver and gold, in the palace's most beautiful apartment. Her cheeks were rosy and her lips the color of coral! She only had her eyes closed for you could hear her breathing softly, and this proved that she was not dead." Thus the princess, fated to sleep for a hundred years, awaits a lovestruck prince, her body fit for love. Meanwhile, the good fairy, who had saved the princess's life by condemning her to sleep for a hundred years, learns about the provisions that the king had made for his daughter. "Being

endowed with great foresight, this fairy thought to herself that
when the moment finally came for the princess to wake up, she
would be quite perplexed to find herself all alone in this old castle." Thus, "with a single stroke of her magic wand," she puts to
sleep "everything that was in the castle . . . right down to the
spits over the fire which were stuffed, to the point of overflowing,
with partridges and pheasant. Even the fire dozed off." Everything, excepting the king and queen, fell under her spell. The
whole process of cooking is literally suspended. The dishes being
prepared (dishes that did not figure on the tale's initial banquet
table) and the courses in the process of being cooked (courses that
went untouched by the magnificent utensils which the king had
provided his guests) are all suspended in a time that is fixed and
immobile from then on: the culinary processes are brought to a
standstill, and the culinary activities that transform wild meats
into edible roasts "doze off" into the permanence of a single,
monotonous, and interminable moment. In a marvelous tale, it is
not the least bit strange that everything and everybody should fall
asleep in such a way, including governesses and ladies-in-waiting,
footmen, stewards and scullions, stable boys, the horses and dogs,
and even little Pouffe; in short, all things live, animal or human.
The suspension of time, an ambiguous figure of death and eternity, could not have been more forcefully indicated. What could
be more powerful than the image of the process of cooking dropping off to sleep? To be more precise, the activity of roasting meat
is stilled into a dormant state. This culinary process is itself situated or caught between two meals, between a banquet at which
nobody eats and, as we shall see shortly, a kind of solitary feast
attended by someone who is deceived about the nature of what
she does eat.

We shall understand the role played by this suspension of culinary processes better once we grasp the communicational implications of the courses included in a meal. The dishes that make
up a meal guarantee a horizontal and vertical communication
between those human and superhuman figures who participate
in the meal by eating it, as well as between creation and destruction, death and life, the heavens and earth, fire and meat. Having
been ignored or postponed, it is as though this communication
could be thought and subsequently realized, only once it had
been suspended and brought to a halt. We note the immediate suspension of space within a reserved place, signalled by the wild
meat which, although ceaselessly roasting, does not burn (the

sign of suspended time). Moreover, this space corresponds to that of an inhabited dwelling, surrounded by plants and wild trees that prohibit all trespassing without, however, obscuring the abode (the sign of a reserved place): and in the middle of this reserved space, declines the body of a desiring, yet sleeping Eros who awaits the advent of her lover. Thus the meat keeps roasting without burning, and the castle continues to be visible without being accessible.

The second act of the drama takes place a hundred years later. Out hunting in the vicinity of the castle, the king's son spots some towers sticking out above a very large and thick forest; he makes some inquiries about them. We shall focus only on two of the many answers that he receives: the first and most common response is that the towers belonged to "the dwelling of an ogre who took all the children he could possibly trap there, to eat them in peace, without having to worry about anybody pursuing him since he alone was able to forge his way through the forest." The second and true response was that "the castle sheltered a beautiful princess, the most beautiful in the world and that she would be awakened by the king's son to whom she was destined." The two answers are symmetrical and diametrically opposed to each other: according to the first, the castle is the forbidden site where a monstrous eater, the ogre, engages in the cannibalistic consumption of fresh meat. According to the second answer, the castle is the place reserved for the erotic consummation of the princess's amorously reclining body, a consummation that is to be enjoyed by her privileged or destined lover, the king's son. Yet if we look more closely, we discover that these two answers are not quite as opposed to each other as they appear at first glance: a tiny sign provides us with an inkling of the tale's end without actually giving it away. Just like the alleged ogre, the young prince possesses the power that gives him access to the castle "without anyone being able to follow him." Moreover, the prince is consumed by passion as he listens to the words of the peasant who evokes the presence of the sleeping princess. For the time being, we have no idea whether or not the ogre roasts the children that he catches. Yet we quite readily assume that the advent of the prince and his suddenly aroused passion will cause the culinary fire, which fell into a state of slumber a hundred years earlier, to be revived in the form of erotic fire. We expect the prince to awaken the desiring body of Eros to his own desire, to that of the lover. This awakening is to take place in the ambiguous place

Illustration of Perrault's "Sleeping Beauty in the Forest," by G. Doré

(for which the suspension of the culinary process, the suspension of time, seemed to be the most appropriate sign) where life and death meet: death which was able to chill with fear the fiery being of the prince; life which announces itself in the drops of wine that cling to the cups of the guards.

At this point, the princess awakens. This is an exquisite moment of happiness in which, just as in the harmony of a symphony or in the complex unity of a flavor, an exemplary dialectical process marries a variety of elements: dishes, discourses, and caresses; *Sitos*, Logos, and Eros; food sublimated into courses, the exalted language of words of affection and recognition, desire gratified during the pleasures of a wedding night. In fact, it all starts with speech: "Is that you, my prince, she says to him, I have long awaited your arrival. Charmed by these words and even more so by the way in which they had been spoken, the prince was at a loss as to how to express his happiness and gratitude. . . . His words were jumbled, yet pleased her all the more as a result. . . . In the end, they talked for four whole hours and they still did not say half of the things they wanted to say to each other." After or during the words of love comes the culinary experience, the meal. The whole castle is like a vast kitchen: "The whole palace wakes up at the same time as the princess; everyone looks to their duties, and since they are not all love-sick, they feel famished; the lady-in-waiting, in as much of a hurry to eat as the others, becomes impatient and, in a loud voice, tells the princess that the meat is on the table. . . . They then go into a room of mirrors where they have their dinner." Finally, it is time for the wedding night to crown the conjunction between discourses and meals, words and dishes, language and kitchen, marriage and its consummation: "After dinner and without wasting any time, the grand chaplain married them in the castle's chapel, and her lady-in-waiting drew the curtain for them; they slept very little for the princess was not in need of it." Thus the affectionate and appreciative conversation between prince and princess brings to an end the baptismal speeches and feast, as does the wedding dinner. In matrimony, the amorous bodies bring back to life the gifts granted by the fairy godmothers. This is the point at which the second act ends. Recent editions of Perrault's tales frequently interrupt the author at this point and amputate his very strange and interesting conclusion to "Sleeping Beauty in the Forest."

Act three begins the morning after the wedding night, when the prince leaves his wife to return to town where his father anxiously awaits him. The prince, however, behaves like an overgrown little boy caught in an act of mischief. Feeling that he owes some account of his whereabouts and doings, he tells his father, his king, a story that paints a wholly imagined picture of another place or space. This third setting is opposed to that occupied by the ogre, which is equally fictive (even if nobody seems to be aware of this), as well as to the real place that accommodates the princess. It will be recalled that the first fictional space was said to be occupied by a monstrous eater who transgressed the rules governing the consumption of meat. The second nonfictional space accommodates the prince as he consummates the princess's amorous desire according to the rules of marriage; it is at this moment that cooking and speech recover their rules and norms. The third setting is just as fictive as the first, although it involves a lie, whereas the first simply turned on ignorance. It is a stage without the beastly and monstrous castle of the ogre or the noble and sumptuous castle of the princess. Instead, these two castles have become the hut of a coalman "who had given the prince rye bread and cheese to eat." In other words, in his generosity, the coalman offers neither the forbidden fresh human meat characteristic of the ogre nor the roasted wild animal meat characteristic of the nobility. Instead, the proffered food is without meat and consists of coagulated or fermented milk and black bread, characteristic foods of country folk. We shall soon witness how this fictive hut and its food are made real; related to the two castles in a particular way, this lowly abode will be realized as a result of borrowing and transforming some of the traits that characterize the ogreish and noble castles, as well as their respective foods.

For two years, the prince lives secretly with the princess and, during this period, he spends at least two or three nights in the castle hidden in the depths of the forest. The result is two children, an elder daughter named Aurora and a younger son called Day. At this point, the reader is quite befuddled: what in the world is the reason for all this secrecy? We soon learn that the prince has strong reasons for his behavior: his mother, the queen, is an ogress and his father, the king, married her only for the sake of her money. "At court it was secretly whispered that she had the same inclinations as ogres and that she had a terrible time restraining herself from pouncing on little children when she saw them go by." Thus, although the prince loves his mother the queen, he dreads the sight of his children being devoured by their grandmother. This is the second time a member of the ogre species appears in the tale. The first manifestation occurred in the fiction based on hearsay that figured in the tale's first act. Unlike the first ogre, the second one is quite real and appears in the form of an ogress, the prince's mother. This ogress does not live in the castle deep in the woods, but in the royal palace in town. Between the moment of the first ogre's appearance and that of the second, something like a marvelous ogreish reversal has taken place: from one sex to another, from a distant strangeness to close kinship. The opposition between the ogre and the ogress is almost complete, with the exception of a single shared trait: they both eat children, and there is nothing to say that the ogress does not eat them raw, just like the fictive ogre. In both cases, it is a question of omophagia and allelophagia. Yet in the case of the ogre, one may go so far as to say that it is also a matter of exocannibalism, of the form of cannibalism diametrically opposed to the ogress's endocannibalism.

Only upon the death of the king, when he becomes master of the kingdom, does the prince make his marriage public. Only then, and with great ceremony, does he go and fetch his wife from the castle. Thus the acquisition of absolute political power sets an insuperable limit, which is simultaneously a prohibition that cannot be transgressed, to the desire to indulge in monstrous eating habits. This is a desire that manifests itself in a taste for the fresh meat of little children, even hungering after the offspring produced within the sphere of immediate kinship. It seems, then, that the wielding of an absolute political power establishes a particular kind and little-known relationship between ogres and kings. I have tried to characterize this relationship elsewhere, particularly with respect to "Donkey-Skin," the prologue of which announces an ogre who remains absent throughout the story, unless we agree to consider the absolute monarch and the incestuous father as figures that double for the ogre. In "Sleeping Beauty in the Forest," the son/king would be more like the ogre's inverted image. Not only does this opposition underscore the twin event involving the prince's seizure of power and simultaneous proclamation of his marriage, it also brings out the ambivalent nature of his feelings toward his mother: love, appropriate to the norm of affiliation, and fear, a consequence of a maternal perversion. Thus the political order and its absolute monarch, along with all the signs and effects that accompany and manifest them, come up against a kind of figurative double that reveals their features, albeit negatively. This figure has its home in the domain of orality, a domain that boasts of its excessive eater who puts in question culture and society as a result of transgressing the rules of cooking, as well as the very norms of the alimentary system that provide the art of cooking with its specificity.

Unfortunately, however, the narrative stasis will be short-lived. It is not long before the king has to leave to wage war against his neighbor, the emperor Cantalabutte. He delegates the crown to his mother, the queen, and particularly commends, with the involuntary irony of wishful thinking, his wife and children to her care. Having previously been separated like the two sides of a coin, political power and oral desire, absolutism and monstrosity, perversion and transgression are now all brought together in a single figure for the duration of a summer. "As soon as he had left, the queen-mother sent her daughter-in-law and children to a country house in the forest so she could indulge her terrible desire in peace." At that point, the apparatus governing spatial and local relations is entirely in place, at both the fictive as well as the real levels. This is what a diagram of this apparatus looks like:

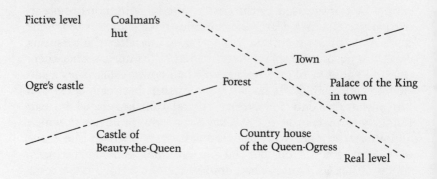

This apparatus is also a culinary one, because a lie states that the prince eats rye bread and cheese in the coalman's hut, food which is virtually natural and socially undervalorized; in the castle of Beauty-the-queen, the prince and his betrothed eat roast game, wild animal meat that is socially overvalorized; in the ogre's castle, the ogre eats little children raw, human meat that is socially prohibited as food. It is not difficult to infer what will happen in the country house belonging to the queen-ogress: in opposition to the coalman's hut, and as in the castle of Beauty-the-queen, it is meat, not milk or rye, that will be consumed. As in the ogre's castle, the meat will not be roasted and will not be animal. Does this mean that the meat necessarily will be raw human flesh? At this point, the tale takes a new turn; the turning point is complex, since it is situated in the woods as opposed to the city, where the coalman's hut has been elevated to the status of a country house, while the castles belonging to the ogre and to Beauty-the-queen are subject to a proportional depreciation.

The queen ogress "went there [to her country house] a few days later and one evening said to the steward: 'Tomorrow I want to have little Aurora for dinner.' 'Oh Madame!', exclaims the steward; 'That is my wish,' said the queen (and she said it the way an ogress does when she really feels like eating fresh meat), and I want to eat her with a Robert sauce." We know how the poor man dropped the knife at the sight of little Aurora and how he finally "went to the farmyard where he slit the throat of a little lamb, which he prepared with such a good sauce that his mistress assured him she had never eaten anything quite as good." Our storyteller adds that, in the meantime, little Aurora had been hidden in the cook's apartment in the far corner of the farmyard. We know that the same episode repeats itself twice more: once with respect to little Day, whom the queen-grandmother claims for her dinner and for whom the cook substitutes a very tender little goat "that the ogress found to be quite excellent." The second time, it is the queen herself whom the ogress "wants to eat, . . . with the same sauce that accompanied the children"; the cook substitutes a doe, which he prepares so magnificently that the queen eats her supper with such gusto, one would have thought she was eating the young queen herself. The conclusion to this series of allegedly cannibalistic meals is a kind of ogrish self-congratulation for a job well done: "Her cruelty made her very pleased with herself and, upon the king's return, she was prepared to tell him that wild wolves had eaten his wife, the queen, as well as his two children."

It is striking that, in each of the three successive episodes, the ogress, repeatedly and to a certain extent, diverges from her customary diet, which dictates the devouring of raw human meat. To recall what was whispered at court: word had it that, when the ogress saw little children go by, she had an incredibly difficult time restraining herself from simply throwing herself upon them. The ogress transgresses transgression itself, for she herself tells the head waiter to prepare her first victim, Aurora, in a Robert sauce. She ought to have devoured or, at the very least, simply eaten the meat raw. Instead, she demands to have the meat cooked (and it is human meat to boot). In fact, her orders are more excessive still than an already excessive action, and this quality is magnified by the repetition of "I want," underscored by the tone of the ogress's voice. She wants to apply the art of cooking, the Robert sauce, to its antithesis, raw flesh, and seeks to subject to the rules of a culinary recipe, a meat, human meat, which necessarily would involve a transgression of the recipe's specifications. Partly because of the ingredients it utilizes (vinegar, spices, and so on), Robert sauce serves a dual function: as a marinade, it is used in the preparation of game or wild animal meat, while also being served as a sauce that accompanies a given dish. Thus, when the ogress insists that Aurora be prepared *à la sauce Robert*, she implicitly considers her to be game meat, readily assimilating her granddaughter to a wild animal, that is, to an animal that has not been raised within a cultural sphere, having instead been hunted within a natural sphere. Moreover, it seems to me that one could consider the steward's wholly culinary response—he does not permit himself to discuss anything with or even to speak to the ogress—to be a matter of the distortion of a rule pertaining to normal human cuisine. This distortion corresponds to the transgression of the ogre's monstrous diet: the steward applies a sauce meant for game meat to a domestic animal, to the lamb that substitutes for the little girl. There is no point in underscoring the fact that this substitution realizes one of the metaphorical names given to every child, "it's a lamb." This distortion is straightened out during the next two episodes: the very tender little goat that is substituted for little Day is less domestic than the lamb which was palatable only as a result of the sauce ("he prepared [the lamb] with such a good sauce that his mistress assured him she had never eaten anything quite as good"); and the doe that replaces the queen is wild meat in every respect. Yet the transition, effected by cooking, from the domestic to the wild is motivated by exclusively culinary reasons: "The young queen was more than twenty, not to mention the hundred years that she had been asleep! Her skin was a little tough, although white and beautiful; and how was he to find an animal quite that tough in the menagerie." We may remark, then, that the grandchildren of the queen-ogress are substituted for by domestic animals; her endocannibalism is deceptively satisfied by the meats raised within the sphere of the household. Her daughter by marriage, however, is replaced by a wild animal. We could even go so far as to say that she is replaced by an object which, in the manner of bait, attracts the ogress's impulses for exocannibalism. Finally, the queen-mother (ogress) prepares herself to provide her son with reasons explaining the absence of his wife, the queen, and of his two children. Within the untruth of her lie resides a moralized metaphor for what the ogress has done: "some wild wolves ate them." The justification simultaneously provides us with the truth about ogres, who are a kind of living metaphor for a wild and ferocious bestiality that has been deviated into culture and society. In this respect, the fiction that the mother ogress concocts for the benefit of her son, the king, is the precise inversion of the one which the king's son presented to his father, when the latter was still alive and ruling: the ogress tells a tale about wild wolves that devour raw human flesh, and the son invents a coalman who hands out rye bread and cheese.

What becomes manifest, then, is the importance of the culinary sign par excellence: the sauce, particularly Robert sauce. For it is prima facie the sauce that makes it possible to mediate between fresh human meat and fresh animal meat, between the little girl belonging to the royal family and the little farmyard lamb. Thanks to Robert sauce, the one passes for the other, the animal for the child. One could even go so far as to say that this complex process of *significance* characterizing the culinary sign is caught up in an exchange of requests, orders, and services. The modality of this exchange is that of an obligation at the level of deontics and that of certitude at the epistemic level: by virtue of the culinary sign, the sauce that he prepares, the cook makes the ogress, who is responsible for ordering the monstrous meal, believe that she definitely is eating the human meat of a child rather than domestic animal meat. But can we go so far as to say that the Robert sauce causes mutton to be taken for child? This would be the equivalent of saying that, in this instance, the culinary process does anything but elevate the raw food—the meat of a domestic animal, lamb from the farmyard—to the dignity and value of a dish, "lamb à la Robert." Instead, it transforms this raw food into unnatural and even anticultural food, into "little girl." What this reveals is that the cultural sign of cooking (Robert sauce) transcends the opposition between human meat and animal meat. It renders both the former and the latter unrecognizable, at least from the perspective of the ogress. Speaking literally, the sign transsignifies, rather than transubstantiates. It transforms both what is inedible according to social prohibition, as well as what is edible according to the rules governing culture, into a prepared dish that is ready to be eaten. The lamb does not turn into a little girl for the ogress, any more than the little girl becomes lamb for the cook. Yet both meats, what the cook knows to be lamb and what the ogress presumes to be little girl, become meat in a sauce, lamb meat as far as the cook is concerned, Aurora meat following the queen-mother. Earlier, I cited from *The Logic of Port-Royal* the famous example of the warm cinders that reveal in the form of a sign the object they conceal. The culinary sign is, however, unlike this example, since it conceals the object, both as object and as sign, and does so without there being any analytic relation, iconic or mimetic, between the sign and the object. The sign renders opaque the object to which it is joined, and it is more like an ornament than a symptom, more like a mask than the feature characterizing a facial expression. Somehow the object, substance and suppositum, subsists in the sign; contrary to the eucharistic sign, however, which involves bread concealing the transubstantiated body of Jesus, the culinary sign involves letting the sauce conceal the animal meat, which itself continues to exist while it supports the saucy sign: Rather than transubstantiation, we have trans*signifiance*; as I have been trying to show, this is what constitutes the marvelous nature of the tale, compared to the miracles of theology. Considered according to its specificity, the culinary sign, and particularly the Robert sauce in "Sleeping Beauty in the Forest," would be the distinctive mark of the marvelous.

Let us briefly consider the Robert sauce from a different perspective, that dictated by a representational apparatus that defines the significance of the sign in terms of a process of substitution. Situated at the border between a semiotics of terms and a propositional semantics, the Robert sauce would play out its meaning by virtue of the substitution of the sign for the object, a process that marks all the arts of make-believe and trompe l'oeil. At this point, the Robert sauce would be the rhetorical *signifiant par excellence,* for it would cause lamb to be taken for little girl, even if, in reality, it is the lamb that is eaten and not the girl. According to the teachings of Plato, cooking is one of the treacherous arts of deception and should be opposed to medicine, just as the rhetoric of the Sophists should be opposed to philosophy. In this case, however, the culinary sign, in the form of Robert sauce, realizes what is just and appropriate by deploying all the savvy contained in a lie, by persuading in favor of falsehood as opposed to truth. In spite of herself, the ogress eats the meat of lamb, goat, and doe in a Robert sauce, instead of the flesh of a little girl, a little boy, and a young woman, all of whom were to have been served in the same sauce. The crafty art of cooking deceives the ogress about certain tangible features. As a result, without knowing she is doing so, without wanting to do so, the queen-mother abides by the cultural rules governing a civilized meal, as well as by the social norms of an acceptable diet.

To recall the end of the story: after having made three meals on "meat in a sauce," the queen, who also is mother and regent, is overtaken once more by bestial impulses and unnatural instincts:

> One evening she, as usual, prowls around the castle's courtyards and farmyards where she hopes to smell out some fresh meat. There she hears little Day crying in one of the lowly sheds. . . . She recognizes

the voice of the queen, his mother, as well as that of Aurora, who begs forgiveness for her brother. She becomes furious for having been cheated. Early next morning in a dreadful voice she ... orders a big vat to be placed in the middle of the courtyard. She has the tub filled with toads, vipers, snakes, and serpents and subsequently intends to throw into it the queen and her children, the steward, his wife, and her maid.

At precisely this moment the king returns from war, and "the ogress, livid at the sight of what she saw, threw herself head first into the tub." The narrator adds, as one would expect, that she was devoured immediately by the vile beasts that she had put in there. The narrator does indeed use the word "devoured." In a narrative moment, we see toads, vipers, snakes, and serpents transformed into savage wolves, carnivorous animals. Two levels operate here, an alimentary and a culinary level. The former concerns primarily the foods that are eaten: we note that the queen-mother, regent and ogress, *falsely believed* herself to have eaten her daughter-in-law and grandchildren in the form of a cooked dish. In the conversation which she anticipates having with her son, she intends to say that all this human meat had been eaten raw by the wolves, which would figure in her lie. Released from her deception by the signs of language and by the voices that convey them, she decides to let the queen and her children be eaten raw by animals which, as a result of their very nature, cannot eat them. On a culinary level, which primarily concerns the manner in which some food is prepared, the ogress once more reveals herself to be a monstrous and perverse eater who transgresses food laws and the rules governing a meal. For she tries to install an anticuisine by beginning to boil (this is the technical value of the big tub) human meat with cold and humid animals that are the carriers of an anti-sauce, toad dribble and serpent venom. The sudden *dénouement* of the tale leaves us with no doubt whatever about its outcome: as a result of an abrupt reversal of subject and object, of the active and the passive, the ogress herself turns out to be the only dish prepared following her cooking methods, the only course accompanied by her sauce. An eater of raw meat, she herself is consumed without further ado or preparation; in short, the devouring cannibal is herself devoured.

10   Recipes of Power ("Puss-in-Boots")

This essay can be viewed in a number of different ways: it may be considered as a contribution to the long and respectable intellectual tradition that studies the history of ideas and ideologies as they find expression in literary texts. It also brushes against the study of myth, in that it provides an element that appears to make possible the comparison of myths and tales belonging to different cultures; as an example, the analysis of a tale by Perrault includes an approach to a theory of the text, of reading, and of their respective effects, an approach roughly characterized by the use of some procedures pertaining to structural analysis. Finally, the essay may be considered an attempt to define a kind of logic that is not the logic of truth as representation, as *adequatio rei et intellectus*, but the logic of willing and desiring or, to be more precise, a logic proper to minorities, to the weak and marginal, a logic, that is, of deceit, trickery, simulation, and lies, a cunning logic that serves as a weapon against the powerful and as a way of capturing their power while simultaneously subverting it.

With these themes in mind, I propose to elaborate a reading of Perrault's "Master-Cat, or Puss-in-Boots." This will not be a very serious reading: it just deals with a tale, a children's tale from which I shall extract only what seem to me to be the most pleasurable, the most delightful features of the story. At the same time, I can imagine some very pedantic subtitles for my essay: "Power of Signs, or Signs of Power," or "How to do Things with

Words," or "Language as Representation and Power," the latter being a kind of Schopenhauerian parody. Donning the hat of the historian of ideas and with a nod in the direction of my earlier analyses of the logic of Port-Royal and of Pascal, I might be tempted to rephrase these subtitles so as to make them even more explicit and pedantic (if this is possible): "Deceptive words, powerful speech: a mythical eucharist in a French seventeenth-century tale."

In reading the tale, I am struck by the important role played by a certain use of language. The main character, the Cat, seems to be the master of words in the following sense: he is forever speaking and always lying, yet in the final analysis, his deceptive words are actually true. Everything he says at the moment of deceiving his interlocutors finally turns out to be just the way he had claimed. The most straightforward way of understanding this process is to consider it to be nothing short of magic. His *"parole"* or speech, by which I mean his use of language, has the power to change his representations and words into real things. In this respect, the tale recalls the basic conception of language developed by the logicians of Port-Royal, as well as their model of the relationships between mind and reality, between thought and words. My purpose is to explore this particular aspect of the ideological and philosophical context of Perrault's text. To put it differently, I would like to show that, in "Puss-in-Boots," Perrault rearticulates the traditional content of the folktale on a literary plane in such a way that he provides us with a good tool for displaying and criticizing the implicit presuppositions of the representationalist paradigm of language and thought, a model that outlines some of the basic problems still of concern to us today. Along these same lines, Perrault's version of the tale is a good tool for pointing out some interesting historical and social changes that occurred during the seventeenth century.

To summarize the basic elements of the tale: Perrault tells of a miller who left three objects as an inheritance to his three sons: the mill to the eldest, the ass to the second, and the cat to the youngest. The three objects are ranked according to an order of decreasing value, which is itself related to the order established by the ages of the sons. The exclusion of the scrivener and the attorney from the legal partition of the estate implies that the family is to be governed by its own rules. Indeed, as the youngest son observes, by putting their stocks together, the eldest and second sons are able to reconstitute a stable self-reproducing social community, from which the youngest son is excluded. With nothing to contribute but his cat, the youngest cannot participate in the social process of production. At the beginning of the tale, he is defined as an individual situated outside the social community, on its boundaries, in a position of cultural marginality. For him, the crucial question concerns survival and not the production of commodities. However, his exclusion from culture makes him a socially unbound adventurer and gives him a kind of absolute freedom vis-à-vis social regulations. Given this state of affairs, his first project has to do with food—with eating his cat, a socially transgressive project since culture specifies that a domestic cat is not edible. To be sure, the prohibition is not very strong; a common story among hunters tells about how an unlucky hunter substitutes a cat for a rabbit when he offers a hunting party dinner to his friends. Yet the cat is his cat and, in a certain sense, we may say that what is a situation of lack in relation to culture is the opposite or the inverse outside of culture, that is, a situation of excess. In fact, the youngest son's freedom will be invested in language, or better yet, a certain use of language will be the natural instrument of this individual. The basic questions—what to eat? how to survive?—are changed into this one: how to transform linguistic use value into economic and social use value? Paradoxically, this investment in language is represented by the cat: when we read the tale, we notice that, contrary to our own implicit expectations and contrary to one of the story's morals, it is not the miller's son, but the cat, who is the actual hero. More important still, the cat is a speaker, since all of his actions consist of talking and communicating with others. We witness something like a scission or duplication of the hero that makes the youngest son into a passive principle, the beneficiary of gifts and things, and the cat into the active one that procures them by, above all else, a certain use of language.

Were I to pursue this line of reasoning a little further into the domain of abstraction, I would say that the cat is an operator of change: he articulates a spatial continuum (he differentiates space) by means of a temporal program or, better yet, by means of a strategy. The cat, much like the trickster figure in the North American Indian myths, is a nomadic figure, perpetually wandering all over the world. Yet, in our tale, his trips cannot be separated from his tricks, that is, from his use of language. In the tale, the particularities of the cat's linguistic usage are evidenced by the fact that he never fails to anticipate or imagine the itinerary that will lead his master toward the apex of the cultural (social and economic) order, to the site that is its highest or maximal point. It is as though the very fact of the master's arrival in a certain place actualizes what his feline servitor said just before his appearance. Textually speaking, the cat is the representative of narrative modalizations (mainly the modality of desire) and his master, the vehicle of narrative assertions or wish fulfillments.

The cat, the real hero, is endowed with a couple of qualities that pertain to two different levels of the tale's semantic content. As far as the cat's qualifications are concerned, we see that he is depicted as a liar or as a trickster. What is more important, however, is that the very mark of his deceptive nature is related to language: the cat hears his master's bitter remarks—which concern him directly, since he is in danger of being eaten—but he pretends that they go unnoticed. The modality of his behavior is that of the *as if:* he responds to the real situation as if he had not understood it. Integrally connected to language, the cat is also inextricably related to pretense and dissimulation, to the domain of appearances as opposed to truth and reality. As for the level of narration, the cat is transformed from being a gift given by the miller to his youngest son into a receiver of gifts, and through this transformation into a potential donor. This turn of events is made possible by the fact that the cat asks his master for a bag and a pair of boots as if he had not heard his master's expressed intention to eat him. Moreover, the cat receives these gifts because he pretends that the future may see a potential giver in him. The cat offers his master a contract. Its acceptance stems from the master's knowing his cat to be a player of tricks.

Following immediately upon the cat's proposition, we read about how he catches a young rabbit not yet acquainted with the deceitful ways of the world, and thus we are inclined to conclude that the contract between the cat and his master undoubtedly will be fulfilled: the cat, we imagine, will be able to bring his master the captured rabbit, a gesture that would imply the successful substitution of an edible object for the one threatened by the prospect of being consumed, that is, for himself. Thus the cat could be said to transform himself from a nonproductive object of consumption into a productive instrument that promises to benefit his master greatly. Thanks to their deceptive illocutionary force, the cat's words would effect a transformation at the very lowest level of the cycle of exchange: death (by starvation or by incorporation) becomes life (a minimal survival).

Rather than opting for this closed cycle of exchange, however, the cat offers his prey to the king. He institutes someone else, other than his master, as the receiver of his gifts. He chooses as the receiver a figure situated at the top of the social scale, on a level that is the exact opposite of the one occupied by the miller's son. The cat's communicational strategy consists of substituting the level that is highest for the one that is lowest. It is only with the help of deception that he can play his hand properly: first, he behaves in a deceptive manner vis-à-vis his master, since he does not observe the terms of the contract. Second, he speaks deceptive words to the king, since it is not the Marquis of Carabas who gives the king a rabbit from his personal warren. However, his behavior with respect to the king is true enough: it is true that a cat gives the king a rabbit from a warren. The episode is repeated three times with a quantitative amplification at each step: one rabbit, two partridges, game. Each time, the king responds to the gifts with countergifts that have the value of signs: words of thanks and money. At this point in the narrative, some interesting transformations occur. First, we note that the cat's master is excluded from the cycle of exchange. Second, this cycle is a matter of exchanging words and things that can be eaten: natural things (game) are exchanged against arbitrary signs. Third, that the natural gifts (hunted prey) are signified by deceptive words allows the transformation of natural things into arbitrary signs to take place: the rabbit ceases to be simply a thing that is good to eat and becomes instead the social sign of the feudal homage that the marquis pays his king. Fourth, this transformation has the effect of reintroducing the cat's master into the cycle of exchange, not as a person but as a name, the Marquis of Carabas, a proper name that is also a social title. In this sense, the Miller's son does indeed receive a gift from his cat, a name: "the Marquis of Carabas was the name the cat was pleased to give his Master." It is, of course, a false name that does not actually denote anybody. However, we do not know the true name of the youngest son. Following the terms proposed in the *Logic of Port-Royal*, the cat's designation is a nominal definition: of my own free will, I am pleased to name as "the Marquis of Carabas" this man whom I pick out in the world, I am pleased to announce that "this is the Marquis of Carabas."

At this stage in the discussion it is useful to recall some passages from the *Logic of Port-Royal* on the definition of names. The definitions have three basic characteristics: First, "they are arbitrary. For every sound being indifferent in itself, I may be allowed, for my own use and provided I forewarn others of it, to select a sound to signify precisely a certain thing" (Arnauld and Nicole [1683] 1970, 121). This is the cat's first trick: he explicitly names his master "the Marquis of Carabas" ("from now on, I shall call my master the Marquis of Carabas"), and he conforms in the story to the basic logical requirement imposed on a correct or proper definition of a name: the norm of consistency that specifies that, within the frame established by a given discourse, the definition of the name may not be changed. Second, "because they are arbitrary, the definitions of names cannot be contested, for we cannot deny that a man [here a cat] has given a sound [here Marquis of Carabas] the signification which he says he has given it, nor that the sound in question only carries that particular meaning when used after we have been forewarned of its signification" (Arnauld and Nicole [1683] 1970, 121–22). Third, "since it cannot be contested, every definition of a name may be employed as a principle" (Arnauld and Nicole [1683] 1970, 122). This is the case in our tale. The logicians add: "But we ought not to infer from this idea that, because we have given it a name, it signifies anything real. For example, I may define a chimera by saying that I shall call that which implies contradiction 'a chimera.' It does not, however, follow that a chimera is a thing" (Arnauld and Nicole [1683] 1970, 122). This may be true for common nouns, but what about proper names? If it is the very logical function of a proper name to point out a real individual, then, in this case, says and thinks the cat, the proper name "Marquis of Carabas" does indeed designate someone real for it refers to "my master." Yet in naming his master "the Marquis of Carabas," the cat does more than just name this individual who is his master. He bestows on him a title of nobility and more, as we shall see in a moment. Essentially the cat employs a deceptive, though correct, definition of a name as though it were a definition of a thing. However, the tale's subsequent episodes transform this deceptive use of a correct definition of a name into a proper use of a correct definition of a thing.

Let us now turn our attention to the three episodes that figure as the crucial phases within the transformational process that we referred to above: the Master's bathing in the river, the cat's encounter with the peasants, and his dealings with the ogre. These sequences of actions and events represent three ways of providing the name "Marquis of Carabas" with a semantic content by extending it narratively.

The first phase, the swim in the river, is a repetition of the initial contract between the cat and his master, although it also introduces an important difference. In the first contract, the master has to give a bag and a pair of boots to the cat in order to receive something to eat from him in return. Yet the cat deceives his master. In the second contract, the master actually has to surrender himself to the cat (he has to undress and take a bath) without knowing anything about the ultimate purpose of the cat's advice. It is only by giving himself over to the cat that the master obtains the greatest gift of all, a gift that goes unspecified and undefined. The cat has no obligations toward his master, nor does he have anything to give him; the master has nothing to expect from his cat. The master is gradually being subordinated to his cat, he is turning into a servant; as for the cat, he is becoming his master's master. The miller's youngest son really has hit rock bottom, since he can fall no lower on the social scale; yet curiously, language, a proper name that is also a title, ensures that he simultaneously is a member of the uppermost crust. It is at this point that the cat calls out to the king: "Help! Help! My Lord, the Marquis of Carabas, is on the point of drowning." Once again, the cat utters words of deception. Yet this time, we note that the words carry a symbolic truth, since his master is indeed at his wit's end. On this occasion, the cat does not give the king anything. Instead, he asks the king for something: he begs help for his master. In the past, the things given by the cat elicited words of gratitude from the king. Now the situation is reversed, because the king is called upon to match the cat's words with deeds and things. He is asked to put his money where his mouth is: first, by helping the cat's master; second, by giving him his royal clothes. It is at this moment that the name begins to be properly realized and its implicit promise fulfilled: to bear a noble name means to wear noble clothes. There is even a textual sign of this very transformation in the tale itself. Henceforth, the narrator will name the miller's son the Marquis of Carabas. The name that was arbitrary qua word and qua sign without a real referent now becomes a definition of the man who is named by it. With the help of the king's clothes, the marquis's name is fleshed out, rounded out, and given real content. As a result, the cat's master suddenly turns into a beautiful young man who inspires love in the king's daughter. He becomes a potential recipient of a woman, a princess. Having nothing to give, he is now in a position to receive the greatest gift of all.

The clothes are followed by an estate: this is the second step in the transformational process undergone by the name. The transferral of the estate is effected by means of the repetition of three episodes that are ranked according to their incremental value: first, hay; then, corn; and finally, everything. Now, what exactly is the cat's strategy here? He no longer speaks words of deception. Instead, he asks others to lie and insists that those who object or refuse will be eaten: "You will be chopped up as meat for meat pies." In other words, if you do not speak my language, my words, you will be eaten. The cat requests the peasants to speak words of deception that have the particular characteristic of defining the marquis's estate, that is, of defining his very name. The words refer truly to the agricultural products and edible things, but falsely to the name of their owner.

Edible things have to be attached to the wrong predicate, they have to figure as integral parts of a name: this means that they have to be incorrectly named to provide a proper name with a semantic content and a truth value. If the peasants refuse to speak, the speakers themselves become edible things (meat for the meat pie). The speakers have to affirm that food is a part of a given name. In the event of refusal, they themselves become food. The speakers have to change things, food (bread, for example) into a name (Carabas or "my body"). If not, the speaker or his name will be changed into food.

The events described above raise one very important question: Why is the cat's speech so powerful? What is the basis of his linguistic power? Where does it reside? I would be inclined to suggest that the first answer is to be found in something like an empiricism of the text: the peasants are petrified by the cat's threats, because they reiterate and mimic words that are the particular prerogative of the ogre. As we know, it is the ogre who, by definition, reigns supreme in the sphere of eating and incorporation. He is nothing short of the absolute, a kind of super cannibal. The second answer to the question concerning the particular locus of the cat's power is a linguistic one: the force of the cat's speech rests upon the power that accrues to or is inherent in his expression by virtue of its formulaic quality; he utters a curse, the words of which have the power to destroy the people towards whom it is directed.

Now to the sequence of events that takes place in the ogre's castle or in its immediate vicinity. In a sense this episode figures as the third step in the fleshing out of the name "Carabas" by providing it with a semantic content. It is also, however, the moment of truth; the name in question will either acquire its definitive and ultimate truth value, or it will be reduced to nothing more than an empty sound. The castle is the place of truth. Should it become apparent that the estate belongs to the ogre, the king will take back his clothes and the Marquis of Carabas will once again be transformed into the poorest and youngest son of a dead miller.

In this tale, the ogre is not characterized by his usual feature as the greatest of eaters, as a man-eater, although the very name ogre is enough to suggest this particular trait to the reader's mind. By virtue of his name, the ogre is the opposite of the miller's son, for the latter has no name and is characterized as the most minimal of eaters: he did not eat his cat, and this potential object of consumption has not yet made good on the initial contract with his master. Against this implicit background, a crucial feature of the situation is particularly noticeable: the ogre is the richest being ever known to man, woman, or animal. He is absolute wealth and, in a sense, so is the Marquis of Carabas. Yet, while the former's wealth is real, the latter's riches reside in his name, a name that is false and has no referent.

Once again, we are privy to the cat's speech. Whereas he previously uttered formulaic threats, he now has recourse to the language of social conventions: "I could not possibly pass by your castle, without having the honor of paying you my respects." The cat is again a speaker, a donor of words, a master of language. He acts upon things and beings through words. He articulates reality through words; in so doing, he succeeds to some degree in making real things correspond to words. He substitutes names for things; his words stand for things. Now the time is ripe to invert the direction of the substitution: to substitute things for words, to speak a true language instead of a deceptive one.

The ogre is quite the opposite of the cat: unlike the cat, he does not have the natural power of linguistic deception, the gift for a false, yet natural use of words. Instead, he possesses the magical power of real metamorphosis, a supernatural use of his body. In the body of the ogre, supernature and infraculture are conjoined and form cannibalism: the ogre is a god who behaves like a beast. The cat, on the other hand, unites nature (he is an animal, a domestic one) with culture (he speaks very cleverly): the cat is an animal who behaves like a man. Alternately, we could say: the ogre can perform a supernatural transubstantiation of himself by

Illustration of Perrault's "Puss-in-Boots," by G. Doré

negating language; the cat, a representational transubstantiation of things through linguistic articulation.

In the light of the question of the transformational power of language, the cat's two challenges are particularly interesting: the cat invites the ogre to use his power without it being necessary to do so; it will be a matter of a kind of show, just for the sake of being admired. As a result of the linguistic power of the cat's flattery, the ogre puts his power to false ends. The cat successively calls upon the ogre to change himself into the two animals that stand for each of the extremes of the animal order: the lion, the king of animals, and the mouse, a parasite. What is important, however, is this: under ordinary circumstances, the lion can eat the cat, but in this particular situation, the ogre merely wishes to show off his powers to the cat, and so the lion does not eat him. He cannot eat the cat, because the recognition of his metamorphic powers requires the existence of the spectator. The situation is not real, but simulated. However, the cat does eat the mouse: he does not play according to the rules of the game. He acts as if the simulated situation were a real one, that is, he pretends that his encounter with the mouse takes place under ordinary circumstances. What we have here is the ultimate of tricks. What is tricky about the cat's action is that it finds its realization through the exact opposite of a trick, an inversion that finds an echo at the level of the narrative itself. We note that the cat's trick enacts a situation that is diametrically opposed to the one that obtains at the outset of the tale: in danger of being eaten by his master, he escapes death by speaking like a man and by taking the real situation for one of pretense. At the end of the tale, he eats the cannibalistic eater, the god-beast, by behaving like a cat and by taking what is a matter of feigning and play to be reality. The cat eats the cannibalistic eater. The master of words eats the monstrous master of food. The ultimate and true transubstantiation hinges on the power to transform things into words in order to change words into things. The cat's power resides in his ability to substitute words for things, and it is effective precisely because he finally substitutes things for words. Thus, his words of deception become an objectively valid language, since language is power. By eating the ogre as a mouse, the cat gives an objective value to his words of deception. By eating or assimilating the master of food to himself, the master of language, he represents the true metamorphosis of things into words by means of an enactment of the process. Now words and things correspond perfectly.

The cat's actions also provide the answer to one of the questions framed at the outset of our discussion, a question that ultimately is no different from the one concerning the power of speech and language: how can a man, a cultural being who is excluded from culture, reintegrate the cultural world? Moreover, how can a man reduced to a cultural (social and economic) nullity attain not only *a*, but *the* cultural, social, and economic highpoint? How is it that he can come to occupy the supernatural position of the king? Before performing his ultimate trick, the cat, the vehicle of the nature/culture relation, has to transform both a wild and a cultivated nature into culture: first, as we have seen, by changing wild animals into cultural signs; second, by converting agricultural products into the component parts of an estate and, ultimately, into the constitutive elements of a name and a noble title. The cat accomplishes this particular conversion by threatening the producers of the harvested products with being changed into infracultural food, food for the supercannibal or ogre. Language is representation and power. Discourse is a structural strategy pertaining to desire and the will, to a social will as well as to an epistemological desire. Is the Cartesian process of hyperbolic skepticism that culminates in the statement *cogito ergo sum ergo Deus est* really so different from the comings and goings or the tricks of the master-cat? Is the encounter of the philosophical mind with the demon in Descartes's *Meditations* not akin to Puss-in-Boots's encounter with the ogre?

Now we are ready for the final episode: the king arrives at the castle with the princess and the Marquis of Carabas. The cat speaks one last time, offering conventional words of welcome, but now they are true words: "Your Majesty is welcome to this castle that belongs to my lord the Marquis of Carabas." The king responds with words of congratulation that are also words of recognition since they acknowledge Carabas as a marquis. For the first time in the tale, the king addresses the miller's son as "My Lord Marquis." There is no better proof of the validity of our preceding analysis than the fact that the king then immediately goes on to ask the crucial question: "Does this castle also belong to you?" The deictic in the cat's address to the king signals the end of the transformational process that began with the nominal definition of the miller's son as the Marquis of Carabas; the act of naming has now been replaced by an ostensive definition of being.

Shortly after his arrival, the king enters the castle where he, in a great hall, comes upon the most magnificent feast. In a sense, this meal is not necessary to the narrative, although it does satisfy a very real imperative, that of recuperating and neutralizing the negative bodily function that opens the story: the starvation of the Miller's son. The sudden appearance of the spread offers proof that the truth value to be assigned to the cat's words is that of "true" rather than "false": the meal is the concrete eucharist that explicitly realizes what has already occurred in the previous episodes. All the tale's characters share a meal together and, at least symbolically, they devour the cannibalistic ogre. This communal meal is the ultimate proof that the cat's recipes of power have met with a complete success. The performatives that figure prominently within his linguistic activity have been fully realized: not only have words been transformed into consumables, they have been changed into the most delicious foods.

On the other hand, the feast has the interesting function of excluding from the community of true eaters and speakers those who did not participate in the cycle of exchange and in its trans- formational process. The magnificent spread had been prepared by the ogre "for his friends who were to come pay him a visit that very same day and who did not dare enter, since they knew that the king was there." It is clear that the ogre's friends belong to the class of ogres. They are merely eaters, they come only to eat with their friend; but they are excluded from the banquet by the king's presence, just as heretics and pagans are excluded from the Holy Table, from the place where a thing is changed into a word that is God's body, symbolically his body as a priest and really Christ's body, Christ of whom the priest is the representative. The repre- sentational system of signification is at one and the same time closed in upon itself and completely equivalent to the Being it represents.

Much like other tales, "Puss-in-Boots" ends with a marriage. Nevertheless, it is remarkable that it is only "after having downed five or six glassfuls" that the king decides to give the Marquis of Carabas his daughter's hand in marriage. It is only after the meal has been consumed that the ultimate gift, the princess, is be- stowed upon the host: in a sense, she is the last course. In other words, what we have here is a kind of generalized potlatch that finds its expression in the representation of the most complete and ultimate consumption and consummation. In fact, it is none other than the king himself who offers himself to be consumed through the daughter, who represents him genealogically. This is how the king responds to the total consumption of Carabas that is offered to him in the form of the feast; for we know that, ulti- mately, the meal signifies the marquis's castle, estate, clothes, title, name — it stands for everything he is.

One last word about the cat's reward: he became a great lord and no longer chased mice, except for the sake of amusement. To become part of the nobility means that one no longer needs to eat. Life becomes play and ceases to be a vital necessity; it is no longer a matter of survival, but of recreation. At the beginning of the tale, the cat, much like a mouth, comes within a hair's breadth of being eaten by his master. By the end, he does not need to eat mice for vital purposes; he just plays at eating them. Infinite abundance follows upon total scarcity. And now he can assume his most basic nature. The cat is by nature a player of tricks. At the outset of the tale, the cat's tricks were all oriented toward survival, and the pursuit of mice figured only within this scheme of necessity. By the end, however, he performs tricks in order to derive pleasure from hunting. A biological telos is transformed into an aesthetic-aristocratic activity, into a form of purposiveness without purpose.

However, in order to attain his ultimate goal, the state of purposive play, the cat is obliged temporarily to channel his ability for performing tricks into a wholly serious game; a game in which things must be transformed into words so that words subsequently can be changed into things; it presupposes skill with language, the ability to derive a use of things from a play of words, and a consumption of things from their possession.

In the *Phenomenology of Mind*, Hegel insists that the great discovery made by the noble consciousness during the seventeenth century was precisely this complex relation between words and things. He refers to the dialectical phase in question in terms of the transition from the heroism of feudal fealty to the heroism of the courtier's flattery. By giving the king words of flattery, the courtier receives money; yet through this process, the king's self becomes the state and the noble self a pure futility. Perhaps Hegel's analysis provides us with yet another example of the functioning of the representational system of language, a system that has a eucharistic matrix inscribed within it as its central core; maybe it touches on the real stakes involved in the charming tale by Charles Perrault that I have just read; similarly, my own essay was announced as a mere diversion, but this diversion was itself diverted toward pedantic questions and ended up as that half funny and half serious intellectual game called structural analysis. But *serio ludere*, serious playing, may be the only way to conduct a truly radical criticism.

II

Stew and Roast, or the
Mastery of Discourse
and the Illusions of Eros
("Ricky with the Tuft")

Perrault specialists have often pointed to the narrative incoherence of the tale entitled "Ricky with the Tuft." The incoherence is said to arise from the tale's conflation of two stories that stem from different sources and that diverge at the level of content. It is true that the unadvised yet attentive reader is bound to notice some hesitations in the narrative, as though the narrator fails to get a grip on the material or is unable to settle on a specific course. The interpreter encounters knots in the thread of the story, knots that cannot readily be untangled. To employ a culinary metaphor that is more relevant to our context of discussion, it is as though the story's sauce has thickened nicely, but not without lumps. How might this sauce be made more velvety, more homogeneous?

Following other interpreters, I shall focus on two of the knots in the textual material that tangle the shuttle of the reader's loom. We will look at two of the lumps that stick in the reader's throat, interrupting the meal: the name of the tale's hero and the episode involving the kitchen in the forest. These sticky elements may appear to be external to our topic, yet they are related to it both directly and indirectly. Their alleged incongruity has always seemed to me to reveal the weaknesses of those learned, yet artificial, fabrications of the story concocted by critical geniuses. The tale is, in fact, wholly governed by a cultural and ideological opposition between intelligence and beauty: intelligence finds expression in the mastery of words and actions, as well as in a perfect control over the processes of *signifiance;* beauty reveals itself through the given features of body and face. When presented in a diagram, the structure of the tale's agential apparatus is perfectly clear and seems to be constructed in the manner of a machine: on the one hand, we have a son who lacks a beautiful body and face, although he is endowed with extreme intelligence; on the other hand, there are the two daughters, "the one as beautiful as the light of day" and "as stupid as she was beautiful," and the other, extremely ugly, but endowed with "so much intelligence that people hardly noticed that she lacked beauty." This simple sketch of the tale's structure reveals that a lack of one thing or an excess of another prevents a perfect symmetry between its two halves: one side lacks a beautiful and stupid son, while the other has an ugly and intelligent daughter too many. As we shall see, this anomaly will find a somewhat clumsy resolution through the double play of a representation and an effacement: a representation is added here, an effacement effected there, and it is easy to see that, at the cost of a change of sex and physical features, the representation is that of this absence, that representation is absence. I should add that the storyteller has provided himself with the means, which, I repeat, are of a mechanical nature of effecting the transaction between the two parts of the structural diagram: thanks to his fairy godmother, the ugly but intelligent son can bestow "as much intelligence as he himself possesses on the person he loves most dearly." The beautiful but stupid daughter will "have the power to render beautiful whomever she wants." It is this dynamic principle that allows the narrative process to begin and permits it to unfold to its conclusion; the principle involves an exchange of qualities or features and is introduced, by marvelous means, into an essentially static diagram. It will not, however, go unnoticed that the second daughter is refused the potential for transferring intelligence. As a result, she figures as the female double of the only son, minus the gift that is in his possession. These failures, which pertain to the structural diagram as well as to the motor of the narrative process, are not without significance for the deep internal logic of the tale.

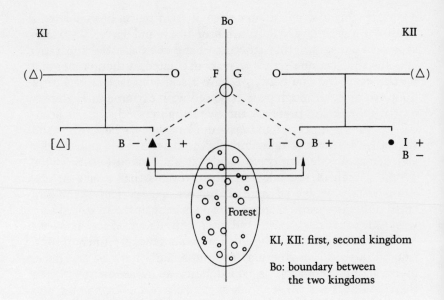

KI, KII: first, second kingdom

Bo: boundary between
the two kingdoms

This diagram reveals the anomalies inherent in the narrative distribution of terms and functions: the text's silence on the issue of the royal fathers designated by Δ; the lack within KI of a masculine term which, in relation to Bo, would be symmetrical to the feminine term in KII; and conversely, KII's supplementary feminine term in relation to KI. By the same token, there is no deployment of the principle of transaction in KII, since the second feminine term does not receive beauty (B) from anybody, and she does not bestow intelligence (I) on anyone; the fairy godmother (FG) functions as an operator who effects the transfer of qualities, since the same fairy bestows the converse gifts granted to the son in KI and to the daughter in KII; the marking of the boundary (Bo) between KI and KII with a forest, which will become the site for a transaction between the story's agents involving intelligence (I+ and I−) and beauty (B+ and B−).

The tale is, then, based entirely on the opposition between a mastery of signs (intelligence) and a possession of (bodily) qualities, as well as on an exchange between these two registers. It is a matter of bestowing bodily qualities on the male or female body which is devoid of them. This must occur without a loss of the mastery of signs on the part of the receiving party. Conversely, a mastery of signs is to be granted to the person lacking it, and this without any loss of bodily qualities on the part of the recipient.

Stated in this way, the tale's argument sets up the transaction in terms of a double figure. Which aspect of the figure dominates depends on the direction the transaction takes and on whether it has already been realized in the past or is to be realized at some future moment. The double figure in question is that of a body-sign and of a sign-body: on the one hand, we have a body, the features of which are signified in a name, and on the other, a process of *signifiance*, which, in being brought to bear on a body, transforms it into a sign. At this point, we run up against the knots in the narrative thread, since this is where we encounter the lumps in the sauce that give spice to our reading and to the food. What we have in mind is, more precisely, the name "Ricky with the Tuft" and the episode involving the kitchen in the forest.

"Once upon a time there was a queen who gave birth to a son so ugly and so deformed that, for the longest time, people wondered whether he was of human form at all." And so the tale is born, as is born a child who, in his ugliness, borders between the beastly and the human. His liminal status is confirmed by the name that he is given a few lines later, after having received the fairy's gift: the child is referred to as an ugly "brat" *(marmot)*, a term which, in French, used to be the name for a monkey before it came to designate a filthy and ill-educated child. At the moment that the gift of intelligence is received by the little prince, with his acquisition of language, the narrator reveals the lad's name, or more precisely, that of his family: Ricky. The family name is styled to individually suit this son of the queen. At his birth, the child exhibits a particular bodily characteristic, "a little tuft of hair on the top of his head." This particularity is the physical sign that is immediately and definitively linked to the prince's name by a nickname, which marks him just as the tuft of hair crowns his head: "and people called him Ricky with the Tuft as a result." The tuft is conspicuous because it figures on the top of Ricky's head; yet it is merely a kind of contingent supplement, since it does not belong to his body in the same way that his arms or legs do. This contingent element is, however, an integral part of a name which, although supplementary, is necessary as a proper nickname. From then on, Ricky is never called anything but Ricky with the Tuft.

The prince's proper name is derived from the tuft that crowns his head. It should be noted that the prince shares, if one may put it that way, the tuft and name with an animal, a bird that derives its name from a similar crest of feathers on the top of its head:

the hoopoe. Thus a linguistic sign, his nickname, situates Ricky
on the border between the animal kingdom and humanity. Ricky
is returned to the site from which his cultural and social mastery
of signs in general and of linguistic signs in particular allowed
him to extrapolate himself. It is true that this reversion is entirely metaphorical (a Mr. Lion or Mr. Rat is hardly a real lion or
rat). Indeed, to be is to have a name, and a proper name appropriates for an individual its own proper being, a comment all the
more appropriate in the case of a fairy tale. Moreover, Ricky and
the hoopoe both wear a crest of feathers or hair on top of their
heads and derive their names from their respective crests. This
crest is common to both of them, with respect to both their
bodies and their names: the tufted hoopoe is to Ricky in one
respect what Ricky is to the tufted hoopoe in another; the
hoopoe called Upupa is a prince in the same way that the prince
called Ricky is a hoopoe. In this tuft, we find the condensation of
a very long and very old and horrible story relating the dreadful
adventures of a prince, Tereus, who was metamorphosed into a
bird. Living at the boundary between the Greek world and that of
the barbarians, this prince was turned into a hoopoe; as a punishment for his crimes against nature: Tereus really does become a
tufted hoopoe; he is not just called Tereus with the Tuft. Yet we
cannot help but notice that, in bequeathing its tuft to the head of
the child at birth and to the prince's name, Tereus-the-hoopoe
simultaneously leaves behind a trace of the story of which the
hoopoe is the last part.

Let us begin by recalling the events of the myth as retold by
Ovid. Tereus is a prince from Thrace and a descendant of Mars,
powerful by virtue of his wealth and many slaves. Tereus marries
Procne, the daughter of Pandion, the king of Athens. The young
bride invites her sister Philomela to come and live with them.
Tereus goes to pick up Philomela in Athens and falls madly in
love the minute he sets eyes on her; he burns with passion,
devours her with his eyes, caresses her with each glance. Seeing
her kiss her father, he wishes he could take the old man's place
and enjoy her affection. Crazed by this passionate love, which he
disguises as the affection duly owed to a sister-in-law, Tereus
finally persuades Pandion to let his daughter leave with him.
Once their boat embarks for Thrace, Tereus is overwhelmed with
joy, so much so that only with difficulty does he postpone the act
which, in imagination, already affords him such pleasure. The
rapist feasts his eyes on his prey, allowing his imagination to run

wild while he fantasizes about the parts of Philomela that he has not yet seen. As soon as they set foot on the domain where he rules supreme, Tereus drags Philomela off into the depths of a forest, where he violently forces himself upon her, uniting them against her will. Thus he violates not only her virginity and the laws of matrimony, but also her father's trust and Procne's conjugal love. And so, against her will, Philomela becomes her sister's rival while Tereus becomes the husband of two women: "I myself will report what you have done, cries Philomela, brushing aside all caution. . . . I will appeal to the people, my lamentations will move forests and rocks; if only the heavens and the gods who dwell there would hear my complaint, even if for just a fleeting instant." Possessed with the frenzy of Eros, the monster cuts out her tongue, thinking that she in this way will always be confined to an eternal silence; he subsequently rejoins his wife Procne and tells her a spurious story about Philomela's death. He builds an empty tomb in Philomela's name and Procne spills many tears — tears, however, which she cries for the wrong reason. As incapable of escaping as she is of speaking, Philomela concocts the following strategy: with a foreign loom, she weaves a tapestry representing the story of Tereus's crime and has it delivered to Procne, who thus learns of her sister's horrible experiences. Sorrow seals Procne's lips; she thinks only of acting; the idea of revenge alone occupies her mind, for she does not give a thought to what is and what is not lawful. She wavers in her hatred for Tereus: should she burn the palace and the tyrant with it, pull out his tongue, his eyes, and his member, kill him by wounding him mortally? It is at this moment of hesitation that Itys shows up. Itys is the son born of her love for the Thracian, and he resembles his father perfectly. Thus a terrible act of revenge suggests itself to her. The two sisters kill the child and dismember it. They boil some of its parts in huge pots and cauldrons, and they roast others on spits. Procne subsequently invites Tereus to celebrate a rite, a kind of ceremonial feast, in which he alone, she says, has the right to participate: she serves him his own child; he wolfs down his own flesh and blood. Exhilarated by his meal, the tyrant orders that Itys be sent to him. "The person that you ask for is already with you," says Procne, and Philomela throws the head of Itys in the face of his father. Tereus, transported by a fit of rage, tries to tear open his own chest to empty it of the infamous food. Then he bursts into tears and proclaims himself the unhappy and living tomb of his son. The two women are unrelenting in their pursuit of him. Finally the gods intervene and they transform Procne into a nightingale and Philomela into a swallow. As for Tereus, the Thracian tyrant, he is transformed into a hoopoe. In her song, Procne bemoans her son Itys, and Philomela's short cries testify to the fact that Tereus cut out her tongue. Tereus on the other hand repeatedly calls "where? where?" as he looks for them. Meanwhile, he is doomed to feed on human excrements.

In this dreadful story, a frenzied erotic desire finds satisfaction at the price of transgressing all the interdictions attached to the social institution of sexuality. It is a tale where a severed tongue, in order to denounce this erotic frenzy, makes itself into a sign. This sign forms a text, a tissue inscribed, a site of writing and reading. It is also a tale where, in order to punish transgression with transgression, Eros and Logos are conjoined in a dish that is monstrous in a threefold manner: because of the nature of the raw foods transformed in it (human meat), as a result of the process employed in its preparation (a mixture of boiling and cooking), and in the very act required in its eating (the guest downs his own flesh and blood). The dish is prohibited and excluded, inedible and indigestible. In incorporating it, what is human necessarily becomes animal once more; to eat the dish is to swallow excrement as food and to put rot in the place of what has been transgressively cooked. What remains of this terrifying tale and of the metamorphosis that brings it to a close? Only a bird's cry ("where? where?"), the erect tuft of feathers that crowns its head, and its parasitical diet of human waste products. What is left, in a word, is a hoopoe, a bird characterized by its tuft, the very word which will provide Ricky with an additional name, just as his tuft of hair crowns his head. Yet the reader will note the extraordinary efficacy and power attributed to signs in the tale, at least in Ovid's version of it. To be more precise, one cannot but recognize writing's power of inscription, the efficacy of the text. For once the voice has been totally stifled, writing and a text become the only means by which a criminal act can avenge the initial crime: a mastery of signs suggests itself here, even if it is misdirected in its ends, straying toward cannibalism and, ultimately, toward the cry of an animal and excremental food. Ricky with the Tuft possesses this mastery to a high degree, so much so that he can share it with someone else. All the other elements of Ovid's story are, however, absent from Perrault's learned tale, everything except the tuft that crowns Ricky's head and perfects his name. True enough, Eros makes its demands felt, just as Logos imposes its laws, but the culinary horrors faced by Tereus, Philomela, and Procne seem to have been effaced. And yet, a rather strange wedding meal is prepared in the depths of the forest, and here we come upon the other rent in the narrative tissue which we signaled above.

"One day the unhappy princess [the beastly beauty] had withdrawn to a forest to bemoan her unhappiness. She saw coming toward her a small man who was very ugly and unappealing, yet magnificently dressed. The man was young prince Ricky with the Tuft, who had fallen in love with her by looking at her portraits dispersed across the whole wide world. He had left behind his father's kingdom in order to have the pleasure of seeing and speaking to her."

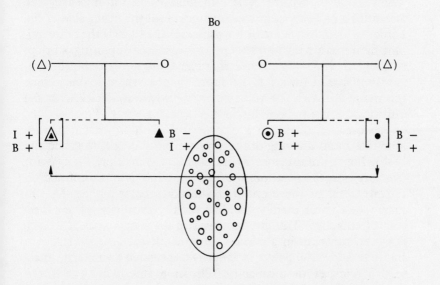

NB$_1$: Once the transaction has been executed, the redundant youngest daughter is excluded, but an extra suitor appears on the scene, in the place of the initial lack.
NB$_2$: Within the masculine register, the suitor is the double of the eldest princess, just as the youngest is Ricky's double within the feminine register.

Ricky does not fall in love with the princess's sister, who is intelligent and ugly like himself. He falls in love with a portrait, a beautiful and silent representation, mute poetry that incites discourse and language. The stupidity of the princess wandering deep in the forest makes her just as mute, or almost as mute, as her portrait. Whence Ricky's proposal of a transaction: "I will give you power over signs if you will grant me erotic power over you. Whether you become as intelligent as one could possibly be is entirely up to you. All you have to do is marry me." Unlike the Thracian prince deep in his forests, Ricky agrees to postpone the satisfaction of his most cherished desire for a year: he grants the gift of a mastery of language in the present in exchange for a promise of marriage at a future date. In this way, the princess suddenly, indeed immediately, acquires "an unbelievable facility for saying everything she wanted to say." From that moment on, the younger sister, who is ugly but intelligent, is wholly dispensable and simply drops out of the story. Structural symmetry is established as a result of the younger sister's disappearance. Yet this newly achieved symmetry is immediately compromised by the advent of a princely suitor who comes from the other side of the border to claim the hand of the princess, just like all the other gallant figures courting her: this prince was "so compelling, so rich, so cerebral, and so handsome that she could not help but be positively disposed toward him." From then on there is one prince too many. As with the younger princess earlier, Ricky with the Tuft now proves to be redundant.

However, to eliminate Ricky with the Tuft from the picture amounts to an undoing of the very exchange or gift that had the bestowing of intelligence as its objective. Not that Ricky with the Tuft is in the position to take back what he has bestowed on the princess. In the event that she takes back her promise to marry, he cannot match the blow with a revocation of her mastery of language. The gift bestowed more than a year ago does, however, function in a certain sense as an antidote to desire in the here and now: power of language, incapacity to marry; mastery of signs, erotic incapacity. "The more intelligent one is, the more difficult it is to arrive at a firm resolution and, in this case [marriage to the princely suitor], the princess, having thanked her father [who leaves the decision to her], begs the prince to give her more time to think it all over. . . . To mull over what she should do, she to goes for a walk in the same forest where she had met Ricky with the Tuft."

At this point, we come across the following unexpected scene. "While strolling along, totally lost in her thoughts, she heard a kind of thumping coming from beneath her feet, as though several people were coming and going and bustling about." The nar-

Illustration of Perrault's "Ricky with the Tuft," by G. Doré

rative moves through three stages describing three different states of affairs, each of which can be characterized in terms of the following aspects: aural field, location, visual field, and action. The first stage is as follows: aural field—noise; location—underground; visual field—invisibility; action—coming and going. With the transition to the next state of affairs, the narrative reads: "Listening more attentively, she hears someone say:

bring me that pot, [and someone else] give me that boiler, [while yet another voice says] put some wood on the fire. At just that moment the ground gapes and, underneath her feet, she sees something like a huge kitchen full of cooks, scullions, and all the kitchen hands necessary for a magnificent feast." We can describe this second stage as follows: aural field—articulate words; location—underground, beneath her feet; visual field—visibility; action—cooking, the preparation of a stew. "Out came a gang of some twenty or thirty cooks who proceeded to plant themselves around a very long table, which they set up in one of the forest's paths. With larding needles in hand and wheat tucked behind their ears, they all set to work to the rhythm of a harmonious song." Third stage, third and final state of affairs: aural field—lyrics sung by several voices; location—above ground, in the forest; visual field—visibility; action—cooking, the preparation of a roast. The reader will be as surprised by this narrative sequence as the princess is by the spectacle which she comes upon deep in the forest. The perfect internal coherence of the narrative sequence and the quasi-mechanical transformations that it effects are equaled only by its incongruity. Even the magical context cannot justify the strong element of surprise: what on earth is this huge underground kitchen, teeming with cooks, doing in the middle of the forest? And what about this very long table that is brought out and set up in a pathway as part of the preparations for a roast? Yet everything in this episode marks the conquest or sublimation of meaning, of even its hyperbolic accomplishment: the noisy thumping becomes harmonious song, rising above intelligible speech; the invisible underground space, a site of indeterminate actions, becomes a visible kitchen above the ground, the place where a roast is in the making. This kitchen is itself the sublimated version of the visible underground kitchen where the stew was being prepared. However, the most remarkable transformation of all is the one that seems to be effected by this sequence, by the events surrounding the kitchen in the forest: from the outset, the princess had her doubts about committing herself to an erotic and matrimonial future with her suitor, the splendid and very intelligent prince; now suddenly, she not only remembers the marriage promise uttered a year earlier, she fulfills it; in doing so, she effects a transaction that is diametrically opposed to the one from which she herself benefited. In a sense, she sets up a relation of identity between Ricky with the Tuft and the princely suitor, and thus she effaces the latter, in much the same way that Ricky, without really intending to do so, ends up neutralizing the youngest sister. In short, structural symmetry is established once and for all, and "the very next day" the festivities celebrating the marriage of the princess and Ricky "were carried out in precisely the way Ricky with the Tuft had anticipated, and according to the orders which he had given much earlier." In other words, the strange kitchen makes it possible to establish a definitive harmony between Eros and Logos, between bodily features and a talent for signs, for now the princess and Ricky are equally equipped. This balance is clearly marked by the transition from the inchoate noise originating from an invisible source underground, to the harmonious song of the visible kitchen hands working above the ground. It is also signaled, although more subtly, by a metaphorical figure and a metonymic process: by the change wrought in the beautiful princess who is paralyzed by indecision because of an excess of intelligence, a transformation effected by the meat which is brought to a boil "beneath her feet," in an underground cauldron above a flaming fire, and which turns into meat that is greased, spitted, and ready to be roasted on one of the pathways in the forest of love, a forest situated above the ground. Witness a princess with her mind made up: not only has she decided to marry Ricky with the Tuft, but she also wants (at Ricky's suggestion, it is true) to bestow on him the amount of beautiful bodily features which

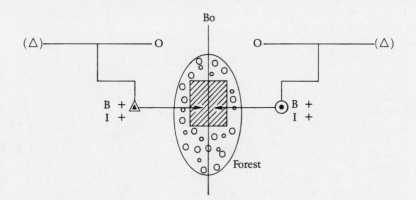

Union between Ricky with the Tuft and the Princess, one brought about by a wedding feast in the forest situated at the border between the two kingdoms.

would equal the intelligence that he had given her in the form of a power over and by means of signs.

Thus Ricky with the Tuft would be a kind of French Tereus who, by virtue of his natural mastery of discourse and language, manages to transform the violence of erotic rapture into the institution of conjugal possession and the cannibalism of a monstrous sacrificial meal into a delicious wedding feast.

12 Butcher's Meat and Game, or the Culinary Sign within Generalized Communication ("Tom Thumb")

"Tom Thumb" figures last in the collection of fairy tales entitled *Histories or Tales from Past Times with Moral Lessons*. The "Perrauldian" economy governing the organization of these tales merits our attention. First is "Sleeping Beauty in the Forest," a tale in which a sleeping princess is awakened by Prince Charming, only to slip into a nightmare involving the conflation of her mother-in-law, the queen regent, and the ogress. The series draws to a close with a tale about a child who measures little more than a thumb upon birth and who is both silent and very delicate; these features notwithstanding, Tom Thumb goes on to contend successfully with the forest, with wolves, and even with the ogre, until he ultimately becomes the king's messenger. If reading Perrault's tales can be compared to the ordered succession of the courses making up a meal, then "Sleeping Beauty in the Forest" would have to be conceived of as a hearty hors d'oeuvre, designed to whet the reading guest's appetite. "Little Red Riding Hood" and "Puss-in-Boots" would be side dishes, "Ricky with the Tuft" a stew or a roast, and finally, "Tom Thumb" would serve as a very rich and savory dessert. During this last course, the guests would already begin to shift from food to speech, from eating to conversation. At base, the story of Tom Thumb is, in its own way, really about this transition. I shall come back to this point. Yet if we are to pursue the comparison between a meal and a collection of tales, between a banquet and the ordering of the tales, feasting and reading, then we must add two additional hors d'oeuvres, both in verse. By including "Donkey-Skin" and "Ridiculous Wishes," we strain our menu somewhat: this inclusion emphasizes the prologue, perhaps excessively so, at the expense of the solid and hearty foods that constitute the body of the meal; moreover, in these introductory courses, we have mixed, in a highly baroque fashion, cake with blood sausage, sweets with meats. We can reintroduce some modicum of balance into our reading banquet by imagining that the words exchanged over dessert imperceptibly come to take the place of a savoring of courses. Without noticing it, the guests slip from one use of the mouth, from one regime of oral pleasure, to another. In short, in eating what they talk about, they speak what they eat.

In the final analysis, this has been my thesis from the outset, not only my strategy as a writer, but also my rhetorical intention. I have been elaborating my analyses in regard to three domains, those of Logos, Eros, and *Sitos*. Within these major paradigms, my readings have focused on issues relating to signs in general, to language in particular, and to the manner in which signs are exchanged. We studied the representation of amorous bodies and their adornments; we discussed how nutritious substances were negated and subsumed within the culinary system. Now it happens that the last tale in the collection presents us once more with all the main figures pertaining to these three paradigms: we encounter ogre and king, mother and child, wolf and thief, forest and house, meat from the butcher's shop and hunter's game, signs and their tricks, discourses and their lies. "Tom Thumb" brings these figures together for us in a figurative narrative deriving from metonymy, synecdoche, and metaphor. It is the last in the series of tales and, as an allegorical fable about the marvels of tales, it comes to stand for the collection as a whole. "Tom Thumb" is peppered with some of the other tales' most salient traits: once more we encounter the meats from "Sleeping Beauty in the Forest" and the roasts from "Ricky with the Tuft." We hear echoed the tender words spoken by mothers and grandmothers; the nagging words of wives and the angry ones of husbands, reminding us of "Ridiculous Wishes." The crowns from "Donkey-Skin" even figure in the tale, and while the fairy godmother may be absent, in the end, the seven-league boots are enchanted and capable of working marvels.

As we know, the tale's beginning consists of two narrative sequences that run parallel to each other, even though they are being presented in succession. The hero in both cases is Tom Thumb, who is happy in the first sequence and unhappy during the second. In the first few sentences, the narrator discreetly tips us off to Tom Thumb's role within the narrative structure. As its operator, Tom Thumb is necessarily a supplement in relation to the narrative's structural organization. This much we know by means of a demographic calculation implicit in the narrative: the woodcutter and his wife have seven children, all of whom are boys. The oldest is only ten while the youngest is seven. As the narrator points out, this means that all but one of the children are twins, the exception being the youngest child who, as a seven-year-old, has reached the age of reason, seven being the number symbolic of wisdom. Now, unlike Ricky with the Tuft, Tom Thumb's silence is anything but the mark of stupidity, and this is perhaps precisely what makes the difference between the king's son and the son of a woodcutter. Indeed, Tom Thumb's silence is "a mark of his mind's excellence . . . for, even if he said little, he listened a great deal." While Ricky masters signs naturally, Tom Thumb immediately grasps the mechanism governing their exchange: he is not part of the communicational process, is neither a sender nor a receiver, and even less a message or a referent. Nor does he occupy a metacommunicational position. Even though he is an auditor, an observer and nonreceiver, he is nonetheless external to the communicative process. It is because of his role within the dialogic structure as that of the silent and concealed third party that he can be the supplement of the process, the excess of the narrative apparatus, the surplus needed for the process to function. The externality of Tom Thumb's position is symbolically disclosed by his status as a remainder within the gemellary line of filiation. It is through him, as the seventh member of the series, that the three couples achieve their fulfillment, the sum of the children being seven, the number "loved by the gods."

In a sense, "Tom Thumb" tells a tale about how a certain mastery is acquired. What is at stake here, however, is not the mastery of signs, as in "Ricky with the Tuft," but their conveyance. The story hinges entirely on this: it hinges on paths and their markers in a first moment; on the exchanging of markers in a second; and, in a third, it is a matter of the transferring of means, so that finally our supplemental hero wins, by virtue of his power over the means of conveyance, a final control over trajectories, exchanges, and transferrals, a final control over all markers and signs.

The tale is less a story about apprenticeship than about mastery: the introduction, which concludes with "even if he said little, he listened a great deal," says as much. Nevertheless, the actual story begins with a lack, which is not that of living speech but of food. "A troublesome year came to pass and the famine was so great that these poor people decided to rid themselves of their children. . . . " There is a negative equation between the modalities of nourishment and the death of the children. Strangely enough, however, helplessness is connected with blindness and food with the loss of life:

$$(I) \quad \frac{\text{The parents} \;\rightarrow\; \text{unable to nourish} \;\rightarrow\; \text{the children}}{\text{The parents} \;\rightarrow\; \text{unable to see die} \;\rightarrow\; \text{the children}} \;=\;$$

This equation is pregnant with the future of the story, thanks to eavesdropping by Tom Thumb, who is in a sense the equation's remainder. Whence the poor parents' decision to lose the children in the forest, a decision which introduces the motif of wandering, even rambling, as well as that of the marking of ground covered, this being possible because Tom Thumb already possesses an extraordinary knowledge of trajectories: during the outward trip, he strews white pebbles along the route and thus plots a path that may be reproduced as a trace on the way home. Here the supplement plays no other role within the apparatus of narrative topography than that of repeating a trajectory by means of its landmarks. He does not invent signs, he does not signify things, he simply retraces a path. This gesture is, however, already a matter of an exchange: a one way ticket—in this case, a real metaphor for death—is exchanged for a return ticket which, in this instance, means life.

A feast awaits the children once they are out of the woods and back in the house of their parents, the site of food and language, of eating and conversation. Is this what constitutes the marvel of the tale? No: "the lord of the manor sent [the parents] ten crowns that he had owed them for a long time and which they no longer expected to get back: this gave them life once more, for the poor folk were famished. The woodcutter immediately sent his wife to the butcher's shop." Thus the monetary signs, which are probably the price attached to the woodcutter's labor, the wages equivalent to his toil, are also the equivalent of the missing food. It is the lord's ten crowns which, in the form of meat from the butcher's shop, will give back life to the family. The monetary signs are converted into edibles and will soon be transformed into words. Or rather, as the narrator tells us, it is the excess meat that will be transformed into discourse: "since she [the woodcutter's wife] had not eaten for a long time she bought three times as much meat as was needed for a supper for two people. Once satiated, the woodcutter's wife says: Alas! Where are our poor children now? They would make a fine meal of our leftovers." The leftover meat, the amount remaining after feeding two people, corresponds to what would be needed for six. The excess meat thus allows an absence to become manifest. The surplus to be eaten amounts to the deficit of one consumer $(3 \times 2) - 1$: Tom Thumb, the supplement of the narrative structure. This surplus is also a matter of excessive speech on the part of the mother. Her diatribe culminates in the following horrifying hypothesis: "Alas! Oh my God! Perhaps the wolves have eaten them. It was really inhuman of you to rid yourself of your children in that way." Finally, the woodcutter loses his patience, for "she reiterates more than twenty times that they would come to feel regret and that she had said as much." The surplus meat to be consumed (3×2), meat which could be eaten by the six children if they were present, undergoes a conversion here. By and through the mother's excessive speech, this surplus becomes six children who have perhaps been eaten by a wolf in the forest, which is where they are supposed to be. Yet the mother's exclusion of Tom Thumb in her calculation concerning the remaining food, allows us to infer that he is similarly excluded from her nightmarish thoughts about the wolves devouring her children. Excluded from eating, Tom Thumb is also excluded from being eaten. By the same token, it is the always supplementary Tom Thumb, who is either an excess or an absence, who will make a liar of his mother. The parents will never have any remorse, and she will be proved wrong. We know the rest. The children, who have been listening at the door, all cry out together: "We're here! We're here! . . . They sat down to table and fell to with an appetite that afforded the mother and father pleasure, and, speaking almost all at once, they told their parents about how afraid they had been in the forest."

Everything is inextricably intertwined here: eating and speaking, speakers and listeners, the irreducibly convivial and familial community, the supplement. Absence is effaced in favor of the eldest child, who represents the whole line of offspring: "My dear children, [says the mother] you must be very tired and very hungry. And you, Peter, how dirty you are. Come here so that I can clean you. This Peter was her oldest son and she loved him more than all the others because he was a little bit of a carrot-top like herself." Here we witness a maternal Eros joining in the game of words and food. Not for long, though.

"The happiness lasted as long as the ten crowns; but once the money had been spent they were plunged back into their initial despair." Hence the parents' decision to lose them anew, and this time (if one may phrase it this way) to do a better job of it. Once again, Tom Thumb overhears the secret, is in the know about the exchange of words. Once more, he is ready to stake out their trail. This he does, although he is obliged to employ different markers this time: not white pebbles, as before, but bread crumbs. These edible markers are in fact eaten. Although Tom Thumb once again makes his way out into the forest, he does not leave the traces of a path behind him. There are no souvenirs of the path taken. As a kind of fraying, his footsteps are repeated at the level of their individual marks. This repetition, however, is a matter of isolated steps, and no synthesis is achieved; it does not amount to a path. His tracks are traceless; in its pure and simple repetition, the way out knows no return. Food can be transformed into a meal and edibles into ready-cooked dishes. It can, in short, be a signified, but it cannot be turned into marks or indexicals: sublimated, raw foods become a dish, but they cannot be turned into markers. It is the essence of the culinary sign to disappear, to have its material reality destroyed in the act of consumption; the proper functioning of a marker depends on its continued empirical existence.

The children thus end up losing their way in the forest. During the night, a strong wind arises, leading them to "believe they were surrounded by howling wolves that had singled them out as prey." The moaning of the wind, the howling of a wild animal, takes the place of the mother's voice. This howling not only prohibits the use of words; it renders comprehension impossible: "they barely dared talk to each other or look around." Tom Thumb is the exception; although he remains silent as usual, he explores the surroundings in search of a path, hoping to set a course. He tries, if not to map the terrain, then at least to establish a route. "He climbed to the top of a tree to see whether he might discover something"; and thus, "having twisted his neck in all directions, he finally, far beyond the forest, detected a faint gleam resembling that of a candle." As we know, a dwelling will indeed welcome the children, but it is not exactly that of the parents; instead they come upon the abode of the ogre, and it is during his terrifying encounter with this figure that Tom Thumb finds his tongue for the first time in the tale. Tom Thumb speaks to the ogre's wife and sets up a crucial alternative — an alternative not between being active or passive, between eating or being eaten, but rather, between two different potential devourers: the wolf on the one hand and the ogre on the other. "The wolves of the forest will surely eat us tonight if you refuse to give us shelter . . . we would rather have your husband eat us; if you asked him, he might even take pity on us." On the one hand, we have the certainty of necessity; on the other, the possibility of realizing an unlikely, yet plausible, plan of escape. Here is a conflict of modalities, a striking aporia; yet a way out can be discerned in the direction of the ogre. So they end up in the perilous abode: "she has them warm themselves by a pleasant fire where a whole lamb is being roasted in preparation for the ogre's dinner." The fire is pleasant, because it is a fire for cooking, because a lamb is roasting on the spit. Indeed, it is not without some surprise that we find the conclusion to the second sequence of forest ramblings to resemble the first sequence in a curious way. In both cases, the dwelling, that of the parents or that of the ogre, is the site of excess meat from the butcher's shop: three times the amount of meat needed for a two-person supper, a whole lamb for one. There is nonetheless a difference between the two situations, for the children stand outside the door of their home and overhear the exchange between their satiated parents; on the other hand, they enter the ogre's house to warm themselves around the kitchen fire or, by contiguity, to be roasted over it and served up to the famished ogre, in the manner of lamb on a spit.

Upon arrival, the ogre immediately takes his place at the table. The lamb is still completely bloody, but seems all the more delicious to him as a result. Sniffing both left and right, he insists that he smells live meat. "It must be the calf that I have just dressed, says his wife. I tell you I smell live meat, repeats the ogre while scowling at his wife." He quickly discovers Tom Thumb and his brothers under the bed where his wife had hidden them. This is an important moment because the ogre reveals that his diet is both bestial and transgressive. Famished, he impatiently interrupts the culinary processes under way to revert to cannibalism: he eats his lamb half raw and sniffs out live (human) meat

Illustration of Perrault's "Tom Thumb," by G. Doré

the way a wild animal pursuing prey would. His wife tries to stop him by holding forth in a culinary vein: she talks about the calf which she has made ready for cooking; here we have meat from the butcher's shop in the process of being transformed into a course, a cooked meal. The ogre, however, pays no attention to her, for on discovering the children, live human meat rather than butchered domestic meat, he immediately assimilates them to game, to wild prey caught in a trap. "This is a timely catch. I'll use this game to treat three of my ogre friends who are supposed to come pay me a visit one of these days." His wife intervenes once again: "You have so much meat already . . . a calf, two lambs, and half a hog." It will be noted that this exchange is underwritten by an arithmetical calculation of portions. There are seven children for three ogres. If the portions are to be of equal size, then only six of the children will be consumed and there will be a remainder, a supplement. And this supplement is Tom Thumb. The response of the ogre's wife indicates that, as far as she is concerned, three and a half animals might be considered the equivalent of the three pairs of twins plus the youngest brother. The ogre disagrees: his adding up is an adding on. This does not, however, efface the minuscule "surplus," for Tom Thumb remains a supplement in that he is not included in the menu.

The exchange between the ogre and his wife inspires a culinary concern in the monstrous devourer, in spite of his cannibalism. Busy gobbling up the children visually, the ogre says to his wife that they "will make scrumptious morsels once she has prepared a sauce to go with them." We must not let the ogre's anticipation of the finished course obscure the fact that he intends to serve human meat, the children, with a sauce reserved for game, for wild animals. "Now what are you doing at this hour? Won't there be time enough for that tomorrow morning?" exclaims the ogre's wife as he prepares to slit the throat of one of the children. "You be quiet," retorts the ogre, adding that the corpses "will be further along" if he kills them now: in other words, the meat will be higher and will have acquired the exquisite perfume of rot. Having trapped themselves, the children are game meat as far as the ogre is concerned, even if he did not have to hunt for them. The perversion and transgression could not be more extreme: imaginary cannibalism, devouring the children with his eyes, is simultaneously a matter of culinary anticipation; the cooking of human meat is presented in terms of the preparation of wild meat; and the cultivated meat from the butcher's shop is assimilated to the wild meat from a hunt.

The ogre is momentarily persuaded by his wife's argument concerning the excess of meat from the butcher's shop. Thus he does not immediately kill the children; and the children do not eat because "they were so terrified" by the idea of being eaten. Tom Thumb, the supplement and operator of the narrative structure, will properly avail himself of this period of narrative respite, entailed by the interruption of the culinary process. He does not eavesdrop the way he did outside the parents' house, nor does he leave behind him the traces of a path, as in the forest. Rather, he substitutes one set of insignia, of distinctive and identifying marks, for another. Thus the seven caps worn by the woodcutter's sons are exchanged against the seven crowns worn by the ogre's daughters. By virtue of their reciprocal opposition, the caps and crowns function as identifying signs. They are also, however, the equivalent of generic names—the "sons of the woodcutter," the "daughters of the ogre"—and in the sole case of the ogre, they are even the signs of what may permissibly be eaten and of what is prohibited as food. These are deontic signs, since the omophagous and allelophagous ogre does not practice endocannibalism. Unlike nominal signs, which establish a necessary connection between the signified and the signifier, these deontic signs can be separated from the entities they characterize, and thus they are subject to manipulation and exchange: once this exchange has occurred, there does still exist a differential relation between the sons of the woodcutter and the daughters of the ogre; however, the terms of the relation no longer correspond to their insignia, and they lose their identity. As a result of the substitution of insignia, one of the terms will be taken for the other and vice versa. In exchanging insignia, Tom Thumb transforms identities into differences and makes opposites interact; he makes obligatory what is prohibited and renders certain the realization of what was ruled out. The ogre gets ready to eat his own daughters and thus spares the game for which he had not hunted. The supplement is indeed the operator of a dialectic of contraries, one which falls under the common heading of ruse. By means of Tom Thumb, the trapped sons of the woodcutter manage to invert the trap, so that the one who in fact was supposed to benefit from it falls into it instead. The ogre duly slits the throats of his own daughters after a brief hesitation over the insignia.

The children flee into the countryside, into the night. They wander about in open terrain. The direction is of no import for anything is better than the enclosed space within the ogre's dwelling. "They were on the run almost all night, trembling at each moment and without any idea about where they were going." Meanwhile, the ogre discovers his tragic error and sets out in pursuit of them. It is then, to his own detriment, the ogre's turn to invert the order of things, for he hunts his game after having caught it and prepared it for cooking. "Having searched far and wide, he finally comes upon the path being pursued by the poor children, who are no more than a hundred feet from their homestead." Both game and hunter make their way forward, the former toward the family home, the latter in the tracks of the children. It is true that the ogre is wearing his seven-league boots, which allow him to step from one mountain to another and to "cross rivers as easily as the smallest stream."

We know about the ogre's nap on top of the hollow rock providing the children with refuge, as well as about the escape of the six brothers to their parents' house. With all of his brothers gone, the supplement of the three pairs of twins is left to confront the ogre on his own; the crafty and unique exchanger of signs and insignia comes up against the universal devourer and assimilator of bodies and meats. All that is needed for the tale to end happily is a simple exchange: the marvelous boots belonging to the hunter of human meat must become the special vehicle of the messenger of signs. There are, however, two happy endings to the tale; one of them is contested by the narrator—in our opinion, quite rightly so—for it involves the accumulation and hoarding of monetary signs. By telling the ogre's wife a story about robbers, Tom Thumb manages to steal the ogre's gold and silver. True enough, stealing is still a matter of an exchange or, more precisely, of substituting one proprietor for another, a gesture that involves the appropriation as one's own of what actually belongs to someone else; as both their means of delivery and their receiver, a thief might be considered a sort of courier of goods and riches. But this outcome essentially puts a stop to all motion, for the dynamic process involving wanderings, trajectories, and itineraries ends up being immobilized into a steady state: "loaded with all of the ogre's riches, Tom Thumb returns to his father's abode where he was welcomed with great joy." In the other ending, the supplementary operator of the narrative structure limits himself to taking the ogre's boots, doing so without any scruples, since they are the weapons of the hunter of human meat. Tom Thumb then goes on to become the king's messenger: he conveys messages and, in exchange, receives money, the correct salary repaying him for his efforts. These monetary signs are not exchanged against objects or goods, but repay the activity of exchange itself: in the tale, money effects a kind of metalevel exchange, and the messenger is therefore a sort of metalevel exchanger. "The king paid him very well for carrying his orders to the army" and for bringing him news back. At this point, we encounter the erotic motif and so conclude in a wholly humorous vein: once again, Tom Thumb is not the sensuous benefactor of bodily consummations of love. Instead, he receives money for being the conveyor of amorous messages and verbal caresses: "an infinity of women gave him anything he wanted so they could have news of their lovers, and this provided him with his greatest source of income."

At the end, by all accounts—since the narrative account is also a kind of accounting—there remain neither food nor courses, meats nor dishes, voices nor linguistic signs. All that is left of the bodies and their qualities is the extraordinarily dynamic, powerful, and efficient dual abstraction that embraces money and exchange value. Money is the equivalent of exchange value, as well as its measure, and exchange value, a pure relation without content, simply allows money to function. It is hardly an accident that this operation—which takes the form of drawing up the balance sheet pertaining to the marvelous tale—should be entrusted to the tiny operator-actor who measures little more than a thumb, is very delicate, and hardly says a word. The supplement is always either a surplus or deficit in relation to the narrative apparatus of representation, but it is nonetheless what allows this apparatus to function at its highest level of transformation and production, that is, at a level where signs become opaque and weighty in the manner of things or bodies, and things acquire a diaphanous and transparent quality by virtue of their signs and simulacra. Within the marvelous narrative of the story, the little Thumb is between the wild meat from the butcher's shop and the words exchanged in discourse. He is between them just as the little word "is," in the miraculous eucharistic formula, comes between the "this" indicating the edible object and the "my body," signifying the Holy Meat of the sacrifice.

Four

The King's Body

13 The Portrait of the King's Glorious Body

The Portrait and Its Name

If there is a scene that sums up or condenses all the signs and insignia of a political power operating at the greatest level of efficacy, it must be that of a king contemplating his own portrait. Such a scene would make manifest to its royal impresario or spectator the imaginary character that affects, if not infects, all power in its consubstantial desire for the absolute. In recognizing the icon of the Monarch that he wishes to be, the royal spectator would recognize himself in the portrait and identify himself with it. The secret that resides within this royal act of contemplation is, then, the disappearance of the portrait's real referent, the canceling out of its model. It is true that the real prince of flesh and blood has not passed through to the other side of Narcissus's mirror. Only a true magic of the image could do this, but death is always the consequence of the mythical climax of self-contemplation. In the present case, the King only imitates his portrait just as the portrait imitates the king: the king of representation and the representation of the king are involved in a process of mutual mimesis that reveals the fundamental figure articulating power and representation; in this process, we are able to discern the chiasmus in which the king and his royal representation reciprocally subordinate themselves to each other, in which they belong to or appropriate each other in a manner that is perfectly reversible. In such a case, the royal representation would be the precise qualification, the most important attribute, and maybe even the effective means of the king's power. The king of representation would be the factitive modality and the processual power that make representations of himself possible. Yet this inverted expression, "the king of representation," already establishes an ironic distance between representation and power, the two terms that make up the adequation. It signals the existence of a critical difference between them, a gap that threatens to separate the terms entirely and already renders the adequation unequal to itself: on the one hand, there would be nothing more than a portrait, a picture; on the other hand, we would discover nothing more than a role, a kind of mannequin. Moreover, the particular body and soul that make up a real individual would be swallowed up by the gulf separating these two poles from each other. Yet the disappearance of the individual allows the "king" to acquire for himself a title that begins with a capital letter—the King.

The story that narrates the life and actions of the king is elaborated in time and across history. This type of story can only represent the prince in a successive manner and necessarily allows for the persistence of a difference that indefinitely and infinitely postpones the real satisfaction of the prince's desire for the absolute, the actual exercise of the law of the will. The portrait of the King will, however, convert this deferred narrative content into the absolute imaginary of the Monarch; the picture of the King will be his real presence, in the same way that the Catholic theology of the Eucharist will speak of the real presence of the body and blood of Jesus in the form of bread and wine.

Theoretically, the constitution of the King's portrait presupposes a twofold belief that is an absolute prerequisite to the portrait's effective presentation. First of all, there has to exist a belief in the efficacy and performativity of the royal iconic sign. It is quite clear why this belief would have to be obligatory: without it, the portrait of the King would be nothing but a simulacrum, and to see his picture in this light would be nothing short of the kind of heresy committed by the Reformers with respect to the bread and wine of the Eucharist. Second, the picture would have to be believed to have substance and real ontological density. The reason for the necessity of this belief is no less obvious than that of the first: were the picture to be considered contingent or merely possible, then the contemplation of the Monarch's portrait would become a form of sacrilege. The body of the King is really present in the form of his portrait. Thus we see that the execution of such an eminent and supreme painting, besides having been simply a matter of political importance, was equally crucial on a theologico-political register. In this respect, the king and his painter engage in a preliminary game that is much like the one played out between the king and his historian, although the expressive medium is different. It is the speech act itself, or in some cases the painterly act, that defines every eulogy in its *epideixis*, every bit of praise in its demonstration, every panegyric in its singular exemplification: this act turns its receiver, the person who views his own portrait or hears his own story into the enunciator of a reflexive identifying utterance: "I am indeed just as you say I am, or just as you show me to be." In this game, a move, like all moves, involves a risk: that of eliminating the crucial difference between the discourse or portrait of praise on the one hand and the discourse or portrait of flattery on the other. Should we, like Hegel, want to accord flattery the positive power of a courtisan's heroism, then it would be a matter of distinguishing between a pragmatically successful flattery and a pragmatically unsuccessful one. By virtue of the excessive nature of its language or images, the unsuccessful form of flattery fails to bring about an identificatory belief on the part of its recipient. To understand this failure fully, it would be necessary to determine very precisely what it is that makes these words or images excessive.

Assume, however, that this risk has been successfully circumvented and that the king identifies with the portrait the painter shows him. The time has now come for the second game, for the second move within the game of representation and power: this move concerns the reader or spectator, that is, the third party who is external to the twin relation that the Monarch entertains (indeed, can only entertain) with his picture or his story; this third party occupies precisely the position we took when we envisaged the narcissistic scene of the king contemplating his own portrait. The move in question is also a speech act, which turns the third party, the spectator or reader, into the enunciator of a transitive utterance of identification: "That is the King," or even "That is indeed the King." By means of "that is," this identificatory utterance makes a King of the portrait and a portrait of the King.

In the *Logic*, the Port-Royal logicians dedicated a careful study to the utterance of "That is Caesar," when spoken in front of the portrait of Caesar; there is an echo here of their famous definition of the sign as a representation, of which maps and portraits are an example. Their explicit aim was to use the example of this proposition to show that the person who utters it is generally understood to be speaking "figuratively and according to acceptation": the proposition is but a manner of speaking, and its utterance requires neither preparation nor ceremony (Arnauld and Nicole [1683] 1970, 205). The utterance can be spoken without further ado, because there exists a visible relation between these kinds of signs (that is, natural signs, of which the mirror's image is the prototype) and the things that they signify. It is clear that when somebody asserts that the sign is the signified thing, they do not mean to say that the sign really is the thing signified. Rather, they claim that the sign is the figure or representation of the thing in question. The portrait of the king will always be a portrait or sign of him; when someone utters "That is the King" before the portrait of Louis XIV, they quite simply employ a figure of speech, just as the royal icon is quite simply an image or picture.

Yet the Port-Royal logicians have quite a specific objective in mind with their study of the example of the King's portrait and the utterance "That is the King." This objective is none other than that of grounding the validity of another utterance. Unlike "That is the King," this other utterance is not spoken by the King's spectator and subject, but by the incarnated Word that is repeated around the world: "This is my body." Just as a spectator will be authorized to claim, without any preamble, that the King's portrait is the King, so Jesus Christ was able to say "This is my body" when speaking of the bread. In the first case, there is a visible relation between the portrait and the King, and this signals the figurative nature of the utterance. The situation is quite different in the second case: "since the apostles did not consider the bread to be a sign of anything and since they were hardly at pains to understand its meaning, Jesus Christ could hardly have given the name of the signified thing—his body—to the bread viewed as a sign, without speaking at odds with ordinary usage and without deceiving his auditors" (Arnauld and Nicole [1683] 1970, 209). From this, we are to conclude that "This is my body" cannot be understood in a figurative sense, and we are told that, as a result, "all the nations in the world were naturally inclined to understand these words literally" (Arnauld and Nicole [1683] 1970, 209). The two utterances are remarkably similar, yet quite significantly different: the Port-Royal logicians insist that contiguity governs the relation between the eucharistic symbols of

Jesus Christ on the one hand and the political signs of the Monarch on the other; but they also establish an insurmountable boundary between the eucharistic symbols and the political signs; to transgress this boundary is at once to commit heresy and sacrilege. Yet it is precisely this boundary that is crossed by the desire for an absolute power that is manifested in the fantastic representation of the Monarch, in his portrait and name, a portrait legitimated by the utterance of a single and unique name which itself is authorized by the representation of the king: a portrait named, the name of an image, itself the manifestation that constitutes the site of the king's fusion with the absolute; it is in this image that he contemplates himself and thus grasps his absoluteness.

The (proper) name and (individual) image intersect in the problematic of the portrait as a representation of an individual. As we know, the proper name is the name of an individual who bears this very name: according to Jakobson, this is a beautiful example of the circularity of the code (Jakobson [1957] 1963, 177–78). "Socrates is the name of an individual called Socrates," "This person is called Peter," "My name is Jack," "You are called Augustus." In the act of naming, there is a shifter, a personal or demonstrative pronoun, a deictic ("this person," "I," "you"), which makes it possible, unfailingly and irresistibly, to detect whether a given being carries a name or can be named. As a result, this being is named in one of a number of ways: as being the means by which names are assigned, as having a name, or as potentially being the carrier of a name. What then would be the relation between a drawing or painting that is an iconic portrait and the written proper name? Could it be that the portrait plays the role of the deictic shifter that figures as an integral part of the act of naming? If we take into account the gesture of pointing, the corporeal *Zeigen* that underlies all forms of deixis, then it becomes clear that the portrait is a very particular form of deixis, a showing forth or manifestation. While the portrait is something that one points to, it also points at something itself; it is shown or exhibited. The gesture of pointing at the portrait involves utterances such as "this person" or "you," while the portrait shows and presents itself in terms of an "I" or a "Me." According to this line of reasoning, the portrait of the King would be a form not only of deixis, but of autodeixis as well. The process whereby the image is reflected back upon itself is perhaps what makes the portrait both an iconic equivalent of the proper name, an autonym ("Socrates is the name of an individual called Socrates," "This is the King"), as well as a form of epideixis, that is, of a positive demonstration, of a unique exemplification, or presentational intensification: "I am the King" or, better still, *'l'Etat, c'est moi.'* In cases such as these, representation hardly serves the purpose of substituting for something that is absent or of making what is dead seem almost alive by virtue of the power of a transitive mimesis. Instead, it redoubles a presence, and this redoubling renders this presence both legitimate and authoritative. In this case, the act of representing involves showing oneself to be representing something. Representation constitutes its subject reflexively, that is, by exhibiting it. It thus effects a process of epideixis that picks out qualifications, justifications, and titles that are to describe the being of whoever is to be made present. Representation reproduces the conditions that make possible the reproduction of a given being and does so both in fact and by right. Thus three utterances can be identified in the portrait of the King: "That is the King," "I am the King," "We are the King."

As a result of the redoubling and epideictic intensification characterizing the form of deixis proper to the portrait, the portrait of the King can be said to be representation. As it is being shown, the portrait shows itself to be showing something. The royal gesture represents that of pointing, whether as the straight line of the gaze which ideally will trace the rection of the imperium, or as the movement of the hand or arm by which it is enlarged. This movement effects an expansion, because it provides the other, the spectator or subject, with the field and program of action dictated by his Majesty, who is the source of order, in the sense that he has the authority of command and provides a rational order of intelligibility. In this respect, the portrait of the king presents to the admiring eye the truth of the name "king, *rex*, he who traces (*oregô:* to extend in a straight line; *regere fines:* to trace a boundary, etc.) and has the authority to draw up the sites of towns, to determine the rules of the law." The king is the person who has the legitimate power to create by means of a pointing gesture, which is nothing more than a tracing of ideal separations and extractions. In a given moment and place, an intense reciprocity is instituted between the gesture of showing that sums up royal power, and the portrait of the King, which shows this gesture in a display of the power that founds his legitimate authority.

The portrait reveals itself to be the iconic equivalent of the (proper) name, while the (proper) name is the nominal equivalent of the portrait. In the portrait's royal name, we come across what we discovered a moment ago in the royal portrait of the name: a remarkable combination of transitivity and reflexivity which, in this case, takes the form of the name's continuity and tradition, both of which serve to designate a lineage, as well as the position and definition of the name that names an individual who is unique within this series. What is at stake in the issue of the name primarily concerns the status of the word "King" and of the "King's name," both of which figure crucially among the utterances of his spectator-subjects as they stand before the portrait of their Monarch. What is meant by "That is the King" is: "Behold the dignity of kingship with all its attributes incarnate, justice, power, majesty, wisdom . . . it is Louis, presently the King of France and of Navarre."

Something more is at stake, however, in the issue of the name. This time, it is a matter of the relation between the King and his name (and his portrait); what must be simultaneously affirmed is the name of an ancestral line, as well as of an individual; the name that marks an ordinal succession, in which king Louis, presently king of France and of Navarre, by definition, is included in the series of predecessors and successors who all were or will be kings just like him. What must also be affirmed is his cardinal position, which consecrates him as the only King "who is comparable to himself," as Perrault will write about the king who figures in "Donkey-Skin." In this respect, we understand the importance of the event of 1672, when Louis the Fourteenth (by name) took on a nickname which individuated him for time immemorial as "the Great," just as his father, Louis the Thirteenth, had been nicknamed "the Just." The transition from one qualifying and individuating nickname to another, from "just" to "great," reflexively marks a tension between two terms that are governed by a conflictual relation, even at the level of their semantic content. One of the terms is the King's name, a name that refers to both his lineage and his legitimacy: he is king of France by right, not by usurpation. The other term is the name that designates the particular quality of the individual King—only Louis, the King of France, is Great: he is no more and no less great than any other king, for he is absolutely Great. The tension exists between the rights that he holds by virtue of his father and ancestors, which he will transmit to his descendants, and the absolute title that he owes to nobody other than himself. The particular task of the

King's portrait then will be to affect its audience in such a way
that the word "King" or the "name of the King" is written or
inscribed upon the consciousnesses of its members, in such a
way that the spectators utter these words out loud. The spectators must also, however, be able to recognize the subject of the
portrait as being particularly and essentially notable, as worthy
of the specific name assigned to him by virtue of a dynastic nomination. The particular task of the King's name will also be to
ensure that the king and the King are shown to be uttering and
listening to his name; the two L's that are the King's initials and
his pictogram, as well as the syllables that make up his first
name, Louis (the equivalent of Peter, John, or William) must all
be transformed and sublimated into the sacred icon of the
Monarch.

The portrait of the King is a portrait of a body and of a face. In
actual fact, only the face, whether seen in profile or from an
angle, is essential to the portrait. The *pro-tractus*, in both senses
of the prefix *pro*, is first and foremost that of the human face, irrespective of the angle from which it is "shot"; the prefix *pro* combines the two dimensions of the representational apparatus, that
of substitution and that of redoubling, "that which takes the
place of" and "that which is placed in front of." One might even
ask whether it is conceivable that a portrait could display its subject entirely from behind, without manifesting an ironic and deri-
sory intention on the part of the painter, or a perfidious betrayal
or act of critical aggression. In addition to the face, the hands are
often represented, for they too, although to a lesser extent, contribute to the goal of individuation and the act of nomination.
How, then, in the portrait does the body summarize itself in the
face-to-face of a face, and what rules determine the construction
of this figure, which is a metaphor as well as a metonym and synecdoche for the physical organism that is its basis? How does a
face come to top and crown a body, which its spectators otherwise (or so, at least, we are to believe) would have thought to be
without a proper name, without a distinguishing mark or feature? How does this face imbue this otherwise anonymous body
with value and meaning? As the face is made visible to alien
glances and stares, the body becomes legible, revealing a unique
substance that the spectator would be hard put to name and
which would incite him or her to endless chatter, were it not for
the fact that a unique name, a simple signal articulating recognition, suggests itself as the appropriate utterance: "That is Louis,"

"That is Caesar," "That is the King." Elsewhere, I have demonstrated the critical and ironic power of Pascal's thought, the humor characterizing his endeavors in anthropology and politics; it is noteworthy that this thinker had an unfailing sense of the point that I have been developing: "A man is a substance, but if you dissect him, what is he? Head, heart, stomach, veins, each vein, each bit of vein, blood, each humour of blood?" (Pascal 1966 [no. 65]). The portrait of a person—the portrait of a body and of a head, of a body that supports a head and of a head supported by a body—would be interminable, since it involves an indefinite list of names, and so the discourse that attempts to describe the subject of the portrait would be much like a kind of infinite anatomy. The process of description will be infinite, unless we adopt a conclusion similar to the one that Pascal sets forth toward the end of the fragment cited above. Pascal notes that a town and the surrounding landscape can be clearly distinguished from a distance. As we draw closer, however, the difference that distinguishes them from each other gradually dissolves into an infinity of differential traits that do not allow us to grasp the fundamental or essential feature that underwrites the specificity of the particular city and landscape in question: "All of this is comprehended in the word 'landscape.'" We could then, following Pascal, say that "everything is comprehended in the name Louis, in the noun 'King.'" Such a conclusion would be difficult, even impossible to draw in the case of the King's portrait. Whereas the common noun "landscape" can comprehend the singularity of this particular landscape within its general scope, the name used with respect to the King's portrait must be a proper name. This name must disclose this particular man, this body in this face; thus it presupposes a primitive recognition that would manifest itself properly and quite simply in the utterance of the proper name in question; the act of naming is perpetually forestalled in function of the endlessness of the discourse that aims at articulating the singular substance which is presented by the portrait. To say "That is Louis" or "That is the King" in the presence of his portrait is probably, as the Port-Royal logicians claimed, a matter of using figurative speech in such a way that the interlocutor will understand the figurative nature of the utterance without further ceremony. Yet these exclamations also presuppose a primitive encounter with Louis, with the King, in flesh and blood, in body and face. This is what authorizes me to rely on the "visible relationship" that obtains between the portrait and the person who serves as its model, allowing me to speak about the image in a figurative manner: "That is Louis," "That is the King." In the event that this encounter were to be alethically impossible, ruled out for epistemological reasons or deontically forbidden for any number of conceivable reasons (death, geographical distance, social hierarchy . . .), then we would have to presuppose what may be called a lateral process: the spectator who is confronted with a particular portrait will allow his or her gaze to wander, following a trajectory that brings it into contact with a whole series of portraits of the same "person." The spectator would, moreover, have to know, have been told, or be able to infer from a group of authorized and convergent testimonies that these portraits are indeed of Louis the King. Thus he or she will be able to compare the series or the elements within it with the initial portrait, the conclusion being "That is Louis," "That is the King." This line of reasoning belongs to a philosopher or a logician, or someone pretending to be one; it may also be an anthropological, aesthetic, or linguistic discourse about the portrait in general. The above argument does not amount to a theologico-political discourse about the portrait of the King. As faithful subjects of Louis XIV, the Port-Royal logicians were fully aware of this fact and revealed as much by default, that is, by the brevity of their discussion in the *Art of Thinking* of what is involved in the utterance "That is Caesar" when this phrase is spoken in front of his portrait.

The King's portrait is immediately recognizable as such, "without preparation and without ceremony," whether it is of his face only or of his whole figure. This immediate recognition is sparked by some majestic air, by the nobility and greatness that marks the face and body of the King. This is an appropriate place to recall Voltaire's description of the young Louis, as he was returning from Vincennes in 1665, dressed in a hunting outfit and on his way to reprimand Parliament, to inform it that it was no longer to debate his decisions: "His already majestic stature, the nobility of his features, the tone and air of mastery with which he spoke, all served to impose the authority of his rank, which had been little respected until that moment" (Voltaire [1751] 1966, 310). By means of an iconic effect, the reported speech and the circumstances that frame it constitute the body of Louis as a royal body. Louis suddenly becomes King and is acknowledged as such in much the same way that his portrait is recognized as being of him. However, the body of the King is a suppositum, although not for anatomical qualities, to use Pascal's terms. Instead, this body in its portrait supports the signs and insignia that designate its particular functions; it provides a basis for the privileged status accorded to its own representation, its most important attributes being communicated to the spectator with the aim of bringing about recognition and admiration. Thus the spectator will be inclined, not only to say "That is Louis," or "That is the King," but also "That is the Monarch in all of his Majesty," "That is the all-powerful warleader and King," "That is the King in all of his infinite justice and wisdom," etc. Many elements contribute to the definition of the King's unique substance, a substance that finds expression in and through his portrait. Thus the decor that serves as a backdrop for his person is crucial. The carpets, tapestries, and curtains, the King's throne and the columns all play an important role, as do the representations, the statues, images, or emblems that they display. The ideograms and ornaments decorating the portrait's frame even contribute to the definition in question. Indeed, in the King's portrait, the identification or identity of the model is not an issue, and the portrait does not even raise it; it is the function of the portrait to ensnare or trick the spectator's gaze in this manner. Assume that the portrait serves a social and ideological function, that of engendering a certain verbal response to the painted object—"That is the King"— just as it tricks spectators into stating the nominal identity of the represented figure—"That is Louis the Great." What makes the portrait function, what constitutes its driving mechanism, is a process involving the identification of the Self. The King's portrait is not Louis the Fourteenth, nor is it even Louis the Great; his portrait is—if I may be so bold—"I." The portrait aims at the spectator's ideological and political subjugation, which is made possible because the spectator-addressee positions him or herself as "I-the-King." This is why the King's portrait first and foremost establishes a relation between the painting and the King himself, his subject being doomed always to the position of a third party, of a distant spectator. Yet it is precisely because the portrait's spectator occupies this third-person position that he or she can be presented or present him or herself as the King's subject. To contemplate the portrait, the spectator probably has to assume the position occupied by the King as he watches himself look at his own portrait. Yet at the very moment of this substitution, which would otherwise be an act of high treason, the King is already his own portrait. The spectator does anything but look at the King's portrait and is anything but a subject caught staring at the king.

Instead, the spectator is the object of the Monarch's gaze; he or she is constituted by and subjected to this gaze, and thereby transformed into a political subject. The scene that we have just imagined, in which the King contemplates his own image, was hardly a rhetorical fiction, designed to introduce a theory of the King's glorious body. The fiction is constitutive of the theory in the strongest sense of the term. The portrait of the King is the theory of the King, it is the theologico-political theory of the royal body.

The Portrait of the King in All of His Majesty

The King's portrait is his body. The King's portrait is the King himself, displayed with impressive self-evidence: he is the King, by virtue first of the agglomeration of royal signs that constitute his being, that determine his presence and produce his identity. His being, presence, and identity are unlike the ones that characterize an individual. Nor does the King's being resemble that of an individual who bears a proper name that articulates an essential difference and thus distinguishes him or her from other individuals and names. Instead, the King's identity and being is that of a dignitary, of a function and role that bear the proper name "the King." Every single element in the painting is an insignia and a sign, a symbolic ornament or a piece of history. Thus everything in the portrait should be seen in this light: everything from the big scarlet and gold canopy to the crimson carpet with its floral design, from the gilded throne covered with blue velvet and decorated with the motif of the fleur-de-lis, from the stool upon which are posed the royal crown and Charles v's arm of justice, to the steps leading up to the dais occupied by the King's throne; from the huge marble column with its pedestal displaying a classical bas-relief, to the heavy royal cape in blue, decorated with golden fleur-de-lis and lined with white ermine, spotted with black; everything from the ritual wig, to Charlemagne's golden scepter and sword, from the collar of the order of the Holy Ghost, worn on top of a broad lace jabot, from the King's billowing cuffs to his culottes, puffed with ceremony, everything right down to his red-heeled white shoes. Thus all of the treasures and ancient regalia of Saint Denis are displayed. They decorate a body which, just like the stool, the throne, and the columns, appears to serve no other purpose than that of presenting them. Moreover, it seems that this body only assumes being and corporeality by vir-

Louis XIV by Hyacinthe Rigaud

tue of its role as a suppositum for these treasures, by becoming a historical body or, rather the real presence of a legendary body of history. This body is given reality and is made present through the signs and insignia discussed above, which serve to construe the represented space as the particular site of the Monarch. Embodied in all of its signs, the being of this body is gradually infused throughout the entire space portrayed in the portrait, beginning with the frame, the dais, and the column and canopy, and spreading from there to the surrounding insignia. Even the light and shadows playing upon the metal, the precious stones, the marbles and sumptuous fabrics help to define this place and the figures that compose it as the refraction of a *numen.* This sacred essence has been placed upon the royal, divine body from above and emanates from it.

This majestically ordered sea of signs and insignia allow the historical painting of the King, which we discussed above, to come together and be condensed into a portrait that captures the Monarch's stateliness. The iconic story that tells about a royal deed is similarly condensed into the epideictic image of absolute power, which is also absolute representation: the width of the horizontal frieze, that is, the historical painting, is replaced in the portrait by the stunning effect of a vertical and tall proposition revealed by the same red and gold curtain that is draped as a canopy above the single figure. Unlike the historical painting, this curtain lends an air of mysterious sublimity to the background and allows the spectator to feel that a divine and immanent transcendence has been realized above this column and in this figure. All the historical actors who, by virtue of either lineage or marriage, war or politics, participated in the miraculous act of the Agent of History, have figuratively disappeared from this "demonstrative scene." They are condensed into the single figure who is the object of a full-length portrait; there, they are reduced to mere signs and ornaments (the cloak, sword, scepter, crown, throne, etc.). They blend into a figure who behaves like a story, into a fragment of history that functions as though it were a full-fledged discourse. Much like a story, this figure shows signs of having been reduced to the implicit subject of the discourse, as opposed to the actual speaking subject from whom this figure is disconnected. Much like discourse, it tends to be reduced to the pure and implicit presence of speaking: as the assertion of a presence outside of all time and beyond the subjectivity of the speaker, the naming sentence articulates a timeless and permanent report.

The naming sentence establishes the absoluteness of a truth that is proffered as such by virtue of the former's authority. This process takes place in a dialogue during which the phrase imposes itself and produces, if we may say so, its own reference, producing itself as its own reference, as the being of an essence.

The royal portrait is an iconic naming sentence: "The King!" The iconic characteristic of dialogue that is always presupposed by a naming sentence is, in this instance, to be found in the gaze of a face that faces its potential spectator, a face that the King looks squarely in the eyes. This description is, however, superficial as a result of the comparison upon which it draws. Even if the naming sentence can be said to presuppose a dialogic discursive relation, this phrase is not a dialogue nor is it structured like one. The gaze that characterizes the Monarch in his portrait is not like the one that an "I" would direct toward a "you," who in turn would contemplate the "I." The portrait of the Monarch has no possible spectator other than the king himself. They look at each other by means of his royal gaze, and in the portrait of his eyes, the king produces himself as the Monarch, just as the gaze of the Monarch in the portrait allows him to proffer and present himself as the King in all of his theoretical reality. It is precisely in this manner that the King is really present in his portrait: the latter is in a certain sense the model, the paroxysm of the king who constantly exhausts himself in his image; the royal portrait would be the excess of a subject who, by negating himself in his image, identifies with it.

From this point on, it is clear that we should no longer say that the royal effigy looks at a spectator who, reciprocally and through the act of contemplation, accords it the status of an object that can be seen; we cannot even say, as we did a moment ago, that the portrait of the King looks at the king and vice versa. As an iconic naming sentence, the portrait inscribes itself within the dialogic. Yet it does not inscribe a visual dialogue between a gaze and a face. What if being present *(prae-sens)* did not mean being there or being before, but rather being ahead, at the forefront, in a state of anticipation or excess, without any discontinuity between the front and the back, between the subject and his or her extremities? What if being there had a temporal meaning, what if it was a matter of immanence, of what is subject to no delays, of what is distinct at the moment in which it is spoken of, although it is not separated from this moment by a single interval? If the king is really present in his portrait, then we shall have to admit that it is not at some spectator that the portrait looks; moreover, we would have to recognize that the portrait does not even take the king as its model. Indeed, in his portrait, the king looks beyond his own face, he looks at nothing, for the portrait's gaze is the most extreme point of his being, the ultimate excess of the royal presence, the extreme passion of the look which, by the same token, annuls all determinate passion in a kind of immanence of being.

The above points help explain why it is that the epideictic portrait is characterized by an ostentatious posing that gives rise to a strange temporal structure. Inspired by Benveniste's approach, we analyzed the prefix *prae* that is constitutive of this structure and were thus able to disclose its immanent and suspended nature. In this structure, we discovered three semantic and pragmatic signs pertaining to the naming sentence, which was shown to be "outside of time," "beyond mood," and "beyond subjectivity." The pose of the painted figure allows the model gradually to emerge in the portrait, leaving the term "model" to oscillate ambiguously between an ideal paradigm (be it political, ethical, or theological) and a referential body (the body that the painter reproduces on his canvas in the form of a mimetic image or representation). Through the pose and its display, the portrait brings into real presence both the one and the other, the King and the king, the Monarch and Louis the Fourteenth by name. It unites these two, reunites them, in the painted figure. Three gestures mark the pose, show it, and signify it: the left hand placed on the hip, the puffed lace cuffs above the hilt of Charlemagne's sword, the elbow supporting the fold that displays the reverse of the royal cape of blue velvet and white ermine; the right hand placed on the scepter, which itself has been installed on the stool's cushion, where the crown and hand of justice have also been put; finally, and perhaps most importantly, the position of the two legs, trim in white satin stockings, and of the feet, neatly fitted with gold buckled and red heeled shoes. The position of the legs and feet is particularly crucial, because to a certain extent it commands and demands the first two gestures. The third and last gesture sketches a figure belonging to the sphere of dance, the so-called fourth position, which is a pause within a flow of movement. It is this pause that begins or ends the future or past execution of a given movement, that marks its imminence and proximity. Although this figure evokes the king's exceptional skill as a dancer, it cannot be considered as a sequence within a ballet: the figure is neither a movement nor a rest, neither the beginning of a story nor its end, neither the premise of an affirmation nor the concluding proposition in a discourse. In other words, the king does not walk, yet he is not motionless either; he does not advance, nor does he stand perfectly still. He poses, he marks a pause within the pose, within a suspended instance that fashions something like a corporeal ideality. In this way, an eternal instance and an infinite duration are brought together in the extreme density of a moment. An epideictic figure, the King turns while being stable, permanent, still. Without turning, he turns around the scepter that is planted in the stool's cushion, the head of the fleur-de-lis downward, much like an elaborate cane. He turns without turning in order to show or rather to present his own presence, that is, the totality of signs and insignia that symbolically represent him through the workings of the imaginary. He presents his majestic gown, the very form of its fold seeming to accompany this immobile turning of the body, and he displays the imperial sword, the stool that carries the regalia, etc. He shows and presents his body as a sign and as insignia; in the real presence of the portrait, he proffers his name, the name (of the) King, a nomination-name: "The King!" As a result of the ostentation of the pose, of the epideixis of a political paradigm and of an individual body, the portrait of the Monarch can be said to be the Name of the King. Thus, does theologico-political power come to be identified with the representation of language and images. In all his Majesty, the King does not rule, he does not govern: this is clearly shown by the fact that the hand of justice and the crown have been set aside and laid upon the stool, while the scepter is held upside down in the manner of a dance cane. Yet in order to rule and govern, the King has only to make himself present through representation; he has merely to proffer himself in the name "King!" since his presence in representation and through nomination is sovereignty itself, in all of its authority and legitimacy.

The right hand is placed on the hip and the elbow holds up, in a magnificent fold, the sumptuous royal gown: we must admit that it is not signs and insignia that are revealed by this fold, but two legs in white silk stockings. These legs are disclosed not as the parts of a physical body, but as the erotic features of a body that promises and enjoys sensuous pleasure. The old king was just as seduced by this erotic body as he was by the image of the absolute Monarch that radiated from the portrait; in this respect,

he is much like the princesses that Perrault wrote about in his
tales at least ten years before Rigaud painted the King's portrait,
princesses who can be vaguely discerned at the end of a long,
dark corridor, through the crack in a door. The King's glorious
body makes itself sensuous and feminine by means of suspenders
and the silky curve of its legs, which are shown to be like those of
a dancer in fourth position, the very figure of suspended movement; the King is like a dancer caught in the imminence of
another movement in the interspace of a single gesture. Using
the example of this royal leg, we should be able to show that the
portrait of the King is also the fetish of representation and that
eroticism and aesthetics, as the sensuous value of taste, are
directly related to politics and, more precisely, to the Monarch's
absolute power, as it is really present in his portrait.

As we know, the fetishist denies that women lack a penis and
does so through an image or a substitute phallus: as a child, he or
she will choose as a fetish the last object seen before the glimps-
ing of this absence. The shoe is an example of a fetish with
respect to the gaze that wanders up the leg, starting at the feet.
The repeated return to this object, the constant repetition of a trajectory that starts from this same point, tends to maintain the
contested organ's right to exist. Gilles Deleuze has shown how
the fetish, far from being a symbol, is in a certain sense a station-
ary image, an arrested image which the gaze leaves only to return
to it forever, to repeat eternally the abnegation of an absence. As
might be expected, the abnegation of inexistence and of absence
is not, however, effected by a sort of mechanics of negativity,
presence, or existence. Abnegation does not negate in a pure and
simple manner. It destroys, but not by means of destruction. In
this particular case, abnegation does not negate absence, yet it
does negate, but not in order to fill its emptiness. Instead, abnegation serves the purpose of "contesting the well-foundedness of
the real," to use Deleuze's phrase. It puts in question Being's right
to be what it is; a transcendental gesture if ever there was one, it
simulates the reflexive dimension of representation, the insis-
tence with which representation not only represents something,
but presents itself representing something in order to justify or
legitimate what it represents, according it the right to be present
within its own delegate and proxy. Abnegation neutralizes this
legitimacy, it suspends this justification. It simulates "what is"
within the connected space that is the site of a particular suspension, that of the belief that Husserl regarded as originary and

foundational for an individual's relation to reality. What is given raises itself to a new horizon, the essential characteristic of which is that it is not given, posited, or perceived.

The portrait of the King, his infinite representation, is the real presence of the absolute Monarch, the accumulation of signs and the quantitative power of ornaments and insignia being no more and no less important than the suspended pose, the neutralization of movement and rest, of gestures and immobility, of duration and the fleeting instant.

The real presence of the Monarch in his portrait is first brought about by the transcendental gesture of abnegation, the abnegation of the limit, which is the abnegation of all possible negation, of indefinite extension, of the infinite expansion of the King's power: "No, I do not lack potency; no, I am not without power"—the hyperbolic value of litotes. The neutral space of absolute power is opened up, a space where the absence or limit of power is infinitely, indefinitely contested and contestable: "No, I do not lack the absolute organ of power." If we paraphrase Deleuze's analysis of fetishism, we could say that the portrait of the King, the fetish of the absolute Monarch, is also a defensive neutralization that is not a forgetting or negation of the real situation (the King is not omnipotent and he is well aware of this fact), but rather its suspension. Who would be better placed to effect this suspension than "I-as-portrait," "the King-as-portrait"? In 1705, the King is triumphant in all of his splendor, despite his illness and his years, despite setbacks, defeats, famines, the rise of English power, and the costs of the war of succession with Spain. His portrait is still that of the greatest King of Europe, of the Sun King who "can be compared only to himself," words that Perrault will use to describe the king in "Donkey-Skin." In this manner, the king finally achieves real presence as the absolute Monarch in his fetish-portrait. Not only does this portrait bring about the defensive neutralization of real history and of the referential body, it also effects the protective and idealizing neutralization of the King: "I am the absolute Monarch." This utterance is a matter of belief and is formulated by the model-paradigm turned portrait. It is entirely without reference, for all reference, be it that of a perfect mimesis, is a real limitation, for the real is an obstacle to the ideological functioning of the King's portrait: in his epideictic monstration, in his ostentatious appearance, the absolute Monarch asserts the rights of what is ideal over and against those pertaining to reality. The desire for absolute power is satisfied through a fetish, through the Monarch's representation. This desire remains suspended in its attachment to an ideal, and thus the blows that knowledge about reality could potentially inflict are more readily neutralized.

We should never lose sight of the fact that the desire for absolute power is but one of many kinds of death drives. As we know, these drives are only presented and presentable to the unconscious when mixed with life drives. In this sense, the King's portrait is a figure of the sublime, that is, a figure that presents what cannot be represented. It is a figure presenting an unrepresentable absolute power. In one of his *pensées*, Pascal defined tyranny as the desire for a universal domination knowing no bounds. This *pensée* simultaneously entailed the most radical critique of tyranny, as well as of absolute Monarchy. For what is this desire for a universal domination which ranges beyond the difference characteristic of its sphere, but a desire for the abolition of all heterogeneity and of all difference? Were such a desire to be satisfied, the result would be a definitive homogeneity; one of the names for such a state of affairs would no doubt be absolute power. Another way to designate it would be in terms of a generalized entropy or death. Tyranny, the desire for absolute power, for all power, is a desire for death, and the portrait of the King is a figure of its realization in the fetish of representation. This fetish serves the purpose of suspending the King's body in a sphere of ideality that asserts itself over and against reality.

Thus the King's portrait is essentially related to abnegation and suspension. To state this point in a formula: the King's portrait will always be the portrait of the portrait, and that is why it is the locus of a paradox. The utterance is abnegated, suspended, and neutralized, yet this entire operation stands in the service of an epideictic ostentation and monstration, in short, in the act of producing an utterance. This paradox is complementary to and the inverted form of another paradox, one that abnegates the apparatus by which utterances are produced. The latter paradox is located in the painting that portrays the King's history, the profile reflected in this mirror being, as we have shown elsewhere, that of a remarkable figure. What does it mean to speak of the portrait of the portrait? Simply this: when the body of the royal model poses in reality, with an eye to being represented mimetically by the painter, this referential body constitutes itself as a "real" portrait (if we may be allowed this expression). At that point, the process of painting the body-model in its real pose becomes one of painting the subject's pose as the subject of a pose. It is to do the portrait of a portrait. As a result of this redoubling, reality's right to be what it is, the referential body's rights to be an exceptional individual, are negatively contested and transformed into an ideal, in order to be presented as the ethical, political, and theological paradigm of the absolute Monarch over and against the real king. The pose is, then, the parameter or rather the operator that effects the neutralization of the king's real body in a "real" portrait, one which will be suspended in the ideality of the Absolute as a result of being represented by the King's portrait. The portrait of the portrait (or portrait²) of the King bearing an exponent that is nothing other than the mathematical and parodic symbol of the pose, is quite simply a fetish, that is, the real presence of the royal body, a body that bears the representative signs of the Monarch.

Following Benveniste, we may say that the difference between a position of *pro-trait and a position of *prae-sence would be the mark of the process by which the portrait of the King is constituted as the fetish of the Monarch. Let us assume that the *protractus* simultaneously refers to what is drawn, extracted, and expulsed from a body and face, as well as to what replaces and substitutes for these elements to cover and protect the vulnerable site. Then if *prae-sens* signifies what is before an object while being continuous with it, if it refers to the object's extremities, to its excess, its paroxysm and imminence, then, as a *pro-tractus*, the portrait of the King will mark the negating dispersion of reality and the defensive neutralization of the image, while the real presence of the Monarch will manifest, with both brilliance and glory, the idealizing neutralization of the icon that would legitimate what is representable—absolute power—by providing it with a foundation.

The king who sits on his throne imitates the Monarch as he is displayed in his image. Before the throne of painting and invested with absolute power, the Monarch contemplates the King who looks at him so as to bring about a fusion of the two before the eyes of the court that repeats his Name: "The King!"

A Caricature by Thackeray

Let us assume that the painted portrait of the King does involve a fetishism of the Monarch and that it is the mark and symptom of the King's masochism, of a King who is seduced by his own

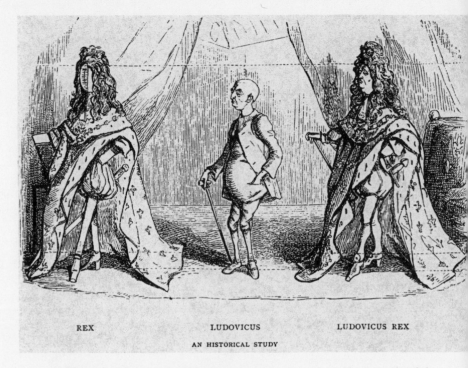

REX   LUDOVICUS   LUDOVICUS REX

AN HISTORICAL STUDY

Caricature by Thackeray of Rigaud's portrait of Louis x i v in *The Paris Sketch by Titmarsh*

image. If our analysis is correct, then Thackeray's drawing, in presenting Rigaud's painting to us in the form of three figures, could be said to have revealed, almost two centuries later, the sadism of the subject who is fascinated by the body of the King. The French painter's portrait of praise presented its object as unified, synthetic, and without ruptures. The caricatural gesture of the English author consists in his presenting this same object, but as a broken, ruptured, and fragmented one. It is not surprising that Ernst Kantorowicz should have turned to this drawing for an illustration of the important theologico-political thesis concerning the King's two bodies. The example does indeed serve a rhetorical and didactic purpose, yet one would also have to underscore its superficial and schematic nature. In fact, Thackeray's drawing does not display the doctrine of the King's two bodies in a satirical manner. Instead, it is, in the strictest sense of the term, an analysis, an undoing, of the King's portrait, of the site where the political theology of the two bodies simultaneously achieved its ultimate realization as well as its most radical transformation. The caricature establishes a rift between what is natural and what is social, between a physical reality and a fictive and symbolic one, between the body and signs. In this sense, the caricature harks back to the doctrine of the King's two bodies, one transcended by the Monarch's portrait. Yet it does so in a manner more akin to a kind of palinode of derision than to an exemplification of the doctrine in question. The caricature decomposes the portrait; the figure at the center of the sketch reveals the natural body of the king. Only in a description oblivious to the laws of the psychology of form would it seem that the spectator has even seen any part of this natural body of the king—the face and part of the legs; but in fact, the spectator of Rigaud's portrait has seen none of this body, since, as we know, the whole is more than and quite different from the sum of its parts; and the face of the King in Rigaud's portrait is not a head (that of Louis of Bourbon, the fourteenth by name) plus a ceremonial wig. The face is not such that the addition of a head and a wig could turn it into the head of Louis XIV that figures in the portrait painted by Rigaud. Nor is this face such that the subtraction of the wig from the face in the portrait would result in a remainder, in the head of the individual who is the king when wearing a wig.

The caricature finds its basis in an analytic, atomistic psychology of association, and, in this respect, it betrays itself as a product of its times and context. In furnishing the exact count of the component elements that make up the model as a referential body, this caricature does not provide a true account of the King's portrait: it offers us something more than and quite different from a state portrait reduced to its component parts; it is almost as if such a portrait is more than its constitutive elements precisely because it brings about their transcendental unity. The political and ideological thrust of the caricatural drawing is that it proposes itself as the decomposition of a portrait of praise: it tries to make us believe that, in reality, the portrait of the King is nothing but a body of miserable and natural organs plus a social body of magnificent signs. In thus subtracting the natural body from the body of signs that it supports, in revealing the two bodies to be separate, the caricature shows the body of signs to be nothing more than a mask, the deceptive disguise of the natural body. In short, it tries to make us believe that the natural body, in all of its pain and suffering, is the truth of the body of signs, represented in all of its glory. The caricature of the king tries to make us believe that it speaks the truth about the King's portrait when it is actually nothing but the sadistic transformation, on the part of the Slave (the bourgeois) of the Master's (the King's) masochistic fetish.

We could also say that the caricature asserts a thesis, develops a discourse, and tells a story. Moreover, it substitutes this thesis, discourse, and story for the portrait's nominal phrase; a straightforward elaboration or explanation does not get us from the portrait's nominal phrase to the complete phrase, a discursive proposition or narrative utterance. Similarly, a straightforward arithmetical subtraction does not get us from a portrait of the King to the caricature. The caricature is a parodic regression from the monarch's portrait to the king's two bodies, a regression that is also a process of decomposition. Yet the caricature is not a straightforward, amusing, and ironic illustration of Kantorowicz's thesis. The caricature does not aspire to demonstrate iconically the validity of this thesis, but that of an entirely different one: the portrait hides its body and the exalted body in a travesty of the natural body. In its portrait, the body of the Monarch is no longer a majestic and ostentatious body that would have the natural body as its invisible support. In this portrait, the face is first and foremost a gaze, and the legs are those of an erotic body, which has nothing to do with a natural and physical body; if we are to believe the caricature, the body of the Monarch is a body of deception. The caricature transforms majestic ostentation, that is, the legitimate sovereignty of the power of representation, into a mask, a body-mask that deceives and disguises and is not simply the support or prop for the exalted body. It fells the natural body and propels it downward, into the domain of the ridiculous and grotesque. The disproportion between the head and the body, between the legs that are as thin as sticks and the bulging belly, the baldness of the head and the many signs of age, all make Louis's body look like that of a grimacing gnome. Yet these features are really only ridiculous and grotesque by virtue of their being contrasted to the two other figures that frame the central one: the one presenting the signs and insignia of kingship, but without the support of a body, and the other representing the fusion and sum of the first two. We shall come back to this point.

The caricature then, is not the representation of the portrait's truth, as the attempt to reveal the deception involved in the King's painting would seem to have us believe. More precisely, even if the caricature succeeds in making us believe that it discloses the truth, the argument that it proposes as peremptory and decisive proof is nothing other than the ugly, ridiculous, and grotesque nature of the natural body. That is the truth underlying the portrait of stateliness and pomp, the caricature seems to exclaim. How could it be anything but the truth, since it is precisely because this natural body is so ugly, ridiculous, and grotesque that the portrait has to play a deceptive role? If we were dealing with a beautiful and noble body, then there would be no reason to engage in deceptive practices. This is what the sophistry underlying the caricature of the portrait looks like when it is spelled out:

  1. The body supports the exalted body that hides it; the latter body hides the natural body.
  2. Everything that could possibly compromise the inadequation of representation and power is excluded or hidden in the power that is exercised by representation and in the representations that are controlled by power.
  3. If the natural body of the king is hidden, it is because its ugliness compromises the majesty of the Monarch.
  4. Since it is hidden the natural body cannot be anything but ridiculous.

This sophistry is highly efficacious: by extracting from the portrait of the King the "real" body that this portrait is supposed to hide, the caricature brings the natural body out into the open; it separates it out and shows it in an objective manner, that is, as an object. Thus the caricature seems to uncover the objective truth about the exalted body in which the natural body is garbed.

It is noteworthy that the caricature should establish an order for the reading of the three figures, whereby we begin on the left with the legendary exalted body REX and conclude with Rigaud's portrait. It is almost as though the caricature provides an account of the existing portrait's genesis rather than an analysis and decomposition of it. It suggests that, to create an appropriate image of the King, the painter dressed up a body decrepit with age and illness (drawing number 2) with the signs and insignia of a royal dignitary (drawing number 1). Thus the caricature adds another element to the thesis concerning the satirical truth of the portrait: the legendary story of its constitution, legendary in the dual sense of the legend of the King's icon and the authorized fable that recounts the details of its creation. If it is true that stories deploy their narrativity only to the extent that they bring about the transformation of an initial state of loss and deficiency

into a final state of completeness or satisfaction, then the caricature proposes that we read the portrait of the King as the final
stage of a process whereby the social state is filled by the state of
nature to compose the state of the monarchic sovereign. The
caricature reveals the institutional history that the creation of
the King's portrait can be said to represent in its own way, in the
movement between the referential model and the finished icon, a
movement achieved through the efficacy of the supplement constituted by ornamentation, decorations, and props. The history
revealed by the caricature is once more a legendary form of history, which in the end is condensed by the portrait into a single
and imposing figure. Thackeray undoubtedly has the ability to
show the signs and insignia of the royal and majestic figure that
precede the presentation of the natural body within the order of
reading. Yet his commentary brings about the constitution of the
King's portrait in a negative manner, as though we were to say: "a
king is not every inch a king . . . and it is curious to see how
much precise majesty there is in that majestic figure of Ludovicus Rex . . . we have endeavoured to make the exact calculation" (Thackeray 1901, 313). Here the story underwriting the order
of the drawings that make up the caricature is largely conceived
on the model of a chemical combination (how much of the substance "majesty" is to be found in the majestic figure of the King?)
before it is reduced to a mathematical addition. Thackeray
continues:

> The idea of kingly dignity is equally strong in the two outer figures;
> don't you see at once that majesty is made out of the wig, the high
> heeled shoes and cloak, all fleur-de-lis bespangled. As for the little,
> lean, shrivelled, paunchy old man of five feet two, in a jacket and
> breeches, there is no majesty in him at any rate; and yet he has just
> stepped out of that very suit of clothes. (Thackeray 1901, 313)

The caricature makes this arithmetical calculation legible in its
drawings by means of the dotted lines that situate Rex, Ludovicus, and Ludovicus Rex on the same scale. However, in order to
calculate the size of this theologico-political majesty, Thackeray,
in his commentary, tells the anecdote about how the King steps
out of this stately and ornamental garb, taking off the wig, the
heeled shoes, and the coat decorated with fleur-de-lis: "He has
just stepped out of that very suit of clothes." He subsequently
enjoins his reader-spectator, in the mode of a prescription or
injunction, to perform the synthesis of the portrait on his or her

own, a synthesis that is at once historical and institutional, as well as artistic and aesthetic: "Put the wig and shoes on him, and he is six feet high; — the other fripperies, and he stands before you majestic, imperial, and heroic! Thus do barbers and cobblers make the gods that we worship" (Thackeray 1901, 313).

Elsewhere, we tried to provide evidence for the at once fictive and transcendental genesis of the King's portrait by focusing on the historical painting that stages one of his actions; we underscored the manner in which the portrait constituted the substantial essence, the permanent truth deployed by the historical agent during the time pertaining to men and things. We see then that Thackeray's caricature proposes a rather different account of this process. While its description of the portrait's history is equally fictive, it purports to be empirical and to represent the process by which absolute power is created. Contrariwise, it also describes the self-evidence of the absolute power of the image, a creation that is itself representative of a positive rather than ideal history of the monarchic institution as the dissimulation of the weakness of the natural, individual body. This deception is understood to be made possible by virtue of the efficacy of the signs and insignia of power, and thus Thackeray's historical narrative discloses not only the originary usurpation of political power, but also the enticing snares that serve to legitimate it.

Yet the caricature also persuades, even though its method involves the illusion of a constitutive or constructive reading of the royal portrait (which begins with the figures that precede it on the page), as well as calculation, the addition and superimposition that produce the portrait as their result: the ordered composition in turn hides an even more primitive decomposition, the construction conceals an initial deconstruction, and the synthetic and genetic constitution proves to be but the enticement of an analytic and negating regression. The sadistic obscenity of the caricature is not difficult to discern. It becomes evident as soon as we refuse to read what the caricature incites us to read, or as soon as we scan the three figures in the opposite direction from that dictated by the order governing the correct reading implicit in the caricature. Its sadistic nature is disclosed once we approach the figures as though they were to be read in the direction that is contrary to that of a written line, or if we consider them all together as a single image. At that point, we no longer witness the construction of the portrait, but its laceration. Obscene, it strips the Monarch of his monarchic dignity by making us believe that the portrait is nothing but the dressing up of a natural body in this dignity; sadistic, it discloses the pain and impotence of a physical body, by making us believe that the concealing of this suffering is all that makes the portrait the portrait of the king.

The caricature is all the more obscene and sadistic, in that it positions its spectator as the only voyeur of a kind of political striptease. Moreover, the caricature claims that power and its representation, representation and its power, dissimulate the permanent performance of this striptease. The spectator is like a voyeur witnessing a sexual aggression against the King's body; that is the true meaning of the imaginary anecdote that Thackeray recounts, that of the King stepping out of his portrait, dropping the majestic clothes that cover his body. The king is like a feminine body, which the caricaturist as voyeur is taking in as an obscene spectacle, an absent third party who is observing the aggression, for which he is, despite his absence, responsible.

Yet this aggressive undressing is also sadistic. The spectator not only witnesses the sexual aggression of the feminine body of the King, he or she also discovers the suffering of this body. The seizure of the body is violent to the extent that it desexualizes it; once a feminine body to be possessed, the king's body now becomes a corpse. The evidence for this interpretation is in the very process by which the caricature is created, as well as in the more or less surreptitious, even involuntary, features that betray its intentions. Thackeray conceals the fact that the point of departure for his meditation on the King is Rigaud's portrait of Louis XIV and not, as he explicitly states, Louis XIV on his throne: "The august figure of the man, as he towers upon his throne," and who "cannot fail to inspire one with respect and awe: —how grand those flowing locks appear; how awful that scepter; how magnificent those flowing robes. In Louis, surely, if in anyone, the majesty of Kinghood is represented" (Thackeray 1901, 313). If the icon to be lacerated is really is one painted by Rigaud, then it is noteworthy that the caricaturist displaces and transforms the only two features in the portrait that manifest the natural body, the face and its gaze on the one hand, and the legs and their figure of movement on the other. The transformation and displacement in question are as follows: first, Thackeray turns the face and the direction of its gaze toward the left. The image thus loses the particular quality of autocontemplation that sublimated the individual, physical body into its theologico-political essence; it loses the look of autoseduction and the dual fascination that together constituted the spectacle to which the spectator was admitted as a third party, as one of the King's subjects. As for the King's legs, they have lost their feminine curve and are no longer positioned as if ready for a dance. Instead, they have been reduced to their shinbones and have become the legs of an old man, if not the shrunken bones of a skeleton. Thus the icon once again loses its power as a fetish; as a result, it also loses its power of fascination. By displaying the decomposition of a physical body, the caricaturist shows us death at work in the living. It is the product of this decomposition that Thackeray chooses to situate in the middle of his historical study, between Rex and the exalted body of Ludovicus Rex, the absolute Monarch (that is, the portrait of the King). He even places this product under a kind of canopy that he, in the upper part of his caricature, has schematically sketched with a few strokes of the pen. From our previous studies of the tapestry in which two Kings meet, we learned just how politically important this canopy is, how full of symbolic significance. In the hands of Thackeray, however, this dais comes to be reserved for this "little lean, shrivelled, paunchy old man of five feet two" (Thackeray 1901, 312). It is this pot-bellied gnome who, in the caricature's unconscious background, is elevated to the supreme dignity of the Monarch, a dignity that has, however, been inverted and turned into its contrary: instead of a divine omnipotence, there is human impotence; an unfathomable wisdom becomes an impenetrable stupidity; a figure triumphant and exalted by power becomes one scarred by the ravages of age and illness; in short, instead of the always adult immortality of the political god in his portrait, we find the natural body mortified by an encroaching senility. The caricaturist does not crown Thanatos with the name of absolute power; he does not exalt the death drive that is at work in all power and of which absolute power is the absolute image. Instead, the caricaturist crowns the decomposition of the life drive in and through power.

14 The Pathetic Body
and Its Doctor:
The "Medical Diary
of Louis XIV"

In this final chapter, we should clearly restate the
historical and theoretical problematic that has been a guiding
thread throughout the essays that make up this book, that is, the
relationship between the body and discourse. We shall attempt to
reformulate this problematic in terms of its nodal points, in
terms of the three ways in which the body and discourse interact
or meet. In the initial stages of this study, we referred to the way
in which a theory and philosophy of language, one profoundly
marked by its historical and social context of production, can be
seen to interact with a given theology of the divine body. We saw
that what was at stake in this particular intersection was the
meaning of the formula "This is my body," which simultaneously presents, accomplishes, and summarizes the Catholic
dogma of real presence, a doctrine that had been challenged by
the Calvinist ministers who insisted that it was based on an
erroneous interpretation of the historical word of Jesus Christ.
We noted that this particular utterance makes use of an ontological assertion *is* to provide the deictic *this* with a predicate that is
the body of the speaking subject, *my body*. The question is then
a matter of determining whether this utterance is anything more
than a figure of speech or whether the thing indicated actually
becomes the act itself, the embodied subject. In other words, can
the thing that is indicated, as if by some institutionalized
Church miracle, become the embodied subject in and through
language itself, *ex opere operato*? Can this transformation be

brought about by the uttering of appropriate words by appropriate persons under appropriate conditions?

The second intersection between the body and discourse is intimately connected with the first and concerns the imbrication of a theology of the divine body with a theory of political power. Thus the chiasmatic relation between power and representation — the representation of the king and the king of representation — contacts the medieval theory of the King's two bodies in a manner that is less strange than it may initially appear. The product of the direct application of the eucharistic model to the imperial and subsequently the royal substance, this theory is radically displaced in the process of its interaction with a power that is inextricable from representation, and vice versa. Kantorowicz has demonstrated the extraordinary role played by the juridical and political model of the divine body in the elaboration of the notion of kingship as it figures in relation to the king's individual person. The displacement is effected in a twofold manner: by the conjunction of the King's two bodies, of the unchanging and eternal body of dignity and of the individual body that is subject to all the miseries and sufferings of nature; and by the incorporation of the referent into the portrait, where it is conflated or confounded with the sign-image that it represents. The sacramental body of the king, the portrait of the absolute Monarch signifies and shows the point of transit that mediates between, on the one hand, the Name (the name of the King), which makes a sign of the body, and, on the other, the historical narrative that makes it possible for the King's laws and rights to take on bodily form. Thus three bodies are united in his image or portrait, in the site that makes possible a remainderless exchange, one that aims at eliminating all possible remainders. The three bodies in question are historical, juridico-political, and sacramental-semiotic in nature.

The third intersection between the body and discourse involves two types of narrative concerning the king — the historiography of the Monarch and his iconography. This intersection coincides with the above exchange and is constitutive of the Monarch's sacramental body and his portrait. According to one of the King's historians, the historiographer relates only in order to make visible, to show the royal body as a "vigorous body, full of variety, of strength and brilliance" (Pellisson-Fontanier 1735, 328). The act of showing, which underwrites the iconography of the King, serves the unique purpose of causing his portrait to be told or related to the spectator in terms of a miraculous or marvelous gesture.

The royal historiography and iconography of the Monarch come together in a metallic history, in historical medals that mint the body of the King in the form of a monarchic host, uniting his image and his deeds, his name and story in a piece of gold or silver attesting to the authenticity of both the deeds and the name by providing them with real presence. The medal is at once historiography and iconography. On one side, it displays the portrait of the King, as well as his name. On the reverse, we see the currency indicated and find the historical event reduced to the matrix of the miraculous act, while the legend articulates in a demonstrative phrase the epiphany of royal perfection corresponding to the deed. In addition to these, there is the exergue, which figures as a kind of hors d'oeuvre by means of which a date and toponymy are inscribed within empirical space and time. It is in the exergue that the King's act of will is recorded and one of his substantial attributes revealed.

The portrait of the king as a Monarch, whether in the form of historiography or iconography, was supposed to effect a remainderless exchange between the historical body and the body politic. In a sense, the historical medal accomplishes this operation: legible and visible on the two sides are the name and effigy of the King, his deeds and perfection, all brought together in a single place and time. A sovereign body coined as a monarchical and a theologico-political host, such a medal has no hidden side. Rather, the absolute reveals and signifies itself in the monumental truth of its dazzling glory. The medal serves as a perfect host, one sacrificed to the omniscience of the Monarch by virtue of historiography and iconography, both of which assume the role played by the verb *is* in the eucharistic utterance. As it is incorporated during a process of contemplation and deciphering, the medal transforms the individuals who have been graciously invited to attend the King's banquet into subjects subjected to his sovereign power. It is he who assumes all of the world's misfortunes: "My Lord, I am not worthy of drawing near unto you."

At this point, I came across yet another intersection between the body and discourse. This fourth point of contact has to do precisely with the remainder of the exchange that takes place between the king and the Monarch in the latter's portrait. This exchange makes it clear that the historical medal has a third side, one that is neither heads nor tails: the pathetic body of the King as it figures in *The Medical Diary of Louis xiv,* which dates from the period between 1647 and 1711 and was kept by Vallot, d'Aquin, and Fagon—Louis xiv's first doctors.

Lost in the shadows of secrecy, this diary describes a very different history of the royal body, which is here presented, not as glorious and solar, but as flesh and blood, suffering from humors, subject to secretions and excretions. What is exposed here is not a dazzling body, but one that has been purged and bled, one worked over according to the art of the doctor, the historian of what cannot be said, what may not be made visible to all, what may find no public inscription. In this diary, we witness a secret and hidden body, which is nonetheless the inescapable and natural condition of possibility of the regal and glorious one:

> Louis xiv, said to be God-given because of his fortunate and miraculous birth, king of France and of Navarre, by the Grace of God, son of Louis xiii and of Anne d'Autriche, was born at Saint-Germain-en-Laye on September 5, 1638 and acceded to the throne on May 14, 1643. He was crowned at Reims on June 7, 1654; after a lengthy war, decked with laurels, having exposed himself from an early age to a thousand dangers, he in 1660 won for his people the peace for which they so much longed; subsequently, he married the infanta of Spain, Marie-Thérèse of Austria, at Fontarabia on June 3 of the same year. (Vallot 1862, 1)

Thus does this other history start. With its emphasis on the miracle of the origin and on God's gift to the peoples of the kingdom of France, this beginning is indistinguishable from any that Pellisson or Racine might have written. In actual fact, however, the doctor's story immediately diverges from that of the historian, for the miracle is a natural exception, the extraordinary element deriving from secondary causes and involving the successful coupling of a faltering and paternal principle and an excellent maternal temperament:

> At a time when all of France had nearly given up hope of such a gifted successor, God, by a special act of Grace, gave us a king who is both accomplished and blessed. Hope for such a succession had waned when his father, blessed be his memory, began to suffer from an extraordinary weakness, caused prematurely by the stubbornness of a long illness, which had reduced him to a state that allowed him to hope neither for a long life nor for a complete cure; thus during the pregnancy of the Queen Mother, one was even given to fear that the weakness of the king, his father, would make itself felt in this royal child. This would indeed, without a doubt, have been the case, were it

not for the fact that the goodness of the queen's temperament and her heroic health rectified the bad impressions of the child's first principles. (Vallot 1862, 2)

The doctor will then write the story of the "preservation of the King's health," for it is in this domain that he possesses mastery and know-how. And just as the royal historiographer, by his writing, sublimates an event into a historic occasion in which the perfection of the royal substance is revealed, so the doctor will show how the successfully applied remedies, prescribed by his art and his knowledge, change a mere accident into the occasion for the preservation of the King's health. Although the process of writing is the same, the end is different in each case, since the historian aims at constituting the story of the King's history into a dazzling and diverse body, into the glorious body of the Monarch, the very sight of which will fill present and future subjects with admiration for centuries to come. On the other hand, the doctor, dare I say, constructs the medical body of the King, a body of prescriptions that match the accidents that have transpired. The repeated application of such cures is meant to produce similar effects and is supposed to bestow on the Monarch a healthy natural life:

> During the preservation of his health, I several times noticed very grave discomforts which I, by the Grace of God, was able to alleviate by means of remedies. These remedies were successful, as I have said in this very book, where I provide a precise description of all the accidents that befell his Majesty. Thus I and my successors may be duly instructed as to how his precious health may be restored and preserved, were future occasions of discomfort to arise during the happy course of his Majesty's life. (Vallot 1862, 2)

The person of the King harmoniously unites history and nature, and thus the two stories—the one about the historical body, the other about the medical body of the King—unfold in parallel fashion, in much the same way that a musical theme is tied to an accompaniment that lies behind its expressive power and meaningfulness. The doctor is responsible for the secret part of the royal symphony, which is nonetheless necessary to the perfect execution of the former. Moreover, he will not hesitate to introduce the accompanying historical sequence into each and every movement of the story. As a result, there appears within this historical narrative a hidden dimension or side, a supplement to the two sides of the historical medal. This supplement stands as a kind of monument representing and marking the

King's sovereign authority, as well as the satisfaction of his desire for the absolute. On the one hand, absolute power is achieved through the writing of royal history, with its representations and marks; on the other hand, this otherwise fully and perfectly established power leaves behind a remainder, which is nothing other than the real body of the King, a body that can never be completely identified with or sublimated by his historical body. All of the doctor's skill, the full force of his art, which is entirely dedicated to the elaboration of the story of the King's health, will be brought to bear on a twofold task: on the one hand, the doctor will pinpoint, mark, and re-mark this remainder, and, on the other, he will seek to eliminate it. More precisely, this remainder, which is the King's real body, only appears within the medical text at the moment and during the process of its elimination. The Monarch thus recovers the transparency of a briefly compromised absolute power, and the brightness of his historical substance is duly restored. From that moment on, the collective beam cast by the admiring gaze of his subjects illuminates nothing more than the two sides of the royal medal.

To use the terms appropriate to the representational paradigm, the "real and natural" body of the King can be said to be installed in the position occupied by the screen of representation, much like a supporting surface upon which the story, the subject of the painting, is made visible to the spectator. The representation of history necessarily implies the existence of a screen, of a representational site and space. It requires a painting that functions like a material screen capable of drawing together the various gazes of the spectators so as to fix and stabilize their point of view. It is also crucial to the representation of history that the screen be neutralized by the represented space and by the figures that avail themselves of its stage for the production of their story. In short, the screen must be perfectly transparent. No stain or mark, no accident or event can figure or arise on this screen without compromising the story and its contemplation. The function of the doctor is to clean and tidy up the *tavola*, story by story, to guarantee and preserve its absolute transparency. The story of the King's diarrhea, which lasted eight months, with occasional symptoms of dysentery and mesenteritis, is particularly striking in this respect, because it allows the reader to witness the very act and event that intertwine the two bodies of the King. Fully apparent here is the unceasing and difficult process of sublimating the natural body into the historical one, of transforming the former, a body governed by the rhythms of indigestion and dejection, into the latter, a body held under the sway of desire, the will, and glory:

Toward the end of the month of March of the current year, the King felt particularly weak in the stomach, where he experienced a strong pain. This pain set on after several attacks of fatigue suffered during a ballet repeatedly danced by his Majesty. These bouts were themselves combined with a number of disorders concerning the King's diet. Indeed, they followed upon the excessive consumption of sugared and artificial drinks, particularly of lemonades. They were also the result of his Majesty's having eaten too many Portuguese oranges; however, the King, contrary to my advice, insisted on religiously observing Lent as was his custom. As a result, after Easter, his Majesty was seized by such strong diarrhea that all foods were rejected undigested in the King's faeces, which were full of glair and other vile substances. This illness became progressively worse as the days wore on, yet it did not stop his Majesty from shortly thereafter embarking on one of the roughest campaigns that he had ever undertaken. He was unable to reconcile himself to the idea of peacefully undergoing the treatment and remedies that I had suggested. It is indeed true that I some days previously had started him on a kind of diet that had done him some good; but his Majesty's impatience for war and for exposing himself to extraordinary degrees of weariness quickly undermined the relief that he had experienced as a result of my remedies. As he pursued his journey, his illness visibly aggravated itself. Indeed, his illness would have been even greater and more uncomfortable, were it not for the fact that he and his men remained several days at Ribemont to await news of his enemies' advance, for they were believed to have the intention of attacking Saint-Quentin. I availed myself of this opportunity to administer some special remedies to him and thus afforded us some relief that made it possible to withstand more readily the drudgeries and travails of war. Some days later, his Majesty's discomfort increased and gave rise to great consternation amidst the most important figures of the court. I was obliged to have recourse to my remedies upon our arrival at Montmédi, where I was forced to give him an enema as soon as he had dismounted from his horse. His Majesty still wore his riding boots as I administered this treatment in what surely must be the most uncomfortable and desolate place that the kingdom has to offer. The effect of this remedy was to instill in the King some strength and courage, so that he was able the next morning to leave Montmédi and pursue his plans and his march. Throughout the travails and discomforts of his long and trying campaign, the King, unable to do exactly what was necessary to restore his health, and unwilling to forego a single military opportunity, did at the very least agree to live as regularly as possible. During this

time, he was unable to spare the time necessary for the remedies that
I proposed and so postponed everything until after his campaign and
until his return to Paris. Indeed, in response to my remonstrances concerning the consequences of his illness, his Majesty frequently told
me that he would prefer to die than to miss the least opportunity for
enhancing his glory and consolidating his State. This statement gives
us reason to admire the greatness of his soul, as well as the extraordinary patience that this King combines with a remarkable will; he did,
however, agree to let me deprive him of all the foods that I considered
detrimental to his health, and he agreed to eat only what I advised
him to consume; he also recognized the necessity of retiring for the
night earlier and at more regular hours than was his wont. Indeed, for
eight months, his Majesty forbade himself the consumption of raw
fruit and salads, as well as of all meats that were difficult to digest; it
is true, however, that he was sometimes obliged to eat cold meats during those halts when he was unable to draw on the services of his
cooks in the usual manner.

And since God has bestowed upon me the light of those remedies
that I have invented exclusively for restoring the King's health, I have
every reason to be grateful to Him and, as a result, I deem myself
obliged to render a precise account of the way in which I administered
them to his Majesty. The same remedies may serve him once again,
were he to fall similarly ill. At the very least, this record will allow
his children to benefit from them, were they to be beset by the same
illness as their father. (Vallot 1862, 15–18)

We note that the last phrase of the story about the King's diarrhea makes reference to the royal lineage, to the natural and institutional permanence of the royal house and of the sovereign, both
of which are embodied in the Monarch and in the person of the
King. In 1653, Vallot had no idea of the problems that he would
face two years later on precisely this score:

The perfect health enjoyed by the King last year has provided us, by
the Grace of God, with a beautiful and hopeful beginning to the current year. Indeed, there was much to suggest that his Majesty would
enjoy as fortunate a year as the preceding one, for each day we noted
that he had gained in strength and vigor; however, since even the greatest of Kings are hardly exempted from the onslaughts of illness and
infirmity that plague mankind, his Majesty became subject to a sickness while he was still in the prime of his years and tender youth.
This sickness was so great and unusual that I found myself at my wits'
end and in a state of confusion so great, that I cannot believe that any
of my predecessors, or even the very first doctors, could possibly have
experienced as much consternation as I then did. Nor do I believe

them to have witnessed a mishap as strange and as great as the one
that befell the King at the age of seventeen.

At the outset of the month of May, 1655, just before the King was to
go to war, I was informed by others that his shirts were soiled by a substance that led us to suspect he was suffering from some illness requiring our attention. The persons who initially advised me of this state
of affairs were poorly informed as to the nature and quality of the illness and believed it to be a type of poisoning or venereal disease.
Upon closer examination, however, I felt differently and was of the
persuasion that this accident was of the gravest importance. Indeed, I
was not mistaken on this score for, in granting this great King such a
fortunate birth, God expressed his intention that the soul of his Majesty should be engraved to an exceptionally high degree with all of the
virtues. God had surely inspired in this person such noble inclinations that I had no reason to doubt the purity of his life, nor his chastity, having been assured of the truth of the latter, not only by his own
lips, but also by the fact that his Majesty proved to be untroubled by
the discharge that he produced almost continuously, without pain or
pleasure. Thus I was obliged to inform him that this liquid was a great
inconvenience and that it ought to be duly treated; had I not spoken
in this manner he would for some time have persisted in his ignorance as to the gravity of this symptom. (Vallot 1862, 26–28)

The royal substance is being drained "almost continuously,
without pain or pleasure," thus giving rise to a pure loss. This gratuitous and fundamental expenditure wastes his body, almost as
if it is now nothing more than the perpetually decaying remains
of a human form. The doctor's discourse finds its basis or premise
in the reports concerning the soiled state in which the King's
shirts were discovered each morning. It should be noted that the
persons who furnish these reports remain anonymous throughout and that the doctor takes the particular perfections of the
King as the guiding principle of his diagnostic: the seeds of out-
standing virtue engraved in his soul, which are taken to be the
source of all his good inclinations. The nobility of his impulses is
granted the status of an a priori truth that is twice confirmed:
first by the King's own discourse, and second because "he proved
to be untroubled by the involuntary discharge" of his semen. We
understand, then, the extraordinary gravity of this illness, since
what is at stake is the very possibility of *representing* the royal
substance. The physical complaint inscribes a fundamental ontological contradiction within this substance and thus endangers
its representation, both by the subject who is sovereign and by
the subject who is guarantor and keeper. The royal being may be

transmitted only through the channels provided by the line of the King's descendants and must remain within the parameters established by the ordered, regulated, and rhythmic flux of voluntary generations. It is contrary to the order of things that his being should be dispersed or wastefully expended in a pure loss; that his being, without the intervention of his will, should experience a luxurious consummation that amounts to nothing more than an autoconsummation and a neutralization of his strength and force. His power and his desire for the absolute is also a matter of the representation of potency. Involving neither pleasure nor pain, the perpetual discharge of royal semen serves to undermine this potency, as well as the King's infinite desire, both of which are ceaselessly channeled into a sphere of exteriority, in the manner of refuse or rejected matter.

> Having evoked for his Majesty the consequences of this accident, he mulled over the advice that I had proffered, particularly once I had informed him that he could find himself valetudinary throughout the remainder of his life and in a condition that would make it impossible to have children. My statements took him greatly by surprise, and he begged me with great insistence to provide him with the means that would alleviate his discomfort.
>
> As I said above, the substance flowed from his body without any prickling or painful sensations, and it displayed a consistency somewhere between that of an egg white and pus. The substance was so firmly stuck to his shirt that the stains could be removed only by washing it with soap. The color of this liquid was usually a mixture of yellow and green; it flowed imperceptibly, rather more greatly by night than by day. All of these symptoms very much surprised me and caused me to entertain the idea that such an extraordinary illness must necessarily be related to a weakness of the prostate glands and of the spermatic vessels. Having settled upon this interpretation, God's Grace allowed me to cure his Majesty fully, as we shall see at a later stage in our diary. (Vallot 1862, 28–29)

Although the doctor has decided upon the appropriate treatment for the King's illness, he comes up against an insurmountable obstacle in his attempt to administer it, none other than the King's passion for history, his desire for the sovereign's glorious body. This body wholly sublimates nature, and it is the task of the historians' writings, of their representations and marks, to preserve it in a wholesale and monumental manner:

> As for the measures that needed to be taken in order to stop the flux and strengthen the afflicted parts of his body, I admitted to his Maj-

esty my embarrassment and explained that I was incapable of immediately satisfying his wishes to be cured. I also admitted my inabil-
ity to tell him exactly what the nature of my services might be on this
particular occasion. I assured him, however, that I would apply myself
to the task of finding a remedy and would do so with all the assiduity
that his Majesty could possibly desire. To these assurances, I added
that the illness was all the more difficult to cure because it appeared
to be quite unusual and without precedent. Moreover, I suspected
that the remedies to be applied to his Majesty's body, with the purpose of curing it, would be interrupted, since he appeared resolved to
die rather than allow the occasion for a campaign to go unseized. And
everything suggested that the campaign would be long and very pain-
ful. Indeed, no sooner did I wish to begin some treatments than I saw
myself obliged to cease them in order to satisfy the King's desire to
tend to matters of State. I can truthfully say that we progressed very
little during this period. All our efforts were aimed at simply bringing
the illness to a halt at its present stage of development. Upon closer
examination, I realized that there was no time to lose, and I began to
treat the King in Paris, only a few days before his Majesty's departure,
and I was firmly resolved to persevere in my efforts until such time
that God would bestow on me the particular strength and lucidity necessary to treat his Majesty in accordance with the regime that I had
envisaged. Meanwhile, I in no way discussed these matters with anyone in my profession, for I had been explicitly told that a matter of
such importance could be divulged to nobody.

I was, however, worried at all times, for there seemed to be no way
to ensure that his Majesty would accept treatment. He continuously
postponed his cure until a later date, and he assured me that he would
never undertake to deal with his illness unless he had fully carried
out his plans and found himself in a place of peace; he preferred to die
or suffer his affliction for the rest of his life rather than allow such
promising opportunities to go unexploited. Since I at that point was
not permitted to do more, I resigned myself to preparing for him some
remedies that would strengthen the afflicted parts of his body and put
a stop to the further development of the illness. First I resorted to my
iron tablets, which contained my March salts, my stomach medicine,
and crushed crayfish shells, as well as crushed pearls and corals. Every
morning, without telling anybody, I made him take these tablets
while he was still in bed. I pursued this treatment for some time, and
then I on occasion made his Majesty take other remedies which were
designed to refresh his intestines, a bloodwort drink, for example,
which he took during times of great heat. Although the flux had not
entirely disappeared, I noted that his Majesty had greatly benefited
from this mixture of medicines, as well as from some rest. After his
travails in foreign countries were over, the King arrived in Paris on the
seventh day of September. It was then that I decided to speak to the

King and to tell him that it was out of the question that He should postpone his cure any longer. (Vallot 1862, 30–32).

The most important remedy proved to be the waters from the King's ironworks, which he drank once he had been "prepared by bleeding and after a purge." Thus was the King, in the final analysis, relieved of an illness which was all the more sensitive an issue by virtue of its being intimately related to his health and happiness, as well as to his chances for having children, as we are told in the doctor's digression on the inconveniences and discomforts suffered by the King:

It would have been impossible for the King to have children had I not, by a special heavenly Grace, courageously undertaken to stop the continual flux of corrupted and infected seminal matter, which was hardly the venom that young and debauched persons typically contract in their dealings with lewd women, for the King had never slept with any girl or woman. Nor had this illness been caused by dirty and infamous infections for the King lived a life of complete chastity, which was without equal. I can, however, say that two main causes were at the source of all our worries: the first was the weakness of the spermatic vessels, a weakness that I had taken note of with the greatest precision possible and for which no reasons and explanations need be provided in this context. Suffice it to say that, thanks to my care, his Majesty's afflicted parts were so fully restored to health that nobody in this kingdom could possibly have greater reason to congratulate himself on having recovered from a weakness that was entirely natural to him. This infirmity would certainly never have been overcome, had it not been for the fact that I possessed knowledge about certain things and thus was spurred to apply myself to the task at hand with the greatest commitment imaginable.

What, then, was the other cause behind this flux and continual loss of corrupted, infected, and multicolored seminal matter, behind this liquid that escaped his Majesty's body at all hours, during the day and night, without pain and entailing neither pleasure nor a prickling sensation? The second cause is to be found in the strenuous actions in which the King daily engaged himself when he went horseback riding and particularly when he brought the horse to a gallop. He also undertook very rough and long journeys during seasons that were very uncomfortable because of the excessive heat and cold. He made it a point of pride to go to war on horseback and not in a carriage, and he preferred strenuous exercise to all the comforts that his Majesty could have enjoyed on many an occasion. These reasons adequately explain the cause and severity of his illness. (Vallot 1862, 45–46)

At several points in the above texts, we note that the doctor's story, which is written year in and year out, is constitutive of the medical body of the King. We also note that this story has a hidden or secret nature. Not only is the King's doctor sworn to professional secrecy, which is normal enough, but the story he writes is destined for the King's eyes only. The diary that records all of the illnesses befalling his august patient, as well as all the remedies administered to him, is to be read by the King and by nobody else. The historical writings that describe a material body, opaque with all the heaviness incumbent upon flesh, with all the viscosity of blood and humors, with the natural and organic life of the King, this historiography must remain quite private. Only the King has the right to contemplate the body articulated by means of medical signs and symbols and fashioned through the writings of the doctors; only his Majesty has the power to think of himself as a body made of flesh and blood. Only he has the right to tell himself, through the act of reading, the story of his organic life. Only he is privy to the story of his bleedings, enemas, purges, and vomiting, all of which are construed as so many responses or reactions to the sufferings inflicted by the illness that plagues him. Many other battles unfold in this manner, each having the King's body as their battlefield, unlike the wars in Flanders and the Franche-Comté. These wars made it possible for the King's great deeds, much like all the events that make up history, to be described in a process of writing that thus constitutes his glorious body. This latter type of history is written only to be made public; the former in order to remain private. Although the two types of historical writings have different orientations, I see expressed in them the same desire on the part of the King for an absolute appropriation of the self. The King attempts to achieve this self-appropriation by having recourse to a fictive double of himself, who provides him with the perfect representation of this process. The historiographer and doctor both serve this particular function.

Perhaps we should pursue the idea of a parallel development between these two types of historical writing one step further. These two histories are constitutive of the King's two bodies; we may thus usefully begin this part of our discussion by contrasting these bodies to each other. The historiographer never writes anything before the fact and he construes events as the marvelous deeds of the King. Thus the historian describes the present moment pertaining to the person who makes history in terms of a permanent monument to a fully realized past. The writing about the glorious body of the King can never be anything other than retrospective. The doctor, on the other hand, is something of an astrologer: he predicts the future, not it is true, the particular illnesses, the accidents and events, which will afflict the king, but the general and popular maladies that will spread throughout the kingdom, throughout the body with which the glorious body of the King is eminently coextensive. He is responsible for the prognosis concerning the general state of health in the kingdom, and his futurology involves schemes, plans, resolutions, medical strategies pertinent to the natural body of the King, health regimes, diets, and preventive medicines.

Yet the medical strategy that concerns the future is restricted to a book that presents itself as an account of the history of the King's health, a book that exalts the doctor's know-how, his science, and his perfect mastery: the specialized servant appropriates for his own benefit the glory of his master. There is a ruse at work here in this general prediction of the medical future of the kingdom, even if the ruse is to be attributed to the doctor, rather than the historian. The doctor only predicts the medical future of the kingdom to dispose the King favorably to the health plan that he wishes him to follow, to win a more complete administrative control over the King's health. Is it not true though that the diary is supposed to be read only by the King? Yet Vallot, the King's doctor in 1669, assumes that, at some point in the future, it may be read as a book of history. He invents a future public for the diary, the private narrative. He imagines an audience that would indeed read the narrative about the future as though it were about the past. Such an audience could not, in fact, read the story any other way. At that point, the post-factum prognosis presenting itself in the guise of history will seem like a hoax on the part of the doctor, unless the King himself were to use his doctor to glean some assurance of his total mastery over time, if only with respect to his natural organic body, with respect to the life of his organs. We witness, then, the doctor caught between the desire of the King, who is his only reader, and the simulacrum of a future public. From the perspective of the King, the doctor is nothing more than an instrument of his power, even if this power is imaginary; from the point of view of the latter party, the doctor is doomed to be a charlatan for all times. Whence Vallot's resolution in his "Remarks for the Year 1669":

The King has explicitly ordered me to begin my remarks about each year with precise observations concerning the prediction of those illnesses which are bound to be inflicted upon the kingdom. I am to present an accurate account thereof in the book, just as I did until recent years. In spite of these orders I have, however, decided to include nothing along these lines in this work since the envious typically assume that I made my predictions after the fact, it being very easy to guess about things that have already taken place. Without the express instructions of his Majesty, it would never have occurred to me to write these predictions in this book which is destined for the King only; I would have abstained from all such accounts were it not for the fact that the king each year recognized the accuracy of my predictions, about which I informed him some time during the first or second month of each year. To escape from the vain presumption of which one may accuse me, I shall in the future be concerned only with providing an accurate report of all the illnesses, as well as the cures to which our invincible Monarch will be subjected. I shall concentrate on all the circumstances surrounding his illnesses and on the remedies necessary for curing him, as well as for preventing like afflictions. And since the current year will be subject to far fewer unfortunate and popular illnesses than the preceding one, we have reason to give thanks to God for having allowed his Majesty to embark on this year in such a favorable condition that we are warranted in hoping he will see it out without experiencing severe discomfort, and we hope that God will grant him all sorts of blessings and prosperity.

The King has left Paris in perfect health to complete a number of projects in his two castles and to spend a large part of the year with the queen and the royal family. (Vallot 1862, 100–101)

What emerges from these passages is the centrality of the King's two bodies: the glorious body described by history and the infamous, doctored body; the public, transparent, and exalted body, and the private, hidden, and secret body; the body of history, legend, representation, and inscription, a body given permanence in the monument erected to its glory, and the bled body, purged, and emptied, which becomes the object of discourse only on those occasions when it rejects its waste products, serosities, liquids, and humors, when it is muted in the silence of its organs. On the one hand, we have the medal that records one of the King's deeds and thus sublimates the event in an epiphany of one of his many perfections; grouped together in a series, such medals constitute the eternal revelation of the royal substance in historical time. On the other hand, we witness the diary documenting the misfortunes that besiege the organic body, disturbing its perfect silence with attacks of pain, a silence which is also disrupted by the words and gestures pertaining to a medical practice that is intended to efface the ravages of illness.

It so happens that the historical story pertaining to the King's glorious body, and the medical diary concerning his natural body, meet as a result of the occurrence of an event that was both an historic occasion and an organic misfortune. The event in question is the King's falling ill in Calais in 1658, the history of which is told by the doctor, while the historian (that is, the members of the *petite académie*) is responsible for commemorating it in a medal, coined almost forty years later.

From the beginning of his "History of the King's Illness in Calais in 1658," Vallot insists on a diagnosis, which he will reiterate in other remarks concerning that particular year: "The discomfort of the place where the King was staying, the vileness of the air, the polluted waters, the large number of sick persons, the many deaths, and a thousand other circumstances all were responsible for the [King's] gradually having contracted a hidden poison" (Vallot 1862, 52). Subsequently, when the "terrible illness" is raging most violently, Vallot will describe its salient symptom, the swelling of the entire body, a symptom that he compares to those that typically accompany a snake bite" (Vallot 1862, 54). This comparison is taken up once more in his remarks concerning the misfortunes that have befallen the King: "His body was bloated, just as if it had been bitten by a scorpion or by a poisonous snake" (Vallot 1862, 54). In Vallot's medical story, the serpent provides a term of comparison for the organic sign of the sick royal body.

Between 1694 and 1695, the *petite académie* prepared a medal commemorating the historic event of 1658. Its emblem and legend, however, as well as the formula employed in the exergue, all represent and mark, not the King's illness, but his cure, not the event of the accident or misfortune, but that of its cancellation. It is by implication and presupposition alone that the allegorical representation of the goddess Health is suggestive of an anterior state of illness. The same can be said for the representation of the term *convalescent* (from *convalesco*, meaning to grow, gain strength, recover from an illness). The doctor's narrative, on the other hand, focuses on the illness and draws to a close once the unfortunate period is over:

The body continued to discharge in this violent manner for nine
days . . . but this process had such favorable consequences that it
brought about the cure of his Majesty without entailing any further
misfortunes or causing a relapse. This cure was even effected without
the slightest sensation of discomfort. (Vallot 1862, 63–64)

The medal's legend, as well as its translation and commentary,
underscore the identification of the royal body with that of the
kingdom, and do so in a manner that plays upon both senses of
salus and *imperium*. *Salus Imperii*, the health of the supreme
power, is *salus Imperii*, the health of the area where this supreme
power is exercised. In other words, the health of the King is the
health of the kingdom. In this respect, then, the following is an
instance of the historiographical operation par excellence: the
Aufhebung or sublimation of the organic, natural, and empirical
body of Louis into the political, transcendent, and distinguished
body of the King, a sublimation leading toward a perfect representational identification. Thus *Salus Imperii est Salus imperii*, or I
= the State, and vice versa. For such a sublimation to be possible,
however, it is necessary that no accident or misfortune compromise the transparency of the organic body, tamper with the perfection of the royal substance, or break the absolute silence of its
nature. To be more precise, such mishaps may arise; indeed, it is
imperative that they do arise, since it is their effacement or cancellation that allows the process of identification to take place.
Such is the dialectic of power in its desire for the absolute. It is
crucial that the absolute, which is identical to itself, should
always have inscribed within itself a split, an imbalance or failing. For in eliminating the difference that arises in this manner,
the absolute recognizes and experiences itself as both absolute
and unified. The medal's legend is at once the trace and the
expression of this movement of differentiation and identification, which is proper to power. Engraved on the flip side of the
medal, *Salus Imperii* refers to the formula, both homonymic and
disemic, which is tautological with respect to its signifier and
heterologic with respect to its signified: *salus imperii* is *salus
imperii*. The organic health of the King's body is coterminous
with the political health of the kingdom that is his body; in this
arrested movement, the natural body of the King becomes a political body, and his political body becomes his natural body, a body
that was always already political.

The nouns that constitute the noun phrase on the medal make

it possible for its legend to both produce and preserve this particular movement. Similarly, the medal's type makes the movement
visible and comprehensible. It represents Health allegorically
and in the manner of the Ancients, as a woman standing near an
altar around which a serpent has wrapped itself. The roundness
of the altar, and especially the snake coiled around it, makes it
possible to recognize this woman as Health. The serpent serves
as a comparative term for the organic sign that stands for a sick
royal body. In the historical story represented by the medal's type,
this term becomes an allegorical term, an iconic sign that refers
to a cured royal body in full possession of health. And yet, this
metaphor (or metamorphosis) is not a perfect or complete one,
for the serpent of health retains something of the serpent of illness. The serpent, the iconic sign of the King's health and of the
health of the kingdom, acquires its particular meaning only as a
result of having effaced and sublimated the serpent that is the
organic sign of the royal illness.

In the final analysis and at the end of the King's reign, an
exchange took place during the period between the coining of the
medal commemorating the King's recovery at Calais in 1694 and
the writing of the King's medical diary describing his illness in
the same town in 1658. This remainderless exchange takes place
between the suffering body of the king and his glorious body. All
medals, portraits, and stories can be said to bring about this same
kind of exchange, although each accomplishes this task in its
own way. The King's desire to appropriate himself and his representations completely, as well as to have his icons assume complete control over the king, manifests itself in the monuments
erected to his glory, as well as in the writings that document his
excretions. The transaction between these two media of exchange
is effected with recourse to a figure that functions as the
sovereign's fictive and instrumental double, one made possible by
the process of writing and engraving, by images and stories.

This is the appropriate place to focus once more on the state
portraits of the King, having discussed in the previous chapter
the one painted by Rigaud in 1701. This is also the right moment
to reveal the portrait that figures on the hidden back of this regal
painting. That portrait has been meticulously drawn, year in,
year out, by Louis xiv's successive doctors. Yet the materials used
for this hidden portrait are different from those employed in the
publicly oriented one. Instead of the strokes of a crayon or a
brush full of paint, they are the incisions made with a medical

stylet, with spurts of blood and trickles of pus, with the colors of the king's excretions, the odors of his breath and secretions. Such a process gives rise to a portrait that is highly paradoxical, for the explicit intention motivating it is that of effacing the very strokes that make it possible. By rendering these strokes invisible, the doctors bring that other painterly portrait into the foreground, the one that the king contemplates in the site of the screen of representation and in the serenity of the absolute.

As we saw in the previous chapter, the painterly portrait makes it seem as if the body of the King has no other reality, no other corporeality than that provided by his being a basis for the totality of signs and insignia that wrap a legendary historical body around him as if it were his own.

The medical story, and the image of the king that it sketches and depicts from year to year, reaches a kind of conclusion in 1693 with a portrait for which Fagon, the last of the king's doctors, is responsible. Fagon's portrait, much like the preceding sketches, reveals a mysterious and disturbing flaw in the king's identity. We may gather from this that the doctor's story, and the king's subsequent reading of it, will provide the grand occasion for exorcising this particular obstacle to the King's perfect identity.

Let us, then, turn our attention to one of the remarks that d'Aquin entered in the diary in 1673:

> Although very healthy, his sleep was agitated and fitful, a little more so than usual. He often spoke out loud, and he even left his bed a couple of times, an action that I took to be a sure sign that he was suffering from some heated bile in his entrails, as well as from the strain caused by the many important matters about which we had been deliberating during the day. During the night, the memory of the events of the day reawakened the soul to activity, even though the body was at rest. (Vallot 1862, 117)

This remark is interesting. The reader will note that the king's fitful sleep is attributed not only to the heat of his bile, but also to the repercussions of his glorious body, with all of its passion and political desires. The King's glorious body makes itself felt by disturbing the nocturnal intimacy of the king's physical body.

Another entry in the diary, this time from 1675, bears the title "reflections on the King's vapors" and significantly sharpens the sketch of the earlier pathetic portrait, since it attributes a specific humor to the king:

The king has been subject to vapors for seven or eight years, although much less so than previously. These vapors stem from the spleen and from a melancholic humor, the characteristic signs of which are the instilling of sadness and the desire for solitude. These vapors travel through the arteries to the heart and lungs, where they provoke palpitations, anguish, listlessness, and considerable choking. From there, they continue all the way to the brain where they, by agitating the spirit in the optical nerves, cause bouts of dizziness and make the head spin. Moreover, by striking at the very base of the nerves, they weaken the legs to such an extent that help is needed in walking. Although these effects are bothersome to everybody, they are particularly so in the king's case, for he greatly needs a clear head to be able to contend with all the matters requiring his attention. A number of factors made it possible for this illness to afflict his Majesty: his temperament quite inclines him to be melancholic, his life is sedentary most of the time and largely spent in councils, and his natural voracity encourages him to eat a great deal. Indigestion caused him to experience heavy and inveterate clogging of the veins which retained and blocked the melancholic humour and thus hampered its flow along habitual passageways. This standstill caused heat and fermentation and engendered a great turmoil in the king's body. . . . These thoughts, as well as my fear that this tiresome illness could repeat itself, made me believe that his Majesty ought to be able to resolve himself to bringing order into his life and to undergoing a systematic treatment that could undo the damage caused by the old cloggings of his spleen, thus relieving it somewhat of the melancholic humor. (Vallot 1862, 130–31)

In 1680, the same entry figures once more:

To this we must add the heat of his bowels, which disposes the patient to be unsettled by the slightest event. Such a disposition can be readily detected by the following symptoms: a more fitful sleep, disturbed by dreams, a hot and heavy head, listlessness of the body, melancholy, and even sorrow without cause. The king quite frequently complains about these discomforts, the causes of which are to be sought in the infrequent rest that he allots to himself. Too much on guard, he sleeps too little for a man whose mind works as much as his does. (Vallot 1862, 131)

In 1693, d'Aquin is disgraced, and his assistant, Fagon, becomes the King's chief doctor. It is at this point that Fagon creates the pathetic portrait of the king's unhappy body. He does this to distinguish himself from his predecessor, to whose downfall he had greatly contributed, and to ensure that, in the eyes of his King, he now fully occupies the throne that accompanies the role that he is to play.

First of all, Fagon settles accounts with d'Aquin and with his thesis concerning the King's constitution. At the same time, he provides an epistemological justification for the King's portrait, as well as for his own proposal for a new diagnostic. Thus we come across the following phrase: "when one has no other passion than that of attentively pursuing all that reason, study, and experience may reveal about the greatest subject in the world" (Vallot 1862, 209).

The hypothesis elaborated by Mr. d'Aquin "presupposes that the King was naturally bilious, and he speaks only of the bile that was removed during his Majesty's purges. Yet his Majesty's temperament is quite different from the one that makes the body and spirit vulnerable to dispositions that are quite different from his" (Vallot 1862, 209).

Subsequently, Fagon goes on to elaborate a portrait of a general type of person, as well as of someone who is an average representative of it. It is against the backdrop of this description of a generality, of the bilious person, that the individuality, singularity, and uniqueness of the King's portrait will be discerned, first in a negative manner, then positively:

Bilious individuals have fiery hair and eyebrows, and their skin is very often a yellowish color. They are inclined to vomiting and to feeling sick as soon as it is slightly warm or they are hot themselves. They naturally have a mediocre appetite, the stomach generally being empty, more so than it should be. They are inclined to be transported by anger, and they are rarely able to master the intense and sudden passions that it excites. . . . Not one of these features or symptoms applies to the King. His eyebrows and brown hair are virtually black. His white skin, more perfect than that of the most delicate women, is combined with the most beautiful rosy tint and has only been somewhat changed by smallpox. It has retained its whiteness and shows not the slightest trace of yellow. Nobody has ever been less inclined to vomit than the King . . . only rarely does he feel nauseous, not even during those periods when he is severely ill, and his appetite is great at all hours of the day and during all seasons . . . his stomach is sometimes constipated, and his bowels are never loose, except as a result of eating certain foods, of mixing them together or eating too much. Nobody in the whole world has been as much a master of himself as the King. He has never lost his patience or composure and has always been wise. His mind has always been lively and quick, causing him to speak very quickly and allowing him to react immediately with a surprising clarity and precision that would remain unequaled by even the longest and most assiduous preparation. He never uttered a word that displayed anger or an evil temper. To these characteristics we must add that his courage remains unshakeable before sorrow, danger, or the most perplexing and important matters that could arise. Without even wavering and despite the numerous occasions that would allow him to satisfy his passions, he keeps his resolutions in a manner that is unrivaled in its exemplariness. Given these features, can one possibly entertain any doubts about whether the King's temperament is that of heroes and the greatest of men? (Vallot 1862, 209–10)

Let us once more briefly consider Rigaud's portrait of the King, a portrait in which political power and representation function at a level of maximal efficacy; let us imagine once again a situation where the old king comes face to face with his majestic icon; imagine the reciprocal look exchanged on this occasion, the one identifying himself with the other and imitating the other as Monarch, just as the Monarch in the portrait imitates the king. The look exchanged is of an absolute serenity, transcending all physical accidents, all moral passions, all intellectual thought. It exhausts itself in itself, and, in the suspension of a pose, it ranges in the direction of emptiness. What we have here is absolute power looking apathetically at its own representation.

If we cast another glance at Fagon's portrait of the king's pathetic body, we discover that the King's two bodies are involved in a process that tends toward the elimination of their duality and toward the establishment of an identity between them. The two bodies are, as we know, the glorious, political, and solar body on the one hand, and the natural, physical, and nocturnal body on the other; by virtue of an extraordinary mimetic capacity, the painter shows what the doctor describes with the means of his art and science. In the doctor's portrait of the Monarch, the king is a melancholic figure:

Can one possibly entertain any doubts about whether the king's temperament is that of heroes and the greatest of men? It is clear that in times of well-being, the blood's tempered melancholic humor is constitutive of a healthy equilibrium. While it underwent change during times of illness, the melancholic humor has always been dominant, as we clearly note from the slowness with which his body revealed symptoms of the most severe illnesses, such as the one that befell him at Calais. The dominance of the melancholic humor can also be detected in the various attacks of fever and gout that besieged him, as well as in the tumor followed by a fistula. Mr. d'Aquin was obliged to admit that this fistula had been caused by the king's melancholic humor, which was why it had been so slow to manifest itself and so difficult to bring to the point of suppuration. (Vallot 1862, 211)

The dispute between d'Aquin and Fagon really concerns the King's bilious temperament, although one could also say that it concerns a faulty reading of the King's purges: d'Aquin detected too much bile in them. The two doctors are nonetheless in profound agreement, since they both claim that the "King is melancholic." Indeed, it is almost as though they cite Benjamin's *The Origins of German Tragic Drama* two centuries before it was written; this German thinker claimed that "the king is the paradigm of the melancholic figure." Benjamin develops this proposition by means of two of Pascal's *pensées*, one of which is as follows:

> Is not the dignity of kingship sufficiently great in itself to make its possessor happy by simply seeing what he is? Does he need to be diverted from such thoughts like ordinary people? I can quite see that it makes a man happy to be diverted from contemplating his private miseries by making him care about nothing else but dancing well, but will it be the same with a king, and will he be happier absorbed in such vain amusements than in contemplating his own greatness? What more satisfying object could his mind be offered? Would it not therefore be spoiling his delight to occupy his mind with thoughts of how to fit his steps to the rhythm of a tune or how to place a bar skillfully, instead of leaving him in peace to enjoy the contemplation of the majestic glory surrounding him? Put it to the test; leave a king entirely alone, with nothing to satisfy his senses, no care to occupy his mind, with no one to keep him company and no diversion, with complete leisure to think about himself, and you will see that a king without diversion is a very wretched man. Therefore such a thing is carefully avoided, and the persons of kings are variably attended by a great number of people concerned to see that diversion comes after affairs of state, watching over their leisure hours to provide pleasures and sport so that there should never be an empty moment. In other words they are surrounded by people who are incredibly careful to see that the king should never be alone and able to think about himself, because they know that, king though he is, he will be miserable if he does think about it. (Pascal 1966, 71–72 [no. 137])

This line of reasoning shifts our thoughts from Fagon's pathetic portrait of the King to Rigaud's majestic portrait. And yet, what is underscored in this process is that the portrait fairly clearly sketched by the doctor is not, as we momentarily believed, the hidden side of the one painted by Rigaud: the two are one and the same. This point is clear as long as we do not forget that the saturnine acedia that characterizes the melancholia of the absolute Monarch and despot, the indolence and listlessness of which d'Aquin speaks, is the source of slowness and indecision, as well as of psychophysiological features, such as the metaphysical apathy of absolute power or representation. In the final analysis, it is this saturnine acedia that is at the heart of what we spoke of as the King's pose in the portrait of the Monarch: as the king comes face to face with himself, a figure or fiction is sublimated or suspended in a process of vertiginous self-seduction, giving rise to a kind of ideal body, the fiction in question being that of the tragic solitude that Pascal sees as the salient characteristic of a king without distractions. It is this ideal body that the king's successive doctors construe in terms of an apathetic pathos, in terms of a melancholia which, as it characterizes the king's natural and physical body, equates it with the divine body belonging to the heroes of history and myth.

Afterword:
Portrait of the Translator

If we speak of a translator's preface or afterword as a genre or type of discourse, such rhetorical devices as apology, self-denigration, and *dichologia* (excusing a failure by pointing to its necessity) would have to figure among the defining criteria. In spite of their differences, contemporary translators' remarks find a common ground in their emphasis on the ultimate impossibility of a successful completion of the translator's task. Consequently, these prefaces and afterwords serve a dual function: they make explicit the regulative ideas governing the work of translation and move on to underscore the impossibility of fully realizing these norms. Such skeptical conclusions are not limited to prefaces and afterwords: recent theories of translation often take a fundamental discrepancy between actual practice and ideal conception as the object of their study. Thus the necessity of this gap or difference is made the basis for an argument questioning the validity of idealist models of translation; in some versions, this line of reasoning is held to figure within a more general critique of metaphysical thinking. As far as the continental tradition of philosophy is concerned, this intersection between skeptical theories of translation and metaphysical critique is most apparent in what is commonly known as deconstruction. Within the analytic tradition, it figures within the work of Willard von Orman Quine.* Thus an imposing

---

theoretical literature is readily available to those who wish to contribute to the genre of the translator's confession.

In a sense, the central question raised by the problem of translation today is but a variant on the age-old issue of the relation between theory and practice. Are the explicit views on translation, entertained by poststructuralist and skeptical thinkers, consistent with the institutional conditions, norms, and expectations that inform the practices of readers, authors, and translators of translated texts? If there is a contradiction between theory and practice on this issue, then what conclusions are we to draw? Must we conclude, as Gayatri Spivak did in the introduction to her translation of *Of Grammatology*, that translation is an impossible task? Must we assume that we are most faithful to the best theories of language and meaning when we cease to believe in translation? Is the authentic translator's maxim, then, to be some variation on Samuel Beckett's threnodic "I can't go on, I must go on"? As the work of translating *La Parole mangée* progressed, I became increasingly more dissatisfied with such a perspective. I would like to suggest that, instead of providing the basis for a pessimistic view of translation, the contradiction in question may serve to modify our theoretical views. Such a modification may, in turn, allow us to account for some of the intuitions that seem to persist in practice. In fact, I believe what needs to be altered is a certain widespread interpretation of radical theories of translation. Although the philosophical perspectives of Derrida and Quine quite rightly reject the possibility of realizing the goals of an idealist conception of translation, they do not necessarily entail a wholly skeptical or pessimistic view of it. I shall argue, then, that a pragmatic and institutional conception of translation is wholly compatible with a critique of idealism.

I shall elaborate my argument in three stages, the first of which will be primarily expository. In it, I attempt to set forth some of the salient features of a prevalent idealist conception of language and meaning. It is against such a backdrop that the skeptical theories of translation set forth by Derrida and Quine are best understood. In this same section, I present the most influen-

---

of discussions that appeared in Levesque and McDonald (1982). Christopher Norris's account of the similarities and differences between Quine's and Derrida's conceptions of language and meaning are also of interest in this context. See Norris (1983), 8.

tial and most frequently invoked moves in Derrida's and Quine's arguments against idealist conceptions of translation. In the second part of my argument, I turn to a number of documents relating to the reception of translated texts, as well as to the conditions under which these translations are produced. The aim in this second section will be to make clear the contradiction between widely espoused skeptical theories on the one hand, and the implicit ideology informing the contractual bases of translation, as well as the horizons of expectation of prospective readers, on the other. In the final section, I attempt to discuss the role played by institutional constraints and traditions in the process of stabilizing the indeterminacies touching certain translation projects.

What, then, are some of the most general and recurrent features of idealist theories of language and translation? An idealist semantics typically construes meaning in mentalistic and referential terms. Following the tradition that runs, for example, from the logicians of Port-Royal to Condillac, Frege, and Saussure, the meanings of terms are determined in function of the objects they refer to or in function of their reference to ideas or concepts of objects.* Meanings are understood to be articulated in precisely defined terms, and they are considered to be context-independent. Following this view, translation simply involves choosing the foreign language term equivalent in meaning to the term in the original language. This view of linguistic usage is motivated by the dream of a one-to-one correspondence between words and discrete objects in the world, as well as between one language and another. On this view of language, translation would essentially be reducible to a computational task that could be performed by a machine. Such a device would work term by term, translating them independently of any reference to the emergent meanings of the text as a whole. The calculus embodied in a translation manual or dictionary would then determine which foreign language term serves as the semantic equivalent of the original word. This kind of procedure reveals at least two crucial features: it relies on an atomistic and abstract, that is,

---

*On the theories of language developed by the Port-Royal logicians, see Marin (1975). For their theory of translation, see Marin (1976).

context-free, conception of meaning; and it construes the medium making translation possible as wholly transparent and nondistortive.

In a certain sense, the fundamental differences between idealist and skeptical theories of translation have to do with how they construe the medium of translation. In other words, they turn on rival conceptions of the translator (subjectivity) and the nature of language. Where the idealist tradition projects transparency and the possibility of an exact mirroring of terms, the skeptical tradition sees opacity and the efficacy of a productive subjectivity and language. Indeed, the idealist theories of translation repeatedly underscore the necessity of the translator's ability to transcend her own specificity, her own contextual determinations, while the skeptical tradition of thought never tires of underscoring the very impossibility of living up to this imperative, and it thus perceives the translator as being trapped within a double-bind. Underwriting the idealist project of translation is the necessity of self-discipline, of the translator's complete self-control and ultimate autoannihilation. What is at stake in this self-effacement is the emergence of the original text as it was intended and conceived of by the author. To my knowledge, these underpinnings are nowhere more powerfully stated than in Kornei Chukovsky's *The Art of Translation.* Indeed, the text as a whole is a particularly forceful description of the ideals of translation according to an idealist conception of the latter.

Chukovsky insists that the translator must render correctly the style, literary manner, tone, images, ideas, and creative personality of the original author in his or her translation. This task is considered possible because the authors are construed as lucid personages who have full access to their intentional states, ideas, and so on. In their works, then, the authors have carefully and intentionally deposited a specific set of meanings for which an unadulterated equivalent must be found in a different language. It is assumed that authors are consistent with themselves, and thus those meanings that were unintentional, yet wholly consistent with their intentional states and creative personalities, should be rendered in the foreign tongue. Since the meaning of a text is considered to be partly determined by stylistic elements, it is also the translator's duty to capture this dimension of the original.

Chukovsky literally construes the process of translation in

terms of the painting of the author's portrait. A good, accurate, authentic, and correct translation would elicit from its prospective audience an exclamation such as "That's Marin, all right!" According to Chukovsky, what is at stake in the art of translation is the revelation of a being, the disclosure of the author's presence. These ontological implications become wholly apparent in Chukovsky's discussion of bad translations. An incompetent translation is defined as an "act of slander which is all the more repugnant because the original author almost never has an opportunity to repudiate it" (Chukovsky 1984, 18). Chukovsky points out that the particular "nature of this slander" (Chukovsky 1984, 18) may vary significantly from case to case. He insists, however, that it most frequently involves the presenting of "a personality unlike the original author's" (Chukovsky 1984, 18). The persona disclosed in the translation frequently lacks any similarities to the author and may even be diametrically opposed or hostile to his true nature. Indeed, the bad (in the sense of incompetent as well as evil) translator is said to "shunt the original author aside" (Chukovsky 1984, 20) by putting "an entirely different face" on him or her (Chukovsky 1984, 19); in this way, the author is displaced and supplanted by a mere simulacrum. Chukovsky defines the main threat posed by bad translators as follows: "they pervert not just individual words and phrases, but the very essence of the original author. . . . The translator puts a mask of his own making on the author, so to speak, and he represents this mask as his real face" (Chukovsky 1984, 19). Indeed, we are told that if we as translators foist our own personalities, ideas, and writerly habits off on the public, then we have turned what ought to have been a careful imitation of the author's original "self-portrait" into our own "self-portrait." Instead of the portrait of the author, we produce a narcissistic product—the portrait of the translator. A good translator functions as a membrane allowing the original author to shine through and become fully present. The similarities between this conception of the act of translation and Marin's discussion of the manner in which the Port-Royal logicians construed the proper and ideal functioning of the sign testify to the widespread nature of such idealist doctrines.

We need pursue no further our discussion of idealist views on translation, for their salient features are quite evident at this point. Rather, let us consider the skeptical alternatives to the tradition of Chukovsky and others that are available on a widespread

interpretation of the philosophical writings of Derrida and
Quine. Over and against the idealist view of language, Derrida
proposes that we are born into a language that we can never fully
master; its terms resonate with meanings that are beyond our pur-
view as individual language users, whether we are authors or
translators. Such a noninstrumental and nonvoluntaristic view of
language insists that an individual's utterance is always excessive, calling into play a whole semantic field and not just the
intended meaning. Language is thus always a matter of what Cornelius Castoriadis has called "le renvoi infini." This infinite referral is not the wholly translucent medium of clear and distinct
ideas or thoughts; whereas the idealist tradition dreamed of a one-
to-one correspondence between ideas and terms, the deconstruc-
tionist, as well as the Heideggerian and Gadamerian, encounters
difference and the ceaseless dissemination of nonintentional
meaning, a meaning having no origin. This shift in the basic perception of the nature of language and subjectivity virtually
destroys the possibility of a classical theory of translation. Thus
Derrida insists that translation, in its idealist sense, is impossible. When the idealist view of translation is pushed to its
extreme, we realize that a translation can only be consistent with
the norms implicit in this model if its terms account for the conditions of possibility of the words that figure in the original language (Derrida 1982, 73). Since, however, Derrida follows Heidegger in construing meaning in terms of an explication that finds
its conditions of possibility in a simultaneous implication, the
idealist project for translation is clearly doomed to fail. To translate a term fully, one would have to make explicit the totality of
its implicit conditions of possibility; yet this totality is, strictly
speaking, untranslatable. Translation thus ceases to be the faithful rendition of an original by the means of equivalent terms and
becomes instead a process of unintentional and uncontrollable
displacement and dissemination of meaning.

Although Quine's empiricism ultimately establishes an indis-
putable difference between his views on language and those of
Derrida, their perspectives are compatible up to a certain point.
The first thing to note is that Quine takes radical translation problems as the starting point for his discussion. Such problems
emerge when, for example, an anthropologist or linguist encounters a wholly incomprehensible language and must begin to map
its terms onto his or her own native tongue. Although Quine
acknowledges that the situation is rather different when the

translation at hand is a matter of turning French into English, Danish into Swedish, or Dutch into German, his analysis of radical translation problems has frequently been interpreted as "a strategy for establishing features about our own home language" (Smith 1981, 48). We may legitimately begin by limiting our own discussion to Quine's statements on this matter.

Following Quine, the fundamental indeterminacy of radical translation is the result of an inscrutability of the reference of terms on the one hand, and the underdetermination of physical theory by all possible evidence on the other (Smith 1981, 18). This means that it is impossible to know exactly what someone is referring to when they use a given term; while patient observation of the relation between physical stimuli and utterances may help determine the meaning of certain basic terms, it is impossible to amass the evidence necessary to guarantee absolute certainty on this issue. To prove his case, Quine imagines a tribe where the presence of a rabbit, combined with the linguist's or anthropologist's prompting by the means of pointing gestures, can be correlated with the utterance of *gavagai* on the part of a member of the tribe. Quine goes on to say that this correlation does not warrant us to conclude that *gavagai* means *rabbit*. The term could also refer to an "undetached rabbit part," to a "rabbit stage," to a "rabbit fusion," or to "rabbithood" (Quine 1960, 52). We are reminded here of the story about the early anthropologist in Australia who elicited the word *kangaroo* from an aborigine by pointing to the animal we now associate with that name, while asking "What's that?" Far from being the name of an animal, it later appeared that *kangaroo* means "I do not know" in the aboriginal tongue.

What are the consequences of the *gavagai* example for a theory of translation and meaning? Terms can be said to derive their meaning from a background language and not from unchanging referents in the external world. What terms refer to is a function of the complex découpage established by an entire, interconnected semantic network. When slightly modified to embrace the case of speakers of the same language, the *gavagai* example is understood to prove the impossibility of an absolute certainty as to the precise meanings attached to terms by fellow speakers. While it may be possible to establish a system of explicit rules specifying the translation of one language into another, the result is that there can be no logically binding guarantee that the particular meanings of the original are present in its translated version.

This is taken to be the main thrust of the thesis that "manuals for translating one language into another can be set up in divergent ways, all compatible with the totality of speech dispositions, yet incompatible with one another" (Quine 1960, 27).

With these idealist and skeptical views of translation in mind, let us now focus the issues that they raise on a somewhat more specific case. The following schematic account is useful, since it bears structural similarities to the general context within which *La Parole mangée* became *Food for Thought*. A translator has accepted the task of rendering a text from French into English. She knows that, in the North American context of reception, the author tends to be associated with a general constellation of ideas and positions. For the sake of convenience, let us simply say that his writings are considered to be poststructuralist. Of course, poststructuralism is one of many terms given to the continental version of the critiques of idealist metaphysics just mentioned, and it follows that the author will tend to reject an idealist model of translation. It is also safe to assume that a large part of his readership consists of persons inclined to share his perspective on this matter. As a member of this audience, the translator too ascribes to a skeptical perspective on matters concerning authorship, entirely instrumental conceptions of language use, theories of meaning based on wholly lucid intentional states, and so on. But how is such a translator to proceed? How is she to make a translation of a text written by an author who does not believe in faithful translation (or perhaps in translation *tout court*)? How is she to present this translation to an equally skeptical public? Is her work to orient itself in function of the skeptical theories that in all likelihood enjoy the support of many prospective readers of the translated text?

Memoranda of agreement, as well as reviews of translated texts, suggest a negative response to the last question. For example, in contracting to translate *La Parole mangée*, I signed an agreement stating in its first clause that "the translator agrees to prepare a faithful and accurate translation of the entire Work, as revised by the author, in the English language and to deliver the translation, acceptable to the Publisher, time being of the essence, on or before 1 December 1987." How does this document square with contemporary theories of translation? "Faithful" and "accurate" are terms that clearly suggest a mentalistic and idealistic conception of meaning. The capitalization of "Work" and the importance attached to authorial revisions evoke the kind of idealistic, intentionalist aesthetics that today finds few theoretical defenders. Moreover, the "acceptability" clause evokes processes of verification that rely on a realist epistemology and semantics that seem to be at odds with prevalent ideas about translation.

But memoranda of agreement do not alone an institution make. Let us turn to another kind of evidence by referring to the book reviews of the translation of what everyone recognizes as a key text in literary theory and continental philosophy, Jacques Derrida's *Of Grammatology*. Once more, it would appear that the conceptions of translation underwriting current critical practice are not in line with the theoretical orientations of the readers of poststructuralist texts.* For example, in his review of Gayatri Spivak's translation of *Of Grammatology*, Roland Champagne praises the translator for having "demonstrated her sensitivity to the many implications of Derrida's polyvalent language by explaining whenever a French word had connotations other than the specific words used in English." Champagne goes on to valorize Spivak's explanations of "some of the esoteric references in Derrida's presentation" (Champagne 1978, 741). The first phrase cited suggests the possibility of a full specification of the semantic range of a foreign term, while the second rests on the presupposition that an author's intended reference is available for intersubjective inspection. Some of the statements in Michael Wood's "Deconstructing Derrida" similarly draw on what looks like an idealistic theory of translation:

---

*A notable exception is John Sturrock's recent discussion of the translation of *Glas* by John P. Leavey Jr. and Richard Rand: "'Glas' was not meant to be translated; indeed, it was a book so written as to be untranslatable. Yet now here it is, in an ingenious English translation, and supported by a 'Glossary,' which is for those many readers who would find 'Glas' on its own quite beyond them. But 'Glas' in English is not the same text as 'Glas' in French; the title is the same but the words have changed, and English words cannot be played with to exactly the same effect as French words. Who is to say whether the meanings given off—or 'disseminated'—in the translation match those disseminated by the original? We have no third language somewhere between French and English, against which to test them to see whether they are identical. Thus 'Glas' in English mocks, among so many other standard literary texts, the notion that translation achieves a semantic identity from one language to another" (Sturrock 1987, 3).

But the chief faults of the translation are inextricable from its principal virtue, which is a persistent literalism. This means that for a
reader prepared to imagine a sort of shadow-French behind the text
(and I suppose we can do this whether we know French or not—I do it
all the time with translations from Russian), a good deal of Derrida's
tone is kept and some of his finest phrases come through. (Wood 1977,
28)

Here the author Derrida is defined in a manner wholly consistent with Michel Foucault's archaeology of this term, as a consistent stylistic unity (Foucault 1979). The translator satisfies our
expectations when he or she proffers a shadowy text: the English
language version, however, must be full-bodied, for it must incarnate the stylistic and semantic equivalences of the elements constitutive of the original text; the extent to which the English
elements are accurate is the extent to which they are able to
evoke the ghost of the original, the shadowy outline of its original form.

Daniel O'Hara also praises Spivak for her translation of *Of
Grammatology* and claims that "now uninitiated American readers will be able to determine for themselves what lies behind all
the fuss made over the name 'Derrida'" (O'Hara 1978, 361). Once
more, the reviewer implicitly adopts a realist perspective. He
assumes that there is "a fact of the matter" determining the validity of our statements about a given referent, in this case, the ideas
and philosophical positions of a French philosopher called "Derrida." Let us conclude our list of examples with a final reference
to a somewhat more critical review of *Of Grammatology*. Hugh
Davidson's discussion is priceless within this context, because
his opening paragraph is a veritable specification of the *doxa* surrounding the normative procedures of translation:

Spivak has given us a painstaking English version of *De la grammatol-
ogie*, a very difficult book to translate. She has consulted experts; she
has had her text checked by bilingual readers; she has discussed it
with Derrida himself; and we are told by the dust jacket that he has
given his approval to her work. To her a vote of thanks is certainly
due. (Davidson 1979, 167)

This passage reads like a list of the various precautionary or
enabling mechanisms set in gear by a translator who implicitly
measures his or her product against the regulative ideals that
demand an absolute one-to-one correspondence between the original and its versions. Yet the citation also bespeaks an attitude

commonly held about the translator, whose competence is typically assumed to increase in function of his or her familiarity
with an author's work and person. The closer the translator is to
the author, the more accurate the translation is likely to be. It is
no accident that the most highly regarded translations have been
executed by individuals who are closely associated with the ideas
and positions of the original author. Esteemed as authors in their
own right, such translators as Thomas McCarthy and Barbara
Johnson are assumed to be exceptionally competent in their
capacity as translators, precisely because they profess close intellectual affinities for the original texts that they transform into
English. During a team-taught seminar, students at Northwest-
ern University remarked on the virtual fusion between Thomas
McCarthy and Jürgen Habermas, as the former completed the
sentences of the latter, in a manner that met with the German
master's assent and approval.

Our unanalyzed background beliefs, as evidenced by reviews
and other widespread practices and institutionalized norms,
seem to tell us that the ideal translator would be the "original
author + an additional, invisible language," a kind of improved
double. What the reviews and contract suggest is that most translators continue to work within a context that remains largely
untouched by the most far-reaching contemporary theories of
translation. I do not, of course, wish to imply that skeptical theories of translation are something that we can either choose to
apply or simply ignore. According to these theories, the real
results of translation processes are not fundamentally affected by
the particular self-understandings of the translator or public. It is,
however, clear that variations may occur in the extent to which
the norms governing translation are defined in accordance with
these skeptical theories, rather than along more idealist lines.
Moreover, it appears that the practice of translating even theoretical texts of a poststructural orientation remains at a great
remove from the specifications of the theory.

It is not difficult to understand why the terms under which
most translators continue to be hired remain in keeping with an
idealist definition of the translator's role. While unmastered displacements of meaning may be heralded in some theories, the
translator's semantic transformations of the original are largely
discouraged. For the traces of the translator to have any inherent
interest, he or she would typically have to occupy an institutional site of power and prestige, one that predisposes the public

to adopt a fetishistic attitude toward all signs of this person's presence. Only under certain very specific conditions do such departures from the original text, intentional or otherwise, seem to win any legitimacy. Ezra Pound's "translations" of poems "by Sappho" are an obvious example. The acceptance of radical transformations depends on the extent to which the translator is considered to be more than a translator in a more traditional sense; but in regard to such instances, skeptical theories of translation are mobilized.

Having evoked the existence of a contradiction between the dominant skeptical theories of translation and the actual practice of translators, we must now decide on the nature of its significance. The discrepancy in question suggests the following points: (1) the need to put in question the particular interpretation of Derrida's and Quine's work that entails statements to the effect that translation is impossible *tout court*, or, in other words, that it must necessarily fail to realize its goals; (2) the necessity of articulating some of the stabilizing conventions that make it possible for the practice of translation to go on unperturbed, as though the skeptical theories were but another instance of Wittgenstein's language gone on holiday. My main point is that both (1) and (2) can be accomplished or recognized without resorting to the particular categories that are the mainstay of the idealist's position. We are looking, then, for a theory of language and translation that refuses to succumb to the illusions of the idealist tradition, while simultaneously providing a framework that explains how a series of transformations from one language to another can be more or less determinate, a matter of stability up to a certain point. Although it is impossible in this particular context to examine the relative merits of rival versions of pragmatic theories of language, it does seem clear that a contextual, institutional, and pragmatic theory of linguistic and symbolic usage best satisfies these requirements.

We may begin to suggest what is at stake in a shift from an idealist theory of translation to a pragmatic one by focusing on the category of the author. Chukovsky, we saw, believed the translator's task to be a re-presentation of the author's self-portrait. Note that this proposition does not acknowledge any discrepancy between the author's private or "inner" self and the one that he presents through the medium of language and hence destines for a public life. Expression is by definition assumed to be authentic in every respect. This metaphor for translation implies, then, that meanings are a matter of an unproblematic reference to unchanging objects or states of affairs (such as the author's ideas and intentions or an inner voice) and that they are unaffected by the context in which they appear.

Let us now contrast Chukovsky's conception of the portrait to Marin's analysis of the pragmatic and contextual features of such a practice. In *Food for Thought,* Marin approaches the political dimensions of representation by means of a detailed analysis of the way in which the painter is related to his subject, the King, in what appears to be a tangled hierarchy. Marin points out that the painting of the royal portrait involves a definite risk for the painter. He is assigned the task of portraying the ideal of kingship as it is incarnated in a given subject and not those specific characteristics of an empirical subject that may contradict or be in tension with this ideal. The goal is not a photographic realism, nor may the painter veer toward an obvious exaggeration of the kingly features. As Marin points out, to commit the latter error would be to indulge in flattery. In some instances, an overly idealized portrait will fail to elicit the King's legitimizing recognition of the similarity between the representation and himself. In other cases, the larger audience for which the portrait is destined will refuse to acknowledge a relation of similarity between their King and his alleged representation. We note that the portrait, as analyzed by Marin, involves a tissue of complex strategies and calculations that totally overturn the idea of an autonomous subject who possesses a full and lucid self-understanding that may be unproblematically projected into the public domain and accepted without further dispute. In lectures on Pierre Nicole's *Essais de Morale,* Marin has pursued the notion of an opaque self in relation to theories of portraiture; on these occasions, he developed the striking image of a portrait having two sides: the back of the canvas portrays the subject as perceived by him or herself, while the front exhibits the public image of this person, a secret to nobody but the person in question.

What is the result for a theory of translation, if we substitute Marin's analysis of the portrait for Chukovsky's perspective on this matter? We note, for example, that in both cases the meanings of a text are legitimately rendered in a foreign tongue when the translation elicits an assent on the part of the author; the crucial difference is, however, that Marin's position does not oblige

us to assume that authorial approval means that the translation
has done full justice to every semantic possibility originally entertained by this person. The affirmation could very well be partially determined by a recognition of stylistic and terminological
consistencies between the translation in question and earlier
translations of other books by the same author. Terminological
consistency may indeed be approved by the author where none
existed in the original text. The pragmatic import of such strategies clearly depends on the particular interests of the author in
question. Such translation techniques are not without value for
those who may be intent on associating their name with a doctrine of their own, as well as on encouraging discipular relationships.* The legitimacy, acceptability, and acknowledged quality
of a translation, however, is also a matter of compelling the conviction of the readers belonging to a certain context of reception.
Such readers may be persuaded of the accuracy of the translation,
not because they were able to check it against the full range of
intentions and meanings supposedly projected into the text by its
author, but because its terms, issues, and positions do not depart
from a particular public conception of this author. The quality of
the translation is no longer an enduring and permanent essence;
for example, what within a given context of reception was considered the only acceptable translation of a text attributed to Apule-
ius will later appear bowdlerized; or again, whereas Freud's uses
of *Trieb* were once rendered as "instinct," many translators and
interpreters now prefer the word "drive," which is more in keeping with their emphasis on Freud's representational and nonbio-
logical conception of the psyche. By adopting a Marinian notion
of the portrait as a metaphor for translation, we shift the emphasis from individually entertained meanings and their linguistic
corollaries to processes of meaning-making, where the possibility of only partially distorted acts of communication is guaranteed by shared and overlapping contexts with their respective
institutions and conventions.

Having indicated the way toward a pragmatic conception of
translation, I would like to focus on the manner in which tradi-

---

*For a far-reaching discussion of the manner in which Michael Holquist substi-
tutes terms of art for Bakhtin's ordinary use of the Russian language, thus encouraging a certain kind of reception of his thought, see the unpublished Master's
Thesis by Jim Nielsen, "Authors as Others and Others as Authors," McGill University, 1985.

tion stabilizes the process of translation in a manner that gives the lie to statements proclaiming the impossibility of translation as such. Hans-Georg Gadamer's notion of a hermeneutic fusion of horizons is frequently rejected for its theological and Hegelian overtones. Yet the basic idea is not without plausibility: the sustained interaction between two linguistic subcultures eventually results in processes of reciprocal acculturation, by which I mean to suggest that both cultures betray marks of their interaction with the other, and not necessarily that the exchange involves parity rather than subtle or explicit forms of domination. The product of such interactions is conventions and norms that themselves constitute a tradition, inasmuch as they are continuously sustained and revitalized by agents who continue to orient their actions in function of them.

Particular examples may illustrate how an emergent and shared culture provides the condition of possibility of partially determinate translation. The full significance of these examples, however, only emerges once we possess an answer to the following question: does a pragmatic view of translation necessarily depart from the skeptical theories of Quine and Derrida, or does it simply reject a certain interpretation of their views? Let us begin to take up this question by referring to some crucial statements in Quine's *Word and Object*. Quine says that "translation between kindred languages, e.g., Frisian and English, is aided by resemblance of cognate words. Translation between unrelated languages, e.g., Hungarian and English, may be aided by traditional equations that have evolved in step with a shared culture" (Quine 1960, 28). Quine uses the term "traditional equation" to evoke the idea that the consistent substitution of one term for another does not necessarily guarantee that the terms refer to "some intercultural proposition or meaning" (Quine 1960, 76). He does, however, concede that such "regulative maxims" do help determine which translation should be adopted according to the prevailing norms operative within a given context. Quine's skeptical theory of translation does not deny the validity of the concept of more or less accurate translations. It is simply that their accuracy is measured in relation to intersubjectively sustained practices and not in relation to the full phenomenal reality of an individual's private understanding of linguistic terms.

To suggest that Derrida's philosophy of language admits of partially determinate translations will seem nothing short of anathema to those who have looked to his writings for a subversion

of reason and a doctrine of free play. It is true that Derrida's
critique of metaphysics repeatedly involves an attempt to demonstrate the impossibility of communication or translation according to their most extreme idealist conceptions. Yet the importance
that Derrida attributes to conventions and shared assumptions
does remain crucial to his understanding of how communication
actually takes place. In a particularly cogent article, Stanley Fish
makes this same point:

> While he [Derrida] is certainly not a believer in determinate meaning
> in a way that would give comfort to, say, M. H. Abrams or Frederick
> Crews, he does believe that communications between two or more
> persons regularly occur and occur with a "relative" certainty that
> ensures the continuity of everyday life. Rather than a subverter of
> common sense, this Derrida is very much a philosopher of common
> sense, that is, of the underlying assumptions and conventions within
> which the shape of common sense is specified and acquires its power-
> ful force. One might even say, with the proper qualifications, that he
> is a philosopher of ordinary language. (Fish 1982, 712)

Although Fish's discussion of Derrida's work focuses on his philosophy of language and not on the question of translation, it is
clear that his remarks are wholly pertinent to this latter issue. In
this context, I shall pursue Fish's line of argumentation by referring to the manner in which Derrida directly addresses the translator and the problem of translation in "Limited Inc.: abc . . ."
Not only do these interjections suggest that the process of translation can be rendered less indeterminate by explicit injunctions
and paraphrases on the part of the author, they also support our
most basic point, which is that a partial fusion of horizons,
within an emergent cultural context, provides the translator
with standards against which the translation may be measured
and which will determine its qualities or failings. Here are three
examples of interjections motivated by translation problems that
have come to figure among the background beliefs of the author
by virtue of a longstanding contact with certain aspects of American culture:

> I decide here and from this moment on to give the presumed and col-
> lective author of the *Reply* the French name *"Société à responsabilité
> limitée"*—literally, "Society with Limited Responsibility" (or Limited
> Liability)—which is normally abbreviated to *Sarl*. I ask that the trans-
> lator leave this conventional expression in French and, if necessary,
> that he explain things in a note. (Derrida 1978, 170)

I cannot imagine how Sam Weber is going to translate "fake-out." For his benefit let me specify that, ever since my adolescence, I have understood the word above all as a soccer term, denoting an active ruse designed to surprise one's opponent by catching him off balance. (Derrida 1978, 213)

Evidently it is regrettable that the distinction made in *Sec* between *possibility* and *eventuality* was not rendered in the English translation. (Derrida 1978, 229)

In the first case, we see the coining of a neologism by means of the importation of a foreign term into the language of the translation, where its semantic range is to be specified in a note or with the help of some such strategy. In the second instance, the author similarly writes with the translator in mind, that is, with the foreign context of reception as a shaping force in the process of writing itself. Here, the accuracy of the translation, its proximity to what the author believes himself to be trying to communicate, is to be assured by the anticipation of a problem and by a process of paraphrase. The idea that paraphrase would allow for the delimitation and specification of the semantic range of the French term clearly implies a realist, although not idealist, perspective on meaning. Such realism also informs the third citation where a hierarchy between two possible translations is established, the one being designated as more accurate, appropriate, faithful, or successful than the other.

Traditions of cultural exchange, debate, and dispute, as well as the history of translated terms themselves, are the condition of possibility of ever-changing processes of meaning-making. Yet they also provide the conditions of stability that guarantee partially successful acts of communication. In conclusion, I would like to provide two concrete examples, drawn from *Food for Thought*, of how standards of translation are embodied within cultural contexts and traditions, thus helping to establish the validity of some options and the invalidity of others.

How should the word *advient* in the following sentence be translated? *Ici, l'homme fabulateur est une bête, un corps (dévorant-dévoré) qui ne parle pas encore, un corps à qui advient, au titre de la morale de l'histoire, le langage, des gestes auxquels est donnée une histoire, en conclusion, en supplément.* The verb *advenir* stands out as a special term to anybody familiar with Heidegger's importance to poststructuralist thought, for in France Heidegger's use of *ereignen* is typically translated as *ad-*

venir. As in the above example, Marin frequently uses the verb in a manner that bespeaks the influence of French Heideggerian-ism, and it is important to convey not only the particular mean-ings of this term, but also to signal its usage as a term of art. Moreover, while Marin's use of *avènement* elsewhere in the text plays on the biblical connotations of this term, it also draws on the significantly different sacred dimensions that attach to Heidegger's *Ereignis*. We know that French Heideggerians typi-cally use *avènement* in connection with a noninstrumental the-ory of language. In order to translate Marin's use of the verb in our example, we must overrule the tendency contained in ordi-nary English usage to adopt a voluntaristic and intentionalistic terminology with respect to language. It would not, therefore, be correct to translate *advient* as *appropriates* or *acquires* — a choice that would be perfectly consistent with idiomatic expressions involving language acquisition. It is true, as Quine would point out, that I can never be sure exactly what Marin had in mind when he used *advient* and *avènement*, but it makes sense to adopt a terminology that is consistent with the semantic range of these terms, as they are used within our context. *Avènement* presents no particular problem because *advent* carries noninten-tional as well as sacred connotations, and, within the context of its use, it has the added advantage of standing out as something of a term of art. In this respect, *advent* is to be preferred over the standard English translations of Heidegger's *Ereignen* as *happen-ing*, or *occurrence*. *Advient*, on the other hand, I have opted to translate as follows: "Here man the fabulator is a beast, a body (de-voured and devouring) which has not yet received the power of speech. At the end of the fable, as its moral, this body comes into language, with the advent of gestures that, as a conclusion or sup-plement, are made into a story."

Another problematic term may help draw out a different dimension of the stabilizing force of contextual determinants. The word I have in mind here is chat translator's nightmare, *le regard*. It is generally agreed that the various terms that have been proposed, such as "look," "gaze," "stare," or "act of behold-ing," fail to capture the efficacy and intentionality that is opera-tive in the French.* All four terms imply a disengaged, third-

---

*Grontkowski and Fox Keller have quite rightly pointed out that some English phrases suggest that the efficacy of sight once was more fully articulated in Eng-lish than common usage now suggests. They cite the "locking of gazes" as an exam-

person spectator stance; the latter option suffers from an additional shortcoming that is much like the one that accompanies the translation of *jouissance* as "bliss."* "Beholding" has serene religious connotations that undermine the ominous and threatening dimension of the French term (Marin, for example, speaks of *le regard* as the medium of "Medusa effects"). Yet when used within a context that clearly bespeaks the influence of French thought, "look," "gaze," and "stare" now resonate with meanings that they did not carry ten years ago. The interaction between two different cultural contexts results in the expanded extension of a given set of terms. The semantic range of these words has shifted dramatically. The situation is now such that a French and English poststructuralist will be more inclined to mean the same thing by "the look" than the English speaker and his or her nonfrancophilic counterparts. There is now a tradition of usage that stresses the efficacy of sight, and so the previously inadequate translations begin to be perfectly appropriate. In *Vision and Painting*, for example, Norman Bryson entitles one of his chapters "The Gaze and the Glance," the former term being used in a sense equivalent to that of *le regard*. If this particular opposition is part of our semantic network, then a consistent use of "gaze," "look," or "stare" will do justice to the French. The intensity of these terms is captured precisely by the way in which they contrast with the more fleeting "glance." Once again, it is foolhardy to believe that we may have access to Marin's exact intentions in his use of this term. However, there is public agreement about an approximate interpretation, and the translator must take this into account.

In fine, if it is the translator's task, in her own way, always to paint the portrait of the author, the art in question is not a matter of some private contract. Nor must it be a matter of a hopeless attempt to attain the ideal of reproducing, in a wholly alien tongue, the author's own perfect self-portrait. The translator's failures— and successes—are situated in quite a different frame. This is a frame where our institutions and habits provide constraints and links that make the translator's task something less than the impossible but necessary burden it has often been imagined to be.

Mette Hjort

---

ple of a less objectivistic and disengaged attitude toward sight.

*Stephen Heath discusses the inadequacies of "bliss" as a translation of *jouissance* in his translator's note to Roland Barthes, *Image—Music—Text*. See Barthes (1977).

References

Barthes, Roland. *Image—Music—Text.* Translated by Stephen Heath. New York: Hill & Wang, 1977.

Bryson, Norman. *Vision and Painting: The Logic of the Gaze.* New Haven: Yale University Press, 1983.

Castoriadis, Cornelius. *Les Carrefours du labyrinthe.* Paris: Seuil, 1978.

Champagne, Roland. "Review of *Of Grammatology.*" *French Review* 51 (1978): 741–42.

Chukovsky, Kornei. *The Art of Translation.* Translated by Lauren G. Leighton. Knoxville: University of Tennessee Press, 1984.

Davidson, Hugh. "Review of *Of Grammatology.*" *Comparative Literature* 31 (1979): 167–69.

Derrida, Jacques. "Limited Inc.: abc . . . " *Glyph* 2 (1978): 162–254.

———. "Moi—La Psychanalyse: Introduction à la Traduction de *l'Ecorce et le noyau* de Nicolas Abraham." *Meta* 27 (1982): 72–76.

Fish, Stanley. "With the Compliments of the Author: Reflections on Austin and Derrida." *Critical Inquiry* 8 (1982): 693–721.

Foucault, Michel. "What Is an Author?" In *Textual Strategies: Perspectives in Post-Structuralist Criticism.* Edited by Josué Harari. Ithaca: Cornell University Press, 1979.

Grontkowski, Christine, and Evelyn Fox Keller. "The Mind's Eye." In *Discovering Reality: Feminist Perspectives on Epistemology, Metaphysics, Methodology, and Philosophy of Science.* Edited by Merrill Hintikka and Sandra Harding. Dordrecht: D. Reidel, 1983.

Lacan, Jacques. *The Language of the Self.* Translated with notes and commentary by Anthony Wilden. Baltimore: Johns Hopkins University Press, 1968.

Levesque, Claude, and Christie McDonald. *L'Oreille de l'autre.* Montreal: VLB, 1982.

Marin, Louis. *La Critique du discours, études sur la logique de Port-Royal et les Pensées de Pascal.* Paris: Minuit, 1975.

———. "La Critique de la représentation classique: la traduction de la Bible à Port-Royal." In *Savoir, faire, espérer: les limites de la raison.* Vol. 2. Bruxelles: Facultés universitaires Saint-Louis, 1976: 549–76.

Nielsen, Jim. "Authors as Others and Others as Authors." Unpublished McGill University Master's Thesis, 1985.

Norris, Christopher. *The Deconstructive Turn: Essays in the Rhetoric of Philosophy.* London: Methuen, 1983.

O'Hara, Daniel. "Review of *Of Grammatology.*" *Journal of Aesthetics and Art Criticism* 36 (1978): 361–65.

Quine, Willard van Orman. *Word and Object.* Cambridge, Mass.: MIT Press, 1960.

Smith, Peter. *Realism and the Progress of Science.* Cambridge: Cambridge University Press, 1981.

Sturrock, John. "The Book Is Dead, Long Live the Book!" *The New York Times Book Review,* Sept. 13, 1987, p. 3.

Wood, Michael. "Deconstructing Derrida." *New York Review of Books* 24 (1977): 27–30.

Bibliography

Aristotle. *Categories and De Interpretatione.* Translated by J. L. Ackrill. Oxford: Clarendon Press, 1963.

Arnauld, Antoine, and Pierre Nicole. *La Logique ou l'art de penser.* 5th ed. 1683. Reprint. Introduction by Louis Marin. Paris: Flammarion, 1970.

———. *La Perpétuité de la foy de l'Eglise Catholique.* Paris: C. Savreux, 1664.

Arnauld, Antoine, and Ch. Lancelot. *Grammaire générale et raisonnée.* Paris, 1660. Reprint. Paris: Paulet, 1969.

Auerbach, Erich. *Mimesis: The Representation of Reality in Western Literature.* Translated by W. Trask. Princeton: Princeton University Press, 1953.

Bakhtin, Mikhaïl. *Rabelais and His World.* Translated by Hélène Iswolsky. Bloomington: Indiana University Press, 1984.

Barthes, Roland. *Le plaisir du texte.* Paris: Seuil, 1972.

———. *The Pleasure of the Text.* Translated by Richard Miller. New York: Farrar, Strauss & Giroux, 1975.

Beaujour, Michel. "Le jeu de Rabelais." *l'Herne* 2 (1969): 89–106.

Benjamin, Walter. *The Origin of German Tragic Drama.* Translated by John Osborne. London: New Left Books, 1977.

Benveniste, Emile. *Problèmes de linguistique générale.* Vol. 1. Paris: Gallimard, 1966.

———. *Problèmes de linguistique générale.* Vol. 2. Paris: Gallimard, 1974.

Blunt, Anthony. *Philibert de l'Orme.* London: A. Zwemmer, 1958.

Choay, François. "Le dehors et le dedans." *Nouvelle Revue de Psychanalyse* 9 (1974): 239–51.

────. "Figures d'un discours méconnu." *Critique* 311 (1973): 293–317.

────. *L'Urbaniste, Utopies-réalités*. Paris: Seuil, 1965.

Desonay, F. "En relisant l'abbaye de Thélème." In *Rabelais, IV Centenaire de sa Mort*. Genève and Lille: Droz and Giard, 1953, pp. 93–103.

Dermenghem, E. *Thomus Morus et les Utopistes de la Renaissance*. Paris: Plon, 1927.

Dubois, Claude Gilbert. *Problèmes de l'utopie*. Archives des Lettres Modernes, no. 85. Paris: Ménard, 1968.

Fontanier, Pierre. *Les figures du discours* Paris, 1827. Reprint. Edited by G. Genette. Paris: Flammarion, 1968.

Freud, Sigmund. *Beyond the Pleasure Principle*. Translated by C.J.M. Hubback. London: International Psycho-Analytical Press, 1922.

────. *The Ego and the Id*. London: Hogarth Press, 1950.

────. *Jokes and Their Relation to the Unconscious*. Translated by James Strachey. New York: W. W. Norton, 1963.

Furetière, Antoine. *Dictionnaire Universel*. 3 vols. La Haye and Rotterdam: A. & R. Leers, 1690.

Guillén, Claudio. *Literature as System*. Princeton: Princeton University Press, 1971.

Granger, G.-G. *Essai d'une philosophie du style*. Paris: Colin, 1968.

Greimas, Algirdas. *Du Sens*. Paris: Seuil, 1970.

Hegel, Georg Wilhelm Friedrich. *Phenomenology of Spirit*. Translated by A. V. Miller. Foreword by J. N. Findlay. Oxford: Clarendon Press, 1977.

Heulhard, Arthur. *Rabelais et ses voyages en Italie*. Paris, 1891.

Husserl, Edmund. *Ideas: General Introduction to Pure Phenomenology*. Translated by W. R. Boyce Gibson. London: George Allen & Unwin, 1931.

Imbert, Claude. "Port-Royal et la géométrie des modalités subjectives." *Temps de la réflexion* 2 (1982): 307–35.

Jakobson, R. *Shifters, Verbal Categories, and the Russian Verb*. Russian Language Project, Department of Slavic Languages and Literature, Harvard University, 1957. Ed. fsc. N. Ruwet in *Essais de linguistique générale*. Paris: Minuit, 1963.

Kant, Immanuel. *Critique of Pure Reason*. Translated by J.M.D. Meiklejohn. New York: Dutton, 1934.

Kantorowicz, Ernst. *The King's Two Bodies: A Study in Medieval Political Theology*. Princeton: Princeton University Press, 1957.

Klein, Robert. *La Forme et l'intelligible*. Paris: Gallimard, 1970.

Kristeva, Julia. *La Révolution du langage poétique*. Paris: Seuil, 1974.

La Fontaine, J. de. *Oeuvres*. Edited by Henri Regnier. Paris: Hachette, 1883–87.

Lefranc, A. *Les Navigations de Pantagruel*. Paris: Leclerc, 1905.

Lenormant, C. *Rabelais et l'architecture de la Renaissance*. Paris, 1840.

Lote, Georges. *La Vie et l'oeuvre de Rabelais*. Paris: 1938.

Lyotard, Jean-François. *Discours, Figure*. Paris: Klincksieck, 1971.

Marin, Louis. "The Culinary Sign in the *Tales* of Perrault." Translated by Beatrice Marie and Richard Macksey. *Genre* 4 (1983): 477–92.

———. "Le Neutre, le jeu: temps de l'Utopie." In *Discours de l'Utopie*. Paris: Union Générale d'Editions, Coll. 10/18, 1976.

———. *Utopics: Spatial Play*. Translated by Robert A. Vollrath. Humanities. Riverside, N.J.: Macmillan Press, 1984.

———. *Utopiques, jeux d'espaces*. Paris: Minuit, Coll. Critique, 1973.

Meschonnic, Henri. *Pour la poétique*. Paris: Gallimard, 1970.

Messac, Régis. *Esquisse d'une chronobibliographie des utopies*. Lausanne: Club Eutopia, 1962.

Molière, Jean-Baptiste. *Le Malade imaginaire*. Paris: Hachette, 1976.

Mollé, R. Le. "La ville idéale." *Bibliothèque d'Humaniste et de Renaissance*. Vol. 33. Genève: Droz, 1971.

More, Sir Thomas. *Utopia*. Translated and introduction by Paul Turner. London: Folio Society, 1972.

Nykrog, P. "Thélème, Panurge et la dive Bouteille." *Revue d'Histoire littéraire de la France* (1965): 385–97.

Paris, Jean. *Rabelais au futur*. Paris: Seuil, 1970.

Pascal, Blaise. *Pensées*. Translated by A. J. Krailsheimer. Harmondsworth: Penguin, 1966.

Pellison-Fontainer, Paul. *Oeuvres diverses*. Vol. 2. Paris: Didot, 1735.

Perrault, Charles. *Contes*. Edited by Gilbert Rouger. Paris: Garnier Classiques, 1978.

Plato. *Five Great Dialogues: Apology; Crito; Phaedo; Symposium; Republic*. Translated by B. Jowett. Edited and introduced by Louise Ropes Loomis. Roslyn, N.J.: Walter J. Black, 1942.

Rabelais, François. *L'Abbaye de Thélème*. Edited by Raoul Morcay. Genève and Lille: Droz and Giard, 1949.

———. *Gargantua*. Preface by V. L. Saulnier. Genève: Droz, 1970.

———. *Gargantua and Pantagruel*. Translated by Sir Thomas Urquhart and Peter Motteux. Chicago: Encyclopaedia Brittanica, 1952.

———. *Oeuvres complètes*. Established by G. Demerson. Paris: 1973.

Rigolot, François. "Les Langages de Rabelais." *Etudes rabelaisiennes* 10 (1972): 9–183.

Sami-Ali. *L'Espace imaginaire*. Paris: Gallimard, 1974.

Scarron, Paul. *Le Roman comique*. Text established by Emile Magne. Paris: Garnier Flammarion, 1981.

———. *Le Virgile travesty en vers burlesques*. Paris, 1667.

Starobinski, Jean. "Je hais comme les portes d'Hadès." *Nouvelle Revue de Psychanalyse* 9 (1974): 7–22.

Telle, Emile V. "Thélème et le paulinisme matrimonial érasmien: le sens de l'énigme en prophétie." In *François Rabelais, IV Centenaire de sa Mort*. Genève and Lille: Giard and Droz, 1953, pp. 104–19.

Thackeray, William. *Works*. Vol. 16. *The Paris Sketch by Titmarsh*. London: Charter House, 1901.

Trousson, Raymond. "Utopie et roman utopique." *Revue des Sciences Humaines* 39 (1974): 367–78.

Les Utopies à la Renaissance Colloque international (avril 1961). Paris: Presses Universitaires de France, 1963.

Vallot, Antoine, Antoine d'Aquin, and Guy-Crescent Fagon. *Journal de la santé du roi Louis XIV,* 1647–1711. Paris: A. Durand, 1862.

Versins, P. *Encyclopédie de l'Utopie des voyages extraordinaires et de la science fiction.* Lausanne, 1972.

Vitruvius, Pollio. *Vitruvius: The Ten Books on Architecture.* New York: Dover, 1960.

Voltaire. *Le Siècle de Louis XIV.* Vol. I. Berlin, 1751. Ed. fsc. Paris: Garnier Flammarion, 1966.

Winnicott, Donald Woods. *Playing and Reality.* London: Penguin, 1980.

Wittkower, Rudolf. *Architectural Principles in the Age of Humanism.* London: Tiranti, 1961.

Xénakis, Iannis. *Musique, architecture.* Paris: Casterman, 1971.

Index